the 34-TON BAT

★ **BAT** ★

the
34-TON
★ BAT ★

The Story of Baseball as Told Through
Bobbleheads, Cracker Jacks, Jockstraps,
Eye Black, and 375 Other Strange and
Unforgettable Objects

STEVE RUSHIN

Little, Brown and Company
New York Boston London

Little, Brown and Company
Hachette Book Group
237 Park Avenue, New York, NY 10017
littlebrown.com

First Edition: October 2013

Little, Brown and Company is a division of Hachette Book Group, Inc. The Little, Brown name and logo are trademarks of Hachette Book Group, Inc.

The publisher is not responsible for websites (or their content) that are not owned by the publisher.

The Hachette Speakers Bureau provides a wide range of authors for speaking events. To find out more, go to hachettespeakersbureau.com or call (866) 376-6591.

Excerpt of "That Famous Yankee Logo" reprinted with permission from Tom Shieber, baseballresearcher.blogspot.com.

Library of Congress Cataloging-in-Publication Data
Rushin, Steve.
   The 34-ton bat : the story of baseball as told through bobbleheads, cracker jacks, jockstraps, eye black, and 375 other strange and unforgettable objects / Steve Rushin.
      pages cm
   Includes bibliographical references and index.
   ISBN 978-0-316-20093-6
   1. Baseball—History—Miscellanea.   I. Title.
   GV873.R87 2013
   796.357—dc23   2013017752

10 9 8 7 6 5 4 3 2 1

RRD-C

Printed in the United States of America

*For Mom, who sent me to the library to get books
and the ballpark to get a job.
And for Rose.*

CONTENTS

the 34-TON BAT

Introduction

THE WALK-IN FREEZER
OF DREAMS

It arrives on a gray November day: a brown box filled with packing peanuts, which I brush away with an archaeologist's care to reveal a caramel-colored catcher's mitt—palm up, so that as I reach for it, it appears to reach for me, as if straining to be exhumed from a cardboard coffin.

The mitt belonged to Jimmy Boyle, who wore it for the entirety of his major-league baseball career, which consisted of a single inning of a single game for the New York Giants on June 20, 1926. With his team trailing the defending world champion Pittsburgh Pirates 8–0 in the top of the ninth inning, manager John McGraw summoned Boyle to replace Paul Florence behind home plate at the Polo Grounds. The twenty-two-year-old Boyle, about to realize his lifelong ambition, quietly slipped this mitt over his left hand.

Eighty-five years later, I remove the mitt from its box and instinctively secure it over my nose and mouth, like supplemental oxygen. I take a deep drag—of leather, sweat, and smoke, of a hot Sunday in Harlem, of late-afternoon shadows slanting across the infield, and forty thousand dry-throated spectators lamenting Prohibition.

And then I slide my fingers into the mitt—its pocket molded by the palm of a dead man—and shake hands for the first time with the grandfather I never knew.

Jimmy Boyle was my mother's father. He died of leukemia on Christmas Eve of 1958, eight years before I was born, but a photograph of him in his home Giants uniform—in a catcher's crouch, wearing this mitt, his short-brimmed cap tugged low across his forehead—hung in the house I grew up in, forever silent under glass.

Jimmy Boyle, with catcher's mitt, New York Giants, 1926.
(Courtesy of Patrick Boyle)

In the photo, Boyle's thick wool socks are pulled high. The Giants uniform is long-sleeved, made of heavy flannel, eight ounces to the yard and spectacularly ill suited to a hot summer in Manhattan, to which Boyle had traveled by Pullman car, summoned there from Cincinnati on the Gothic letterhead of "The New York Base Ball Club, John J. McGraw, Vice Pres. & Manager."

In New York, Boyle signed a contract with the Giants for $250 a month, minus a $30 security deposit for the two gorgeous uniforms he was issued. He couldn't keep the home whites or road grays, but he kept everything else from his one summer in the big leagues, including his mitt, and a letter detailing his travel expenses to New York, and a note he wrote on July 24 from the Hotel Chase in St. Louis, on the fifteenth day of a sixteen-game road trip:

"To the best mother in all of this big world," it said, the Palmer script leaning backward, as if reflecting the sudden speed of his new life. "May I realize an ambition that I have harbored since birth." He signed it "James," then added "New York Giants," as if it were an honorific, like "M.D." or "Esquire."

Which of course it was.

Is it any wonder he saved these things? Having seldom traveled outside Cincinnati—where he and professional baseball were born—Boyle was a big-league ballplayer for forty-three days before that Pullman carriage turned into a pumpkin. Upon his release—he'd only played once in six weeks—he pressed some of his baseball mementos into a small scrapbook, on whose title page he had written, in that impeccable hand:

Little scrap book of mine
When your pages are dusty and gray
Then will your contents call me back
To the days that I've passed away.

He passed the scrapbook to his only son, my uncle Pat, now retired in Reno, who gave it to me as a souvenir. *Souvenir:* a French irregular pronominal verb that means "to remember."

I also got the mitt, and the contract countersigned by Giants secretary Eddie Brannick, whose first job with the club—as a sixteen-year-old in 1908—required him to guard the team's supply of baseballs for the penurious McGraw, who knew that those balls were even then an object of desire to fans, players, and anyone else seeking a piece of the national memory.

These objects—catcher's mitt, contract, and scrapbook—had been playing dead for eighty-five years. Now they were suddenly in my home—shaking hands, sitting up, rolling over.

Could they also be taught to speak?

Jimmy Boyle had a little brother named Ralph, whom everybody called Buzz, and Buzz was the better ballplayer. Buzz was my great-uncle in every sense of that word. Buzz played five seasons in the big leagues, the last three for the Brooklyn Dodgers, playing right field for Casey Stengel at a time in the 1930s when Hack Wilson played left.

On a childhood trip to Cincinnati in the 1970s—by which time Uncle Buzz had spent three decades as a scout for the Reds, then Expos, then Royals—I ascended to an upstairs room of his house, paneled walls filled with yellowed balls and lacquered bats and photographs of men who seemed like famous fictional creations to me but were, to him, colleagues and contemporaries.

On September 21, 1934—in a season when he hit safely in twenty-five consecutive games—Buzz broke up a Dizzy Dean no-hitter in the eighth inning of a game at Ebbets Field. The same afternoon, in the second game of a doubleheader, Dizzy's brother Daffy Dean *did* throw a no-hitter. Buzz made the final out, with Leo Durocher fielding his smash on a short hop and nailing him on a bang-bang play at first.

Buzz Boyle in his Dodgers uniform, the pants soon to be stolen. (*National Baseball Hall of Fame Library, Cooperstown, NY*)

These men, and the tools of their trade, exerted a powerful hold on me. Like the woman in Luke, healed when she touched the hem of Christ's garment, or middle-aged Elvis fans, clamoring to catch his towel, I thought there was transcendence in the very fabrics they wore. I was hardly the first to think so. On February 9, 1936, two Brooklyn cops were walking a beat on Bedford Avenue, in the snow and sleet of a Sunday afternoon. As the patrolmen passed beneath the right field wall of Ebbets Field, they saw an unusual spectacle. From inside the ballpark, six baseball bats vaulted the wall and clattered to the sidewalk. There followed a single pair of flannel base-ball pants, softly parachuting to the pavement. When three teenage boys followed the pants over the wall, officers Herman Nagle and Herman Moeller were waiting, nightsticks idly twirling.

One boy escaped. The other two confessed: They had broken into the Dodgers' clubhouse and stolen a bouquet of bats and my Uncle Buzz's uniform pants, BOYLE inked into the waistband. One of the teenagers, Robert Goldfarb, was arraigned in Adolescents' Court, while the other—fifteen-year-old Solomon Cohen—was sent to Bellevue Hospital for psychiatric observation.

But the kid wasn't crazy to want to possess a big-league baseball player's uniform pants. Or if he was, I certainly understood the impulse.

As a child, I wasn't trying to break out of a major-league ballpark. I was trying to find a way in. Thirty-two years before my grandfather's catcher's mitt arrived by UPS, another baseball talisman had arrived in the mail, changing my life.

It was an embossed plastic card, like a credit card, that identified me on my thirteenth birthday in 1979 as the newest employee of the Minnesota Twins Baseball Club. The card—my rookie card, if they issued them to hot-dog boilers—bore the Twins' mesmerizing logo: two flanneled players, Minnie and Paul, shaking hands across the Mississippi River. It was like the seal of some sovereign nation to which I'd just been given citizenship. With closed eyes, I ran my fingers across my name's raised letters, as if doing so might reveal some secret message.

And it did, unlocking a hidden world. In my first season at Metropolitan Stadium, the Twins' outdoor ballpark in my hometown of Bloomington, Minnesota, I saw Reggie Jackson in his Yankees road grays walking gingerly in his spikes across the polished concrete floor of the interior tunnel where I punched in. "You *suck*," one of my teenage colleagues shouted on a dare, but Reggie walked on, ostentatiously oblivious, exactly as he looked later that day when fans showered him with the candy bars that bore his name, implacable in a fusillade of nougat.

That tunnel was baseball's backstage, filled with the multitude of objects that made it all go round: vaudevillian steel travel trunks, Louisville Sluggers, wheeled batting cages, CO_2 canisters of Coke and Sunkist, laundry hampers littered with stirrups and sanitary socks, industrial bags of yellow popcorn, and sharp-cornered cases of Rawlings baseballs, pristine white in their little rows, as in a carton of Grade A eggs.

As with most circuses, the Twins were a family business, full of lifers—concessionaires, carnies, the tattooed and the too-tanned, men (for there were hardly any women) whose faces betrayed sun-soaked days and beer-soaked nights. My paychecks bore the facsimile signature of Calvin R. Griffith, the Twins' owner, who had a stuffed marlin mounted on his office wall and a parking spot whose RESERVED sign had been hand-altered to read REVERED.

Here, in one cantankerous man, was the whole history of major-league baseball. Calvin was a single degree of separation from the game's beginnings. At age eleven, he was adopted by his uncle, Clark Griffith, Hall of Fame pitcher turned manager turned Washington Senators owner, who had begun his own career in organized baseball in 1887. Clark Griffith invented the screwball (or so he claimed) and was the first manager of the New York baseball team that would become the Yankees. He was born the year before Charles Dickens died. And his son—it scarcely seemed possible—was my boss.

Calvin had been batboy for the Senators during the Coolidge administration. As a twelve-year-old, in Game 7 of the 1924 World Series, Calvin had been charged with guarding the supply of game balls at Griffith Stadium, just as Eddie Brannick had done years earlier for John McGraw with the Giants. But when the Senators beat the Giants for the world title that afternoon, celebrating fans overran Calvin and made off with the baseball supply, leaving the boy in tears.

Calvin Griffith, left, in 1924, age twelve, as Senators ball boy. *(Library of Congress)*

Then, as now, baseballs were the game's most accessible game-used object, and they were prized. Owners employed cops or security guards to fight the fans for possession of a foul ball hit into the stands. Failure to return a foul ball was grounds for ejection and even prosecution well into the 1920s. The objects of the game — as Calvin discovered that day, weeping over an empty canvas bag — were unaccountably intoxicating to a great many people.

There were other intoxicants, too: At the Met, reporting for work on a Sunday morning as a thirteen-year-old, I passed case after case of Grain Belt beer stacked on pallets, the bottles waiting to be decanted into wax cups and then decanted again into Twins fans.

It was a job of proximity. No matter your level, you were granted access to the ballpark. I came close enough to hear the snap and pop of the static electricity on George Brett's powder-blue road pants. Rollie Fingers's face, in person, looked just like the guy's on the Pringles can. Strolling up one of the ballpark's vomitoria—has there ever been a less apt word for something so transformative?—revealed an expanse of grass as green as a pool table.

And all about us in the empty stands of the locked stadium were errant baseballs, hit into the seats during batting practice, waiting to be picked off the walkways like fallen apples from an orchard floor.

With a handful of schoolmates, I was assigned to the seething kitchens of the Met, charged with preparing the food sold by the roving vendors. We were a happy few. To get a job with the Twins in those days you either worked your way up from the fields of A-ball or rode your bike to East Bloomington, to the house of a guy named Smoke. I did neither, because my two older brothers already worked for the Twins. They had a word with Smoke, who was as mysterious and elusive as the name implied. Smoke signaled my approval, just as smoke did with the election of popes.

We were characters out of Dickens: children boiling pots of water to cook the Schweigert hot dogs peddled by vendors. In stadium vernacular, we were "stabbing dogs" and "pulling sodas" and "cupping corn," or popcorn. Our overlords were high school kids, my brother Jim among them. These mercurial manager-gods locked us in the walk-in freezers for insubordination, or for their own amusement. It was *Lord of the Flies*—*Lord of the Pop Flies*—but we didn't care. It was like living in a dream in that walk-in freezer, sitting on a mountain of ice cream and hot dogs and snow cones in a major-league ballpark. I felt like Superman, in his Fortress of Solitude, brooding on a throne of ice crystals.

I couldn't bite into a snow cone because my left front tooth was hypersensitive to cold. It had been broken in half by a thrown

11

baseball when I was ten. As a result, I subsisted on Frosty Malts, $0.75 ice cream treats from the Northland Dairy. They came with wooden spoons that looked like tongue depressors. The lid of a Frosty Malt, when thrown properly, sailed like a Frisbee. On hot Saturday afternoons, the warning track at the Met was lid-littered.

We learned, too, how to snap bottle caps—discarded by the Grain Belt beer vendors—onto the field with a flick of thumb and forefinger. At the same time, an adolescent Tom Shieber was learning to do precisely the same thing with Budweiser bottle caps at Busch Stadium in St. Louis. He would grow up to become senior curator of the National Baseball Hall of Fame in Cooperstown, caretaker of the game's most priceless and evocative objects, guardian of its crown jewels, including the first known protective cup, which crowned the jewels of catcher Claude Berry in 1915.

I had no way of knowing, in 1979, what would become of me, but I hoped it would involve baseballs, and bottle caps, and Frosty Malts, and powder-blue double-knit knickers that threw off sparks when they came out of an industrial dryer.

And tarps. Whenever it rained at Met Stadium—and we prayed with the fervor of drought-stricken farmers that it would—a lucky few of us were called out of the commissaries to pull the tarp. At fourteen, I was running onto a major-league diamond, trying not to get sucked under—by the speed of the grounds crew or the gravitational pull of professional baseball. I was exactly what I wanted to be when I grew up and—better still—I hadn't had to grow up to arrive there.

On nights it didn't rain, we closed the kitchen in the seventh inning and watched the no-payroll Twins teams of Butch Wynegar and Hosken Powell and Bombo Rivera lose another August heartbreaker. It didn't matter: A workday that began with the percussive *thwock* of batting practice ended with a PA benediction—"Drive safely"—and a ballpark-organ recessional.

The logos of various teams loomed over the Met Stadium parking lot, suspended from light poles, reminding the beer-addled fan that he had left his Nova beneath the haloed *A* of the Angels, or the interlocking *NY* of the Yankees. Baltimore Orioles slugger Boog Powell later told me that after games he would set off on foot for the team hotel at the edge of the Met's parking lot and sometimes fail to make it, stopping instead to tailgate with strangers, and then bunking in their Winnebago for the night, one cartoon Oriole drifting off to sleep beneath another cartoon Oriole, suspended from a light pole.

None of these things could happen a mere ten years later, let alone today. But in the late 1970s and early 1980s, they weren't all that unusual.

My hereditary affinity for catchers and their gear was sealed on the night of August 25, 1970, during a scoreless tie against the Red Sox. At 10:13 p.m., Twins public-address announcer Bob Casey informed fans that a bomb threat had been phoned in to the Met. "Ladies and gentlemen, there *will be* an explosion at 10:30," Casey announced definitively—if a tad alarmingly—by way of evacuating the stadium. I was later told that Twins catcher George Mitterwald fled next door to the Thunderbird Motel, where I still conjure a vivid mental image of him in full protective armor—and with the aid of a very long straw—sipping a mai tai through his catcher's mask.

Of course, the only baseball fan who was bombed that night was the drunk who phoned in the threat. Police traced the call to a pay phone inside the stadium, and the game resumed forty-four minutes later, but not before a different kind of fuse had been lit. As I reached school age, baseball was a bomb about to detonate. All its objects—ball, bat, mitt, mask, tarp, hot dog, cartoon bird, beer bottle, ballpark organ—were proving, individually and in concert with one another, powerfully hypnotic.

*   *   *

And so I set out to learn more. In the children's section of my local library was a leather chair shaped like a giant fielder's glove, and I would settle into the palm, like a soft fly, to read about the game.

I would riffle past "Alou" and just beyond "Boyer" in *The Baseball Encyclopedia* to find another, less celebrated baseball family: the two sets of Boyle brothers—Grandpa Boyle and Uncle Buzz, and their uncles, Jack and Eddie.

My great-grandfather, a fireman and brewery-truck driver named James Boyle, may have had two sons who would play in the big leagues—Jimmy and Buzz—but he also had two brothers who played in the majors: my great-great-uncles, Jack and Eddie. Which is remarkable when you consider that the whole history of major-league baseball is in essence a small town. In 140 years, roughly 17,000 men have played it, about the population of El Segundo, California, and just nine times the population of tiny Cooperstown, New York.

And my family was where it started, in Cincinnati, almost from when major-league baseball began, in 1869. On November 12, 1886, Jack Boyle of the Cincinnati Reds was party to the first trade in professional baseball, sent from his hometown team along with $350 to the St. Louis Browns, for Hugh Nicol.

Jack went on to play for the Giants, Chicago Pirates, and Philadelphia Phillies and was briefly—when signed by the Giants in 1892—the highest-paid player in the history of the game, at a salary of $5,500.

His brother Eddie, in 1896, caught for Connie Mack as a member of the Pittsburgh Pirates. These men survive in our family in ghostly objects: an Old Judge Tobacco card of Jack, a newspaper line portrait of Eddie, a sheaf of stories clipped from ancient newspapers. There is also, of course, a genetic inheritance. Jack Boyle—born one hundred years and six months to the day before I was—stood six foot four and weighed 190 pounds, exactly as I do now.

Jack Boyle, St. Louis Browns, on his Old Judge
Tobacco card, 1888. *(Library of Congress)*

All of this is to say that for a full century, from the 1880s to the
1980s, a member of my family was employed by a professional baseball team. We were in 1892 the highest paid in the history of the
game and, in 1982, the lowest paid.

At the Met—as Metropolitan Stadium was universally known, with
appropriately operatic echoes—my wage in dollars went from $2.90
to $3.10 to $3.35 over three seasons. If he moved the decimal point
one place to the left, a child of sufficient imagination could just
believe it was his batting average, climbing.

In imitation of the ballplayers, many employees—grown men and teenagers alike, in a workplace where the women were largely confined to the concession stands—chewed Red Man tobacco. We children sometimes wrapped it in Bazooka or Dubble Bubble, and were profoundly grateful for the arrival of Big League Chew, shredded bubble gum in a tobacco pouch, that gave the cheek a conspicuous bulge without the incipient taste (or mouth cancer).

We were just kids. But we felt the clock ticking. That's because Met Stadium was condemned to close after the 1981 season. The Twins would be moving indoors the following year. Each of us knew, even then, it was the best job we would ever have, no matter what we would do as grown-ups.

The last game ever played at the Met wasn't a baseball game at all—it was a Vikings loss to the Kansas City Chiefs. We closed the commissary early as fans began dismantling the stadium mid-game, picking over its carcass for souvenirs. I took two seat backs. Others pulled down the field-goal netting and endeavored to tear out pay phones. A man climbed the scoreboard and began throwing down oversized letters and numbers, an apocalyptic rain of figures and characters that recalled an anxiety dream the night before an algebra exam.

A cloud of Mace descended on the stadium, issued by police. As we drove away, we passed several fans on foot carrying a piece of the goalpost down Killebrew Drive, like an army of ants speeding a pretzel stick away from a picnic. The foul poles were salvaged and erected at our local junior college. And then what was left of the Met was razed three years later to make way for the nation's largest metaphor. Or, rather, the nation's largest shopping mall, aptly named the Mall of America.

The next season, the Twins moved downtown to the Metrodome, and to unimaginable glories, including two World Series titles. I moved to the Metrodome, too, for a single season, to a strip-lit concession stand. It wasn't the same. For starters, I worked not for the Twins but for a professional "food-service company," which issued smocks the color of the San Diego Padres' uniforms and checks in the name of Volume Services.

If you looked down one of the tunnels leading to the Metrodome grandstand, you could sometimes see, from your cash register, Tom Brunansky appear on a patch of right field, running on nylon, beneath Teflon, while wearing rayon.

But that was it. No one was locked into meat freezers or pretended to enjoy Red Man or was yanked from his dreary post to pull a tarp across a major-league infield. There was no need for a tarp. It would never rain in the Metrodome, a heartbreaking knowledge that eventually broke my spirit.

I'm not a collector, and this book is not about collecting. Rather, it's an effort to see the history of baseball—and to glimpse the history of the larger world it inhabits—in the game's objects. I want to bring them—and, by extension, our ancestors—to life. I want to make these objects talk and dance and even sing, like the teapots and candlesticks in *Beauty and the Beast*. I want that rainy stadium and its shining grass. I want to remember: *Souvenir*.

In short, I want to animate what are always called inanimate objects. Which objects? All the inanimate inamorata that first captivated me as a child and continue to exert a hold in adulthood: balls and bats and caps, of course, but also hot dogs and beer cups and ballpark organs; all the beguiling trinkets hung on Peg-Board at novelty stands—the batting-helmet banks and bobblehead dolls—and the whole bewitching alphabet of baseball: the slanted blue script of the Dodgers' uniforms, the knotted *STL* of the Cardinals' caps.

Boy in his bedroom, with a baseball, glove, and cards, 1965. *(© Bettmann/CORBIS)*

The catcher's mitt that my grandfather wore at the Polo Grounds is on my desk as I write this, palm up, as if bidding me to take his hand and follow him somewhere.

Chapter 1

THE BASEBALL GRENADE

A cross section of a baseball looks like a cross section of planet Earth. The tired assertion that baseball is a microcosm of America obscures the fact that a baseball really is a microcosmos, a little world. It includes an inner core of Indonesian cork wrapped in an outer core of Iberian rubber wrapped in a mantle of New Zealand wool wound tightly in a crust of American cotton thread. Major-league baseballs are assembled by hand in Turrialba, Costa Rica, where this little world's surface—two hemispheres of Holstein cowhide—is joined together by 108 stitches.

The single seam of a cricket ball is called its equator. But a baseball—sometimes sourced from five different continents—evokes the age of exploration whenever it's whipped "around the horn," a long-forgotten reference to the most dangerous voyage in maritime history. When a batter strikes out and the catcher throws the ball to third base, we don't think of the mutinous crew of the HMS *Bounty* rounding Cape Horn at the southernmost tip of South America. But we ought to, for that baseball, on its way back to the pitcher's mound, is taking the long way home, as sailors had to do before completion of the Panama Canal in 1914.

Little wonder that the baseball has been pursued and fetishized more than any other object in sport. When the manager of the

Detroit Tigers asked Pope John Paul II for a personalized autograph, the pontiff—accustomed to holy relics—was more puzzled by *what* he was writing ("To Sparky") than by the familiar sphere he was writing *on* (an official major-league baseball).

Such veneration is not just Catholic but catholic. As Hank Greenberg threatened Babe Ruth's single-season home run record in 1938, his mother, succumbing to leading questions from sportswriters, said that she would make Hank sixty-one baseball-shaped gefilte fish if he hit sixty-one home runs.

He didn't, but plenty of symbolic baseballs *have* been ingested. The presidency of former Texas Rangers owner George W. Bush was bookended by baseball eating. In the last weeks before 9/11, in her husband's first year in the Oval Office, Laura Bush commissioned a cake from White House pastry chef Roland Mesnier, a Frenchman who wheeled his masterpiece—an edible baseball—into the State Dining Room on July 4, 2001, surprising the president two days before his birthday. Seven years later, a torture investigation by the International Committee of the Red Cross alleged a terrible analogue to the president's birthday cake: Interrogators at Guantánamo Bay had forced a detainee, in an act of unmistakable symbolism, to eat a real baseball.

Like the planet it resembles, the baseball has been an instrument of oppression and salvation, of birth and death. It's at the center of the game's most famous nativity scene. When his son Mickey was born in Spavinaw, Oklahoma, in 1931, zinc miner Mutt Mantle placed a baseball in his crib. And at the other end of earthly existence, William Hulbert, founder of the National League, was buried beneath a quarter-ton granite baseball at Graceland Cemetery in Chicago. Except for the 108 stone stitches, it looks like the boulder rolled from the mouth of Christ's tomb.

Hulbert was hardly alone in his desire to ride a baseball into eternity. The knuckleballer Joe Niekro, among many others, was buried

William Hulbert headstone, Graceland Cemetery, Chicago. *(National Baseball Hall of Fame Library, Cooperstown, NY)*

with a baseball in his casket, disproving the notion that you can't take it with you.

Of course, it can also take you. Baseballs have ushered countless men into the ever after. They are such ubiquitous objects in American life that the United States Army, for much of the twentieth century, worked to weaponize them.

With the United States still two years from entering World War I, a soldier named Phil Rader, fighting with the French Foreign Legion in the spring of 1915, imagined having baseball's best pitcher by his side. "What Christy Mathewson could do to the Germans near our trenches!" Rader wrote in a column for United Press International. "The hand grenade is about the size of a baseball and it weighs only a few ounces more." Then, in 1916, six months before America's entry into World War I, an army officer invented a hand grenade that "is the size and shape of a baseball and is thrown exactly as a baseball is thrown." But the United States persisted in using cylindrical or pineapple-shaped grenades, ignoring the notion that nearly every American boy knew how to throw a baseball, but very few knew how to throw a pineapple.

"If America ever goes to war, she will have to have her bombing squads, and already there is a fertile field for recruiting," the London correspondent for the *Washington Star* wrote that summer. "It would be among the professional baseball players of the country." Already, British and Canadian troops, training together, were arguing over which method was "most efficacious" for conveying lit grenades a great distance: bowled, as a cricket ball, or thrown, as a baseball. The first question asked of Americans in the French Foreign Legion was "Are you a baseball player?"

The emblem of the French Foreign Legion was a flaming grenade, whose name derived from its resemblance to a pomegranate: a round fruit that fit the hand quite like a baseball. When the United States entered the Great War in 1917, its soldiers instantly surpassed the French as grenadiers. "Our boys already excel the French at grenade throwing on account of their baseball training," Captain Hamilton Fish of the 309th Infantry wrote to his father from France. The Americans, he reported, were throwing the grenades ten meters farther on average than the French.

In support of the war effort, the great Johnny Evers, then with the Phillies, traveled to Europe in 1919 on behalf of the Knights of Columbus, ostensibly to teach baseball in France. There, he suffered the reciprocal indignity of having a French soldier teach him the art of throwing a grenade. "He threw in a peculiar fashion," Evers recalled, "somewhat as though it were a discus, and the best throw he could make was about seventy-five feet." Later, Evers witnessed American soldiers throwing grenades three times that distance.

One of those soldiers was Hank Gowdy, the Braves catcher, whom Evers watched throw a grenade seventy-three yards in a field drill. "The French officers were immediately struck with the superiority of the American soldiers in the matter of grenade throwing,"

Evers wrote in a first-person piece for *Baseball Magazine* in 1919, "and they speedily connected this superiority with the new fangled game which Americans played."

Baseball grenadier Hank Gowdy, with John McGraw. *(Library of Congress)*

The reverse was also true: Throwing grenades improved one's baseball. Gowdy was in the 166th Infantry in France, on the front line, a position he considered excellent training for his work behind the plate at Braves Field. "This hand grenade throwing is great exercise for the arm," he wrote. "It's a little different from throwing a baseball but it sure does develop the arm and shoulder." The grenades were heavier than a baseball, a fact that buoyed Sergeant

Gowdy, who said, "I believe I can stop the fastest runner in the National League trying to steal on me with nothing to peg any heavier than a baseball." Gowdy, who led the league in caught-stealing percentage in 1915 and 1916—throwing out 55 percent of would-be stealers both seasons—improved marginally to 56 percent in 1920.

And still the baseball grenade designed by an anonymous army officer in 1916 was never issued to American GIs. But then every grenade—no matter its shape—was potentially lethal in the hand of its pitcher, a fact made eminently clearer in World War II.

In 1941, Johnny Spillane, a right-handed pitcher from Waterbury, Connecticut, declined a contract offer to pitch for the St. Louis Cardinals and instead joined the marines, as so many others did that year. On November 20, 1943, the United States was invading the Japanese-held atoll of Tarawa, in the Gilbert Islands of the South Pacific, when Corporal Spillane's amphibious landing craft ran aground on a coral reef and instantly became a sitting duck. "The Japs started lobbing hand grenades like high fouls," he recalled. Spillane threw them back with his pitching arm until one went off in his right hand. When it was amputated that night aboard a naval ship, his first thought was for the death of his pitching career.

And indeed, as he sat in the dugout before a 1944 World Series game in St. Louis—at the invitation of the National League pennant winners—Johnny was in the uniform not of the St. Louis Cardinals but of the United States Marines.

To better serve those soldiers, the U.S. military continued to build a better grenade, more easily thrown by American youths. At the end of World War II, the army's Chemical Warfare Service unveiled a new tear-gas grenade for the Corps of Military Police. The round grenade was 2½ inches in diameter and weighed five ounces, the dimensions of a big-league baseball.

Once the ringed pin was pulled, an MP threw the grenade as he would a fastball. Except that this baseball released a nonlethal cloud of chloroacetophenone on its target. In October 1945 *Popular Science* reported: "The baseball-type grenade, because of its familiar shape and weight, has proved an accurate weapon in the hands of Yankee hurlers." To hammer home the point, pitcher Dave Ferriss was photographed, in his Red Sox uniform, regarding the grenade in his outstretched hand. He looked like Hamlet holding Yorick's skull.

As World War II gave way to the Cold War, American soldiers still lacked a lethal version of the baseball grenade.

Soldiers continued to throw deadly pineapples in Korea. During that war, "communist reds" were ridiculed in the American press for their weak throwing arms. "The Chinese, lacking America's baseball tradition, just can't heave grenades very far," the Associated Press reported.

But five years later, in 1956, Dr. Cecil C. Fawcett patented a lethal baseball grenade the size and weight of a major-league baseball. It fit the hand as a perfect projectile. Like the baseball, or the stone that slew Goliath, it fairly demanded to be thrown at a target. Its payload of 2,300 steel pellets could penetrate an inch-thick pine board from fifteen feet away. And so America found itself on the brink of a new age of warfare, in which its soldiers could throw lethal strikes with an incendiary baseball.

This dream of fireballing grenadiers was not exclusive to the U.S. Army. In April 1961, a week before the American-backed invasion of the Bay of Pigs, the official newspaper of the Cuban government taunted the United States with a reference to a Minnesota Twins pitcher from Cuba. "Pedro Ramos will trade a baseball for a hand grenade," went an editorial in the *Prensa Libre,* "but it will be to silence once and for all the Yankee batteries who attack the fatherland." In Ramos, the paper couldn't have chosen a more shambolic subject. The right-hander, in 1961, was on his way to losing twenty games and leading the American League in losses for the fourth straight year; in home runs given up (for the third time in his career); and in hits given up (for the second time). He also once led the league in hit batters, and perhaps for that reason the *Prensa Libre* imagined Ramos would make a formidable grenadier.

We'll never know, of course. Rather than "silence the Yankee batteries" for Castro, Ramos *joined* the Yankee batteries, pitching for New York for three seasons in the mid-1960s, while U.S. soldiers were fighting Communism on a different front. It was there, in Vietnam, that a lethal baseball grenade was finally employed in combat, in 1969, when the M67 fragmentation grenade became standard-issue for U.S. soldiers. It was used to fight the Vietcong (and to accidentally "frag" U.S. officers) with its five-meter kill range.

The hand grenade of the Vietnam era remained 2½ inches in diameter, nearly identical to a major-league baseball, but its heavier payload made the M67 weigh fourteen ounces, almost three times as much as a regulation Spalding—a fact that did little to prevent the M67 from becoming known colloquially, within the armed forces, as a baseball.

Long before that happened, war was being described as if it were a baseball game. "The man who hit the Pearl Harbor home run for the imperial Japanese navy struck out with the bases loaded" went the first sentence of the Associated Press dispatch when Vice Admiral Chuichi Nagumo committed ritual suicide on Saipan in 1944, three years after he'd led the attack on the United States. The rhetoric hadn't changed late in the Vietnam War. "The Army is working on a...teargas grenade made of rubber that skitters around like a baseball across a rocky infield," the *Washington Star* reported in 1971. It was a nonlethal device designed to subdue civil disturbances, said Colonel Lauris Eek Jr. of the Army Research and Development Office, and would replace "the hard-shelled baseball-type grenade now in use."

The baseball grenade that Red Sox pitcher Dave Ferriss had held in his hand, Hamlet-style, twenty-five years earlier was being ditched—alas, poor Yorick, I knew it well—for one that behaved even more like a baseball.

The truth is, baseballs were weaponized long before the baseball grenade. Charles Howard Hinton, an English eccentric of the Victorian age, turned baseballs into ammunition. In the future, he thought, all baseballs would be fired from a gun, and Hinton was a man who thought quite a lot about the future.

An Oxford-educated science-fiction novelist and mathematician, Hinton was married to Mary Everest Boole, eldest daughter of George Boole, inventor of Boolean logic and thus the father of computer science. But to say that Hinton was an absentminded professor doesn't quite do him justice. At the time he was married to Mary Boole, for instance, he was also married to Maud Wheldon, making him a mathematician who evidently couldn't count to two. Fleeing England after his bigamy conviction, Hinton landed at Princeton University, where he taught math, honed his pioneering theories about the fourth dimension, and spent idle hours watching the Tigers baseball team practice.

"Among college boys," Hinton wrote, "I had noticed many a case of [a pitching] aspirant who had to relinquish all efforts to make the team because his arm gave out." To solve that problem, in 1896, Hinton conceived a device that would save the arms of young pitchers—and, he was certain, eliminate the need for pitchers entirely. He set about building a contraption that would marry two of America's most overriding obsessions: firearms and baseballs.

After experimenting with catapults, "it occurred to me that practically whenever men wished to impel a ball with velocity and precision, they drove it out of a tube with powder," Hinton wrote. "Following then the course of history, I determined to use a cannon." And so he built a baseball-firing cannon that proved wildly temperamental. Sometimes the ball "merely roll[ed] out of the muzzle," as he put it; other times it was expelled with "prodigious velocity."

As Hinton explained to three hundred members of the Princeton Club in 1897, "The baseball is placed in the barrel of the cannon as an ordinary cannon ball, and is expelled by the pressure of air which comes from the rifle when a cartridge in the latter is discharged."

That cartridge was discharged when the batter stepped on a metal plate, sending an electrical impulse through a wire to the cannon, activating the cartridge of powder and, one would assume—a split-second later—the bowels of the batter.

It became clear in its very first exhibition—on its very first pitch, in fact—that Hinton's cannon made baseballs ballistic. "There was a muffled report, a puff of smoke and the ball went whizzing toward the plate," reported the *Boston Daily Globe*. "It appeared so suddenly that the batsman ducked [and] the catcher made a wild leap to one side while the ball sailed directly over the plate and up against the backstop with a resounding crack." Subsequent pitches were less accurate. One of the game's participants, Captain Bradley, was reportedly hit "in the breast and floor," which was surely every bit as painful as it sounds.

Hinton retreated for a year to hone his cannon's precision, and to reduce its bulk to "a handy and portable weapon." He returned in 1897 with a baseball-firing rifle, a gun so accurate he called it Cupid. The papers called it "the Princeton Gun" or "the Baseball Gun." Another exhibition was staged on the Princeton varsity field, between two campus social clubs: the Ivy Club and Tiger Inn. The gun impelled a baseball, with a puff of smoke, at seventy miles an hour. Two finger-like rods inserted by choice into the rim of the cannon barrel allowed the baseballs to curve. Cupid's accuracy was such that only four walks were issued. "It was obvious that a little practice operating the machine would produce almost perfect accuracy," an eyewitness reported. Hinton foresaw the day when a single inaccurate pitch would constitute a base on balls, and pitchers—newly rendered redundant—would remain by Cupid's side to field the position and feed the beast its baseballs.

But in fact the baseball gun was so effective that it rendered itself almost instantly obsolete. As a correspondent covering the exhibition put it, "Batters having accustomed themselves to the pitcher's motion find it difficult to hit a ball delivered by an automaton." Their fears and protests could not be overcome. Hitters, recognizing themselves as cannon fodder, were not eager to face the gun a second time, while the smoke still curled from its turret and the air still whistled with the sound of smoking baseball.

Hinton left his Princeton post within months of demonstrating his baseball gun and would go on to vet the inventions of others as the second assistant examiner in the U.S. Patent Office. It is unlikely that he saw, at the turn of the century, the handiwork of Joseph Beit, a photographer and inventor in West Chester, Pennsylvania, who built a device of his own that shot baseballs out of the Chester County Courthouse on summer days at noon. Beit's targets were considerably more receptive than Hinton's. Crowds of children would gather at the courthouse at midday, awaiting Beit's fusillade of horsehide. There was something gratifying—and deeply challenging—about catching a baseball that fell from a clear blue sky.

Construction of the Washington Monument began in 1848 and continued—off and on, as funding and peacetime allowed—for the next thirty-six years. By 1874, when the unfinished obelisk had risen to nearly half its height, there was a "baseball ground" at its base.

By the time the tower was completed, on December 6, 1884, the monument was instantly recognized as both a towering memorial to the city's namesake and a kind of dare to baseball's finest fielders. Professionals wondered—on road swings through the nation's capital—if any among them could catch a baseball dropped from the top of the obelisk.

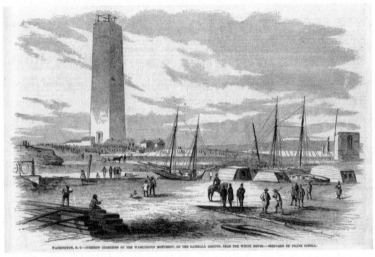

Washington Monument, half completed, in 1874, with a baseball field in the foreground. *(Library of Congress)*

"As regularly as the ball teams visited Washington there would be a controversy that no base ball player could catch a ball thrown from this height to the ground beneath," wrote a correspondent in *Sporting Life.* "It has been held that no man could hold fast to a ball dropped 500 feet in sheer space."

And so, in the spirit of other nineteenth-century quests—Moby-Dick, say, or Stanley's search for Livingstone—an expedition of Washington Nationals set out for the monument on January 9, 1885. The players had waited for only thirty-three days after it opened. A member of their party took the elevator to the top and, one by one, began raining baseballs onto his teammates below. Among them was catcher Phil Baker, who disdained the fairly recent phenomenon of a protective leather glove, relying instead on his bare hands, on which he would break six fingers in his career.

"[A] ball was thrown from one of the small windows with some force," the *Washington Post* reported the next day. "Baker, in one instance, gauged its fall correctly and caught it in his hands, but almost immediately dropped it."

Given that a pop fly seldom ascends higher than 150 feet, and that this ball fell from 555 feet, it should not have surprised Baker that two knuckles of his right hand were broken. But of course it did surprise him. As Baker told an interviewer in 1932, when he was a seventy-five-year-old man in Akron, Ohio, "I decided right then that I'd never try a stunt like that again."

But others were eager to do so. It was the kind of bar bet beloved by idle athletes, nurtured in the hothouse of stifling trains. Chicago Colts player-manager Cap Anson was especially obsessed with the monument, and, on August 25, 1894, at the end of a series in Washington, he volunteered catcher William (Pop) Schriver to attempt an assault on this baseball Everest, albeit an Everest equipped with an elevator.

Teammates Clark Griffith and Wild Bill Hutchinson were dispatched up the elevator, and Griffith—future father of my first boss—dropped a test ball from the north window. When that ball did not burrow into the earth, as some had feared, but instead rebounded ten feet into the air, Schriver was emboldened. Wearing a glove, he caught and held on to the very next ball, at which time a "highly indignant" policeman intervened. "He talked of arrests," *Sporting Life* noted, "but was finally coaxed into a more amiable temper, and the party came up town joyously, with Schriver a hero. Schriver says that the ball was 'hot,' but no more so than if it had come from the bat of a vigorous player."

Alas, Schriver's historic feat eventually faded from memory, and by 1908 two Washington socialites—W. J. Preston Gibson and John Biddle—wagered $500 on whether a man could catch a ball dropped from the monument. On August 21 of that summer, Senators catcher Gabby Street stood beneath the monument and caught the thirteenth ball thrown by Gibson, who later labeled it in black ink: AUGUST 21, 1908, 11:30 A.M. DROPPED FROM THE WASHINGTON MONUMENT BY W. J. PRESTON GIBSON, CAUGHT BY GABBY STREET. 550 FEET, 135 FEET PER SECOND.

In 1964, the ball was discovered by Gibson's son, James, when he sold his family's Georgetown mansion at 3017 N Street to the recently widowed Jacqueline Kennedy, who had somehow not insisted that the ball be included in the sale price.

Street's catch received national attention, and was wrongly but widely reported to have been the first catch of its kind. "Ever since Street accomplished his feat base ball catchers the country over have been talking about it, and not a few of them have confessed a desire to emulate it," according to the 1910 edition of *The Reach Official American League Base Ball Guide*, written with the flair of a Harlequin Romance. "[Billy] Sullivan was among this number, and on each visit of his team to Washington he would spend many hours gazing longingly and speculatively at the top of the big stone shaft."

Armed with a permit from park service police, White Sox catcher Billy Sullivan caught three of thirty-nine balls thrown from the big shaft on August 24, 1910. Within a month, the aviator Charles F. Willard thought it would be "great sport" to fly an airplane fortified with baseballs one thousand feet over Hawthorne Race Course in Cicero, Illinois, dropping them one by one into Sullivan's hungry mitt. Sullivan declined the offer, saying prophetically that he "might as well try to stop a bullet as to be on the receiving end of one whizzing from an aeroplane."

Still, once an airplane was mentioned, it became like the gun in a Chekhov play. It had to go off—and it did, in 1914, in spring training, when Brooklyn manager Wilbert Robinson, for reasons known only to him, agreed to catch a baseball dropped 525 feet from a Wright Model B biplane flown over Daytona Beach. Preparing to take off that day, aviatrix Ruth Law realized she had forgotten a vital piece of equipment. Which is to say, a baseball. A man on the ground with a grapefruit in his lunch offered it to Law as a substitute. And so she brought the breakfast fruit on board instead, unbeknownst to Robinson. When the falling orb stopped whistling on descent and finally hit him in the chest—exploding in a spray of red—Robinson thought, not unreasonably, that he had been killed.

Then as now, the grapefruit was at the upper end of the hail continuum, on which weathermen describe hail as golf-ball-sized, baseball-sized, or grapefruit-sized. And the hail continued to fall from the heavens throughout the next decade, when another attempt was made to catch a baseball from a passing airplane. On July 22, 1926, wearing his National Guard uniform, Babe Ruth circled beneath a biplane at Mitchel Field on Long Island. Such was the allure of these "stunt catches," as they came to be known, that Ruth continued trying to shag flies—necktie knotted tightly in ninety-seven-degree heat—until he succeeded on his seventh attempt.

But because Ruth's ball dropped from a mere 300 feet, the Washington Monument remained the white-marble standard of stunt catches, 555 feet (and 5⅛ inches) of silent Everestian challenge. And so it remained until a group of Ohioans on the Come to Cleveland Committee had a novel idea in 1938. The committee would invite a member of the Indians to break the record shared by Schriver, Street, and Sullivan by catching a ball dropped from the city's Terminal Tower. In doing so, the committee hoped to "let the world know that Cleveland has other things besides Torso murders," as the *Brooklyn Daily Eagle* indelicately put it, referring to the serial killer then decapitating and dismembering his victims in the city.

Babe Ruth in his National Guard uniform, shagging flies dropped from an airplane, at Mitchel Field on Long Island, July 22, 1926. (© Bettmann/CORBIS)

And so on August 20, 1938, Indians third-string catcher Hank Helf, in dress slacks, cabana shirt, and steel helmet, prepared to field balls thrown from the observation deck of the tallest building between New York and Chicago. Terminal Tower rose 708 feet above Helf, and 10,000 spectators gathered behind a cordon. Indians third baseman Ken Keltner—who three summers later would rob Joe DiMaggio to end his fifty-six-game hitting streak—threw the first ball from the fifty-second floor. Keltner let it drop to the sidewalk, and watched with growing disquiet as it rebounded fifty feet into the air.

Two more balls followed until Helf, on the fourth attempt, caught a ball that was falling 138 miles an hour at impact. "They looked like aspirin tablets coming down," he said. "We were dumb enough to think it wouldn't be dangerous."

It may or may not have inspired anyone to come to Cleveland, but the ensuing publicity did attract all manner of copycat catchers. Pedestrians in various American cities might have thought the clouds were seeded with Spaldings the next summer, when Phillies catcher Dave Coble caught a ball dropped from the top of the William Penn Tower in Philadelphia. "It felt as though a man had jumped into my arms," he said.

The same year, in San Francisco, at the Golden Gate International Exposition on Treasure Island, an aging San Francisco Seals catcher named Joe Sprinz caught five balls that fell 450 feet from the expo's tallest attraction, the Tower of the Sun. The stunt went so well that Seals pitcher turned publicity man Walter Mails persuaded Sprinz to up the ante, and field a ball thrown from a blimp.

On August 3, 1939 — the catcher's thirty-seventh birthday, and a mere twenty-one months since the *Hindenburg* disaster — Joe Sprinz stood on the Treasure Island baseball field, before two thousand fans, gazing up at a zeppelin impossibly high in the sky. The first ball it dropped, from a height of 1,200 feet, crashed into an empty section of stands. Sprinz missed the second one entirely, and the ball buried itself in the turf like an unexploded cannonball.

The third ball fell directly into Sprinz's mitt, which could impede but not entirely arrest its progress, traveling as it was at 150 miles an hour. The gloved ball smashed into the catcher's face, breaking his jaw in twelve places and knocking out five teeth. Physicists at the University of California estimated the impact as 8,050 foot-pounds — like catching an 8,000-pound parcel dropped from one foot above. Sprinz was hospitalized for several weeks, and when he finally could speak he echoed Hank Helf. "It looked like an aspirin it looked so small," he also said of the descending baseball, aspirin and other pain remedies then very much on his mind.

Seals owner Charles Graham said, somewhat unnecessarily, "This is the end of that kind of a stunt involving any of my players." And to this day the same has held true for all other players, bar one.

Former minor-league player Jackie Price traveled to major- and minor-league parks, where he fired baseballs into the sky from a pneumatic tube, pursued them across the outfield in a jeep, and caught the "monstrous flies" in his glove hand while steering with his meat hand.

Price could do more things with a baseball than any man before or since. He would hang from a miniature trapeze and take batting practice upside down, lining balls to all fields. He could hold three baseballs in his right hand and pitch them simultaneously to three separate catchers. Or pitch two balls at once, one of them a fastball, one a curve. From the catcher's position, Price could throw two balls with a single motion, one of them to the pitcher's mound, the other to second base.

Jackie Price, upside down like a vampire bat. *(National Baseball Hall of Fame Library, Cooperstown, NY)*

Casey Stengel had managed against Price in Milwaukee and said, "I get mad at the ball players today that can't bunt. This fella could take the bat like this"—Stengel held it out like a rifle—"and *plunk* with the end of it like a pool cue." Price could also lay down a bunt with the *knob* end of the bat, though there was, alas, little call for that in major-league baseball.

Nevertheless, in the closing weeks of the 1946 season Cleveland owner Bill Veeck signed Price to play shortstop for the Indians, despite his having played only two seasons in the previous decade in the minors. An exceedingly skinny man, Price favored leopard-print shirts and often wore a snakeskin belt with the live snake still in it. "He liked his snakes so much that he used to wear them around his waist," wrote Veeck, though Price also kept snakes in his shirts. (At home, the snakes took their repose in his dresser drawer.)

In 1947, the Indians were traveling by train to a spring training game in California when teammate Joe Gordon persuaded Price, whom Veeck had kept on, to remove the snake he was wearing as a belt and loose it down the aisle of the dining car, where a party of lady bowlers was eating. Indians player-manager Lou Boudreau, displeased with the chaos caused by Snakes on a Train, sent Price home, ending his major-league career after seven games.

Price made a meager living throughout the 1950s, invariably billed again as a baseball "clown," but by the following decade there was little call for his manifold skills, and he lived out his final years in San Francisco, where he was reported to have taken his own life on October 2, 1967. He isn't a clown, Veeck said while Price was still alive: "He is an artist."

The sad end to a happy life catching baseballs as they fell from the heavens was one more reminder that the pursuit of these objects was often a fraught and melancholy proposition.

Children have chased after lost balls throughout time, with bad results. At the turn of the last century, New York City newspapers told cautionary tales of boys who hit baseballs into neighboring yards with tragic consequences. In 1902, sixteen-year-old Max Bengersen retrieved a ball from his Brooklyn neighbor's flower garden. The "annoyed" homeowner, cigar maker John Biesel, shot him dead, instilling fear in any child whose ball rolled into the neighbor's yard.

Two years later, on September 30, 1904, fourteen-year-old Christian Koehler climbed a fence in Harlem in pursuit of a baseball that had landed in a vacant lot. There, the great Simon P. Gillis was practicing his hammer throws.

Gillis had competed in that summer's Olympics, and would go on to throw in the 1908 and 1912 Games. Gillis was such a giant figure in every sense of the phrase that he and a group of fellow field athletes had become renowned in the early part of the previous century as the Irish Whales. Coaches urged them to gluttony to improve their throwing distance, and once, Gillis and two other Whales, having phoned in an order of twenty-seven dozen oysters and six steaks, arrived at the restaurant to find their table set for thirty-three people.

"Will you wait for the group?" asked the maître d'.

"We *are* the group," Gillis said.

It was an almost unbelievable misfortune, then, that Christian Koehler clambered over that fence in 1904 just as Gillis released his sixteen-pound hammer. Shouts of warning went unheard. The boy was struck in the head and died instantly. The tragedy left Gillis heartbroken, and served as yet another high-profile reminder of the perils of pursuing a baseball.

Those people who weren't pursuing baseballs in the last century often found baseballs pursuing them. Don Larsen, not expecting to pitch, went out for beers the night before Game 5 of the 1956 World

Series. The morning of the game, he arrived at his Yankee Stadium locker to find a baseball in his left shoe. That's how Larsen—like countless pitchers before him—learned he would be starting on that soon-to-be-famous day.

After jumping into Larsen's arms at the end of the first (and still only) perfect game in World Series history, Yankees catcher Yogi Berra gave the pitcher the ball from the final out, when Dodgers pinch hitter Dale Mitchell was called out looking. Larsen held on to that ball for forty-six years. In 2002, he auctioned it—and the cap, glove, and spikes he wore that day—for $120,750.

By then, historic baseballs had become lottery balls. In 1961, Associated Press photographer Harry Harris, covering spring training, ran into the world's most famous divorcés in a Florida hotel lobby. Harris fumbled for a baseball he happened to have in his pocket, which Joe DiMaggio and Marilyn Monroe—on vacation, attempting to reconcile—agreed to sign. In 2006, the Harris estate sold that baseball at auction for $191,200.

Other fortunes fell from the sky. Philip Ozersky, a research scientist at Washington University School of Medicine, attended a St. Louis Cardinals game with coworkers in 1998. When Cardinals slugger Mark McGwire hit his then-record-setting seventieth home run, the ball bounced off the hands of two different colleagues before it fell, in the left field stands, into the hands of Ozersky, who at the time earned $30,000 a year and lived in a house he rented with his girlfriend.

Enter Todd McFarlane, who made his fortune as a comic-book artist and entrepreneur. At Guernsey's auction house, McFarlane bought Ozersky's baseball for a record $3.05 million, explaining: "Women don't have the same silly wants and needs that men have. Guys can just look at this sedate piece of rawhide and go: 'Whooooa. It's *the ball.*'"

That sedate piece of rawhide, with the right provenance, is

seductive. The writers of *The Simpsons* invented the sexiest possible piece of sports memorabilia when they had Bart marvel, through the fogged glass of a baseball-card shop: "Wow! A baseball made out of Secretariat!"

A baseball need not even be real to be desired. In 1987, Dave Bresnahan, a twenty-five-year-old catcher for the Williamsport Bills of the Double-A Eastern League, had a transformative idea. The Reading Phillies had a runner on third when Bresnahan caught a pitch and then intentionally fired it over the third baseman's head and into left field. When the Phillies runner broke for home, Bresnahan tagged him out with the baseball in his mitt. He hadn't thrown a baseball into left field after all. He had thrown a potato, peeled and then carved. Bresnahan's furious manager immediately pulled him from the game, and the next day, the Cleveland Indians released him, for conduct unbecoming a Double-A catcher.

But the keeper of the Baseball Reliquary, a museum of baseball ephemera in Pasadena, did not let the story die there. So he kept what he claimed were the desiccated remains of the Bresnahan potato spotlighted in a jar of denatured alcohol in his shrine. The reliquary also displayed a dozen major-league baseballs bearing the forged signature of Mother Teresa, allegedly seized in an FBI sports-memorabilia sting called "Operation Bullpen."

The reliquary's Bresnahan potato is a fake. The original tuber is lost to history. And the Mother Teresa baseballs are also bogus— they are forgeries of forgeries. The exhibits are part of an art installation that plays on public reverence for, and fascination with, baseball's artifacts, chief of which is the baseball itself.

America's fascination with the baseball may be explained, in part, by decades of denial. As late as the Depression, many baseball fans were required to return any balls hit into the stands, and most complied, as they still do at tennis matches.

But many did not. As *Sporting Life* editorialized in 1913: "It is rather disconcerting, if not inconvenient, for a fan who is in the throes of the excitement that a close contest entails to have his pet corn trod and trampled on by a big, clumsy, lumbering special policeman, whose feet are as wide as an elephant's, come charging through the aisles and packed side rows in a frantic and usually unsuccessful endeavor to capture a ball from the grasping clutches of a relic-seeking old gentleman or a small boy who wants to show his playmates a 'real dollar-and-a-half big league base ball.' "

Fans sometimes handed foul balls to servicemen seated nearby, as cops and security guards seldom fought soldiers for the safe return of a ball.

In 1916, Cubs owner Charlie Weeghman wearied of fighting his own customers and became the first owner to let fans keep the baseballs. Not every owner followed suit. In 1921, the Giants, as was their custom at the Polo Grounds, ejected a thirty-one-year-old stockbroker named Reuben Berman for failing to turn over a foul ball. Berman sued the team and won $100 for his mental and physical distress.

The following season, at the Baker Bowl in Philadelphia, eleven-year-old Robert Cotter declined to return a foul ball at a Phillies game. The club had a reluctant policeman arrest the boy on a larceny charge, for which he was—it scarcely seems possible now—jailed overnight. The Phillies' business manager, William Shettsline, had been looking to make a test case over a $1.50 baseball. That he chose an eleven-year-old boy as his scapegoat was a tactical error, to say the least.

The judge in the case was not sympathetic to the Phillies. "I don't know whether you or Shettsline were ever boys, for if you were you would know how they cherish the ball they get, and you would permit them to have the ball instead of throwing them into a cell overnight," he told the club's attorney. "Such an act on the part of a boy is merely proof that he is following his own natural impulses."

Shortly after *Phillies v. Cotter,* fans were allowed to keep foul balls and home runs, with one notable exception. During World War II, teams prominently placed barrels on the field for the collection of baseballs hit into the stands. The balls were to be shipped overseas, for use by American servicemen, and any fans who failed to return foul balls to the field of play were often persuaded to do so by their seatmates. The *New York Times* columnist John Kieran witnessed "a one-round knockout of a gent who refused to give. It was a most amusing sight."

Two Barry Bonds home run baseballs—his record seventy-third of the 2001 season and the milestone six hundredth of his career— were the subjects of lawsuits between fans claiming to have been robbed of the ball in the bleacher scrum. But then the quest for an elusive baseball has been a part of American life for as long as the game has been played. John Irving's novel *A Prayer for Owen Meany* centers on a missing baseball that killed the protagonist's mother. Don DeLillo opens *Underworld* at the Giants–Dodgers playoff of October 3, 1951, with a kid attempting to find Bobby Thomson's game-winning "Shot Heard 'Round the World" home run ball. The kid's name is Cotter Martin, an echo of Robert Cotter, detained in Philadelphia for daring to keep the baseball that was hit to him.

By that year, 1951, the annual production of major-league baseballs required the hides of thirty-five thousand horses, most of them American breeds who'd given their lives for "medical purposes," as one contemporary account put it. But with each passing decade, horsehide was getting harder to come by.

For many years, major-league horsehide came from France and Belgium, where young animals were slaughtered for meat. (Babe Ruth was swatting bleached French horsehide into the bleachers at Yankee Stadium.) But the German occupation of those countries in World War II cut off the supply line.

So the major leagues switched first to Bolivian horsehide, then, in 1943, to hide from domestic animals. With Japan occupying Malaya and the Dutch East Indies, rubber had been rationed. So Spalding tried balata at the center of its baseballs. Alas, balata—from the milky juice of the Guyanese bully tree—is inelastic. And it showed instantly.

On Opening Day, the powerhouse Cardinals lost 1–0 in eleven innings. The next day, they lost 1–0 in ten innings. Eleven of the first twenty-nine games in both leagues were shutouts. Reds general manager Warren Giles, in frustration, dropped a bag of balata balls off the roof of Crosley Field onto the sidewalk below. Then he did the same with a bag of 1942 baseballs. The old ones bounced an average of 13 feet, the new ones just 9½. A scientific study at New York's Cooper Union got the same results. By early summer, Spalding acknowledged its mistake and replaced the balata with a synthetic rubber cement that returned resilience to baseballs.

This satisfied the naysayers. But what of the neigh-sayers, the ever scarcer horses who gave their hides for the national pastime? Spalding managed to keep baseballs covered in horsehide until 1974, when the company switched to abundant American Holstein cows.

Rawlings, meanwhile, sewed its bleached horsehides together in Haiti, having moved its plant there from Puerto Rico in 1969. Labor was cheaper in Haiti and workers became skilled with leather. Gucci handbags were made there under the dictatorship of Jean-Claude Duvalier. So were Pierre Cardin belts. After Duvalier was overthrown in 1986, Rawlings left Haiti for the political stability of Costa Rica, and baseballs now make the journey from factory floor in Turrialba to game action at major-league stadiums in as little as two weeks.

All of this started with a lumpen orb. The first baseballs had a solid core, made of lead or another hard substance, wrapped in yarn and covered with a single piece of brown leather. These "lemon-peel" or "rose-petal" balls, their white stitches forming an *X* pattern, resembled a closed rosebud—that evocative word that instantly took "Citizen Kane" back to his childhood.

Because the leather cover wasn't bleached, the balls were brown. They could be ordered dead, medium, or live, depending on the density of the stuffing. The balls were also smaller and softer than they are today: Until 1845, fielders could throw the ball at the runner for a putout, "tucking him out" or "soaking" him.

The great leap forward for the baseball, like the great leap forward for the swimsuit, was the introduction of the two-piecer. The Edison of the two-piece baseball cover is often said to be Colonel William A. Cutler, whose ball went into production by H. P. Harwood & Sons in Natick, Massachusetts, in 1858.

But a shoemaker's son, Ellis Drake, of nearby Stoughton, Massachusetts, also claimed authorship of the two-piece cover. Near the end of his life, in 1909, he told the *Stoughton Sentinel* that the first baseballs he knew had a lead center, were wrapped tightly in knitting yarn, and were then covered in a single scrap of leather chamois.

"One day in school when the teacher was not looking—it was a rare moment—I took a sheet of paper and made a diagram of a baseball cover in its present form. It was just a thought that came to me."

Drake made a prototype but neglected to take out a patent, an oversight for which he sounded both resigned and embittered. "It is a satisfaction to me to think that I have been able to confer some pleasure on the world," he said, "though I have never received a thank you or a complimentary ticket to a ball game."

By the 1870s, London-born Philadelphia Athletics outfielder Al Reach was manufacturing his own baseballs under the brand name A. J. Reach. Boston Red Stockings shortstop George Wright—son of an English immigrant—was manufacturing his own as well. With his partner, Henry Ditson, Wright expanded into tennis, hockey, and golf equipment. To spur club sales, George Wright would design one of America's first public golf courses, Franklin Park in Boston.

The following year, at the National Association's convention in New York, the baseball's dimensions were fixed: Balls should weigh between 5 and 5¼ ounces and measure between 9 and 9¼ inches in circumference, with a two-piece cover in figure-eight stitching. The dimensions have not changed to this day. That Reach and Wright were essentially creating America's sporting-goods industry was not lost on Wright's Boston teammate.

In 1876, Chicago White Stockings owner William Hulbert lured the game's best pitcher, Albert G. Spalding, away from the Boston Red Stockings and back to his native Illinois. Hulbert, with the help

An 1883 baseball being inspected by a U.S. patent officer in 1925. *(Library of Congress)*

of Spalding, set about persuading seven teams, including Boston, to leave the National Association and form a breakaway new league, the National League of Professional Baseball Clubs.

Spalding won forty-six games in 1876, increasing the wattage of his stardom and the breadth of his influence. Spalding was the first star player to wear a protective glove on his catching hand, in 1877, and a year after his move to Chicago, he opened a sporting-goods store in which to sell those gloves, plus his own brand of baseball, for which he became the exclusive supplier to the brand-new National League, a distinction that Spalding would hold for the next hundred years.

But this near monopoly on America was not enough. From October 1888 to April 1889, Spalding traveled the globe, a trip chronicled in a wonderful book by Mark Lamster called *Spalding's World Tour.* Over thirty thousand miles and five continents, Spalding's White Stockings played exhibition games against a team of All-Stars, in an effort to promote friendship among nations— Spalding's middle name literally was Goodwill—but also to sell baseballs to the wider world. "The famous baseball genius has been at work for several months on a plan to carry the game into foreign fields at the furthest ends of the earth," reported the *St. Paul Pioneer Press,* "and at the same time bring back a bountiful store of shekels."

Spalding's raucous party of ballplayers, entertainers, and assorted hangers-on sailed to Hawaii that fall aboard the cruise liner *Alameda.* After losing five baseballs overboard, Spalding forbade all members of his traveling party from playing catch at sea.

That party included comedian Frank Lincoln, a black "mascot" named Clarence Duval, and a one-eyed "aerialist" who called himself Professor C. Bartholomew. At an exhibition in Adelaide, Australia, Bartholomew dangled from a trapeze that in turn dangled from a hot-air balloon hovering two thousand feet in the air. When Bartholomew leaped from his trapeze, and his parachute deployed too late, he hit the chimney of a hotel. The fall didn't kill him, but it did dampen, for the rest of the tour, the professor's enthusiasm for performing.

Ballplayers behaved then as they might today. Spalding's players tried, and failed, to throw a baseball over the Great Pyramid of Giza. They were photographed *climbing* the Sphinx, where one of them threw a baseball at its eye. In Rome, officials declined Spalding's offer of $5,000 to let his teams play an exhibition in the Colosseum. On and on the tour went, for the entirety of an American winter — Ceylon, Naples, Rome, Paris, London, Glasgow, Belfast, Dublin — Spalding attempting to sell his little world to the world at large, hoping an Italian's first experience of the game would prove as captivating as his was, in Illinois.

Spalding's players on the Sphinx, 1889. *(National Baseball Hall of Fame Library, Cooperstown, NY)*

As a boy, Spalding had watched from the sidelines as older kids played baseball games in his native Rockford. One day, a baseball was hit toward him. It was his entrée not only into that baseball game, but into the game itself. "Talk about special Providence!" he wrote years later. "That ball came for me straight as an arrow. Impulsively I sprang to my feet, reached for it with my right hand, held it for a moment, and then threw it home on an air-line to the catcher."

Even as a wealthy man—a wealth built in part on the selling of baseballs—Spalding never failed to be enthralled by the baseball as a physical object. Whenever one of the game's dignitaries died, Spalding would send a funeral wreath composed of white immortelles in the shape of a baseball. When Spalding himself died in 1915, in Point Loma, California, his body was cremated. This was in stark contrast to his partner in forming the National League, Hulbert, who remains buried in Chicago beneath that giant granite baseball embossed with the names of the original National League cities, and figure-eight patterned with 108 stone stitches.

Those 108 stitches recall this world, the ancient world, and—in some religions—the world to come. By happy coincidence, there are also 108 Hindu deities, 108 sins in Buddhism, 108 prayer beads on the *Japa mala,* or Hindu rosary. That number, so fraught in Hindu culture, was introduced in the early twenty-first century as the unifying emergency telephone number in the Indian subcontinent, where 108 is now the equivalent of 911—a number equally fraught, for very different reasons, in America.

In the weeks following the attacks of September 11, 2001, New York firefighter Vin Mavaro was "working the pile" at Ground Zero, sifting through fine rubble for human remains, when he saw what he thought was a chunk of concrete. As he reached for it, he saw red stitching. To Mavaro's astonishment, it was a baseball, intact and emblazoned with the corporate logo of TradeWeb, whose offices had been on the fifty-first floor of the North Tower.

Ball from TradeWeb, whose offices were on the
fifty-first floor of the North Tower of the World
Trade Center, found in the rubble at Ground
Zero, 2001. *(Milo Stewart Jr./National Baseball
Hall of Fame Library, Cooperstown, NY)*

That baseball instantly joined other artifacts—notably, a cast-
iron cross of beams salvaged from the wreckage—as symbols of
hope and recovery in the days after 9/11. Mavaro, a Mets fan, offered
the baseball to the Baseball Hall of Fame, which put it in a traveling
exhibit. That exhibit was called, inevitably, "Baseball as America,"
but might as well have been titled "*The* Baseball as America."

Like Spalding's baseball-shaped funeral wreaths, the baseball
offered token comfort to the grieving. As the twenty-first century
dawned, the baseball—five continents united in a uniquely American object—had become a kind of white immortelle in its own
right.

Chapter 2

STAIRWAY TO HEAVEN

On a map, St. Kitts and Nevis is a Rorschach test: one nation comprising two islands that look like different things to different people around the world.

Depending on what you read, narrow St. Kitts is shaped like "a guitar," "a paddle," or "a pineapple lying on its side." In tandem with circular Nevis, the two islands resemble "a sperm whale swimming away from a giant beach ball," "an upside-down ice cream cone," and "a tennis racquet and ball."

These and other analogies—made in every Caribbean guidebook, cruise-line pamphlet, and travel agent's brochure—tend toward the tropical. They evoke—and are often meant to inspire—vacations. The smaller of the two islands has been called "sombrero-shaped Nevis."

The World Factbook, prepared by the Central Intelligence Agency for the use of U.S. government officials, describes the geography of 266 countries and dependencies without rhetorical filigree—or at least it does until you get to St. Kitts and Nevis.

"With coastlines in the shape of a baseball bat and ball," reads the CIA's entry on that nation, "the two volcanic islands are separated by a 3-km-wide channel called The Narrows; on the southern tip of long, baseball bat–shaped St. Kitts lies the Great Salt Pond;

Nevis Peak sits in the center of its almost circular namesake island and its ball shape complements that of its sister."

To American eyes, the coastlines *do* look like a baseball bat and ball. But they just as closely conjure a turkey leg and dollop of mashed potatoes. Perhaps it was a spring day, shortly after lunch, when a sated CIA officer wrote the *Factbook* entry for St. Kitts and Nevis, and thus saw a bat and ball instead of Thanksgiving dinner.

It certainly wouldn't be the first time the CIA was preoccupied with the physical objects of baseball. In 2003, when George W. Bush, former owner of the Texas Rangers, was president, the United States went to war in Iraq on the testimony of a single Iraqi defector. That informant claimed — falsely, it turned out — to have worked in a biological weapons plant in his homeland. The man's name was Rafid Ahmed Alwan al-Janabi, but he is better known to history by his CIA cryptonym: Curveball.

When Bush's father, the former CIA director George H. W. Bush, was president, he kept his 1945 first baseman's mitt from Yale, a Rawlings Claw, in a desk drawer. He would sometimes pound his fist into the pocket when considering counsel. In 1990, the United States went to war in the Persian Gulf. The first missile fired in Operation Desert Storm bore the oval logo of the Louisville Slugger, hand-painted by personnel aboard the ship from which it was launched, the USS *Louisville.*

Desert Storm was the prequel to the Iraq War. It is a straight line from the Louisville Slugger to Curveball. All of which is to say that where there's a ball, it's in our nature to see a bat. And where there's a bat, it's in our nature to find a ball. The impulse — to judge by St. Kitts and Nevis — may even be in nature itself.

Early bats, befitting that pioneer age, were hewn from wagon tongues and axles. As in golf, specialized implements arose for striking the ball in a specific way. Some bats had a flat face, as on a cricket bat, to better exploit bunting. The short-lived banana bat was curved, like a jai alai cesta, to apply spin to the batted ball.

Many bats didn't taper at the handle at all, so that the batter—like the housewife in a '50s sitcom—appeared to be brandishing a rolling pin at the pitcher. Napoleon Lajoie got many of his 3,242 hits with a two-knobbed bat, the upper knob designed to support his upper hand. That very phrase—upper hand—is synonymous with a dominant advantage.

At the turn of the last century, catalogs offered several brands of mushroom bat, the most famous of which was A. G. Spalding's: Instead of a small knob at the end, the handle appeared to be detonating a large mushroom cloud. The bat industry, likewise, was exploding at the dawn of the twentieth century, most notably in Louisville, Kentucky.

The reluctant father of that explosion came—like Einstein and Oppenheimer, fathers of the nuclear mushroom cloud—from a German family with an eye on America. Johann Frederich Hillerich emigrated from Baden-Baden and settled—after a short residence in Baltimore—in Louisville, where photographs always feature him with a long beard, the worst possible affectation for a woodworker determined to spend life over a belt-driven lathe.

But Hillerich was, in every other respect, averse to risk. His wood-working shop, J. F. Hillerich, Job Turning, opened for business in 1864 and would soon produce wooden bedposts and balusters, ten-pins and bowling balls, porch columns, and other items for the growing middle class. His creations were cozily domestic, if a little sleep-inducing. He wanted to build beautiful staircases for respectable homes. He had great success with a swinging butter churn, the "dairy swing churn," in which the butter was gently rocked rather than hand-agitated. The dairy swing churn could accommodate an attachment for rocking babies to sleep, and Hillerich's story would be equally narcotizing (and long forgotten) if not for the apprenticeship he offered, in 1884, to his seventeen-year-old son, John (Bud) Hillerich.

Bud was American born, with an American nickname and an American passion for baseball. According to the most persistent of the various creation myths that surround his invention, Bud attended a game at Eclipse Park one afternoon, when the eccentric star of the Louisville Spiders, Pete Browning, broke a bat. The loss of that bat was not inconsequential, especially if you imbued bats with personalities, as many players did and still do. According to his biographer, Philip Von Borries, Browning kept a store of his retired bats—broken or otherwise bereft of hits—that he named after biblical figures.

In the grand narrative of his improbable life, Browning knew personal bereavement, which began early, with the loss of both his hearing (to a condition called mastoiditis) and his father (to a cyclone).

He was barely literate and frequently drunk. A typical dispatch— this one from the *New York Times*—began: "Just before the game to-day, 'Pete' Browning, who has been on a howling drunk, was fined $110 by manager Kelley, of the Louisvilles."

Occasionally seized by daydreams on the field, Browning was leading off first base in a game against St. Louis in 1886 when pitcher Dave Foutz walked over to the bag and tagged him out for an exceedingly rare unassisted pickoff.

The next season, with his team bound for Cincinnati and a weekend series, Browning was left behind in Louisville when he was "too intoxicated to find his way to the train." He arrived in Cincinnati in time for the Sunday game, "but he was still suffering from the effects of his debauch." With his team down 2–0, Browning hit a double to lead off an inning that day. But "he played about fifteen feet off second base," an eyewitness wrote, "and fell asleep there. The ball was passed to McPhee, who walked up and put him out to the intense disgust of the spectators."

Browning had literally been caught napping off second, but considered the drink essential to his game. "The Gladiator drank more than was necessary to 'keep his lamps in good trim,'" according to an 1890 newspaper account, referring to Browning's extraordinary eyes, which he called his *lamps, lampterines,* or *peepers.* "Still, he played good ball."

Browning became one of the best ballplayers of his day despite — he would have said *because of* — these and other eccentricities, which were myriad. He fielded fly balls on one leg, refused to slide into bases, always stepped on third on his way to play the outfield, and thought gazing directly into the sun improved his eyesight. He once held his head out the window of a moving train all the way from Louisville to Cincinnati for the benefit of his lamps. For the same reason, he bathed his eyes daily in buttermilk.

All of which is to suggest that Browning was open to experimentation, a different way of looking at things, when Bud Hillerich approached him after a game and said he could turn a new and customized bat to replace the one he'd broken. Which Bud promptly did, down at his father's shop, the white wood shavings collecting on his forearms like fallen snow.

Bud Hillerich turning a Louisville Slugger. *(National Baseball Hall of Fame Library, Cooperstown, NY)*

It's a legend long burnished, if unconfirmable, so that it now resembles a lacquered bat spotlighted in a museum: Browning got three hits with Bud's bat the next day, told his teammates about it, and thus began a sideline for young Bud Hillerich, who made bespoke baseball bats over the strenuous objections of his father, a man loath to associate his business with the rogues and ne'er-do-wells who played baseball professionally.

J. Frederich Hillerich had every reason to fear the game. That same year, 1884, Terry Larkin had signed with the Richmond Virginians despite the events of a year before, when he had shot his wife and slit his own throat. The 1884 season also saw umpire Billy McLean, a former boxer and the first professional ump, throw a bat into a crowd of hecklers in Philadelphia. When the Baltimore Orioles put up a barbed-wire fence on June 13 of that summer, the club aimed to protect the players and umpires from the paying customers, though the fence also worked to protect the paying customers from umps like McLean.

And so J. Frederich Hillerich wanted to make balusters, not baseball bats. But the ballplayers came, and neither he nor the professional ballplayers could long ignore the growing reputation and undeniable quality of the "Falls City Sluggers" turned out by his shop. By 1894, the bats were rebranded — and trademarked — as the Louisville Slugger, a nickname bestowed by newspapers as early as 1891 on Pete Browning. J. Frederich, who enjoyed turning a profit even more than a bedpost, made Bud a partner in 1897, renaming their company J. F. Hillerich & Son.

Bud loved haunting ballparks and hanging out with ballplayers and befriended Louisville Colonels star Honus Wagner, among many others. By the time Wagner was a Pittsburgh Pirate, and perhaps the game's preeminent player, Bud signed him to the company's first exclusive endorsement contract, branding Wagner's signature on the barrel of the bat and selling that model in retail stores.

That was 1905, the same year Louis Rogers (Pete) Browning died, aged forty-five, after serving a two-week, court-ordered tenure in a lunatic asylum. He was buried, not entirely forgotten, beneath a headstone that managed to misspell his name as Lewis. He had lived his entire life in the house in which he was raised, a house he shared, until the day he died, with his mother, Mary Jane. He never took a wife but kept—as he once told the *Louisville Courier-Journal*—that harem full of customized baseball bats, which he stored in the basement, "all oiled and rubbed."

As an official endorser of the Louisville Slugger, Wagner was followed by Ty Cobb, who was followed by the Philadelphia A's Harry Davis, who was followed by Nap Lajoie, who abandoned his Wright & Ditson double-knobber for the single-knobbed sublimity of J. F. Hillerich & Son.

While they were turning out custom bats for the game's biggest stars, the Hillerichs were also making cheaper bats, under private labels, for the recreational market. Their biggest buyer was Simmons Hardware, a national behemoth whose 1909 catalog ran to five thousand pages, and whose young salesman Frank Bradsby so impressed J. Frederich that he sold him the entire business in 1911, for $125,000, essentially cutting his own son, Bud, out of the business he had helped to build.

Bud knew all the ballplayers, and Bradsby—who did not—instantly sold him back a stake in the company, installing him as president of the newly named Hillerich & Bradsby. In 1918, H&B signed left-hander Babe Ruth of the world champion Boston Red Sox for $100 and began manufacturing his R43 bat. In 1919, with Ruth leading the league in home runs and RBIs before his sale to the New York Yankees, Hillerich & Bradsby sold 276,000 Sluggers and started an ad campaign targeting boys. In 1923, when the Babe was a Yankee, and the Yankees opened "the House That Ruth Built," the company sold nearly 1.7 million. Hillerich & Bradsby was the top bat seller in the world. The Hillerich name was branded on a product that all of America was swinging, and that product was not a swinging butter churn.

On January 2, 1924, Johann Frederich Hillerich, recovering baseball skeptic, slipped on an icy street in Louisville, fractured his hip, and became ill. He died two weeks later, aged ninety, his surname forever synonymous with the game he initially sought to avoid.

By then, the bat and its most famous endorser, Babe Ruth, were enjoying twin peaks of popularity. Within a few years, the Yankees batting order would come to be called Murderers' Row, an apt if indelicate description, as bats had been instruments of murder almost since their inception.

Unlike baseballs, bats never had to be weaponized. They were created as weapons, and always used as such. In 1907, when the Louisville Slugger was securing its celebrity endorsers, a man in Washington, D.C., twenty-five-year-old Delaware Ross, fractured another man's skull with a baseball bat in an argument over which one of them owned the bat. The victim, Arthur Reed, died three days later, to little public notice.

For years, the only bat-wielding "murderers" that captured the nation's attention were baseball sluggers. For every home run he hit in 1927 at the heart of Murderers' Row, Babe Ruth carved a notch on the label of his Louisville Slugger. The notches appeared to grow out of the bat's oval brand, like a series of eyelashes, or the rays of an egg-shaped sun. He gave one such bat—with twenty-one notches—to Hillerich & Bradsby, and it's displayed to this day in the Louisville Slugger Museum, where the notches are often described as resembling those on a gunslinger's belt.

While America's most famous baseball slugger unintentionally emulated a gunman, its most famous gunman emulated a baseball slugger. Ruth hit a home run in the Yankees' 6–5 win over the Browns in St. Louis on May 7, 1929. That night, three hundred miles away in Chicago, Al Capone threw a dinner party, ostensibly to honor three members of his crime syndicate: Joseph "Hop Toad" Giunta, Albert Anselmi, and John Scalise. The evening, by all accounts, was a bacchanal, whose honorees ate and drank until well after midnight, at which time Capone produced, to a deeply apprehensive group of guests, a baseball bat.

The three men, whom he suspected of plotting his overthrow, were bound to their chairs in the gathering silence. At least one biographer says Capone "took up a batter's stance." And then, one by one, he bludgeoned Giunta, Anselmi, and Scalise, before a gunman shot each in the head. In the film *The Untouchables,* Capone wielded his bat while delivering a sermon on the sanctity of team play.

If the incident occasioned any civic self-examination in Chicago, it was quickly forgotten. To this day, outside the city's Social Security Administration building on Madison Street, there stands a 101-foot-tall baseball bat designed by Claes Oldenburg. Its official name is *Batcolumn.* As the plaque affixed to the sculpture reads: "Oldenburg selected the baseball bat as an emblem of Chicago's ambition and vigor." It was dedicated in 1977, the summer the city's White Sox became celebrated as the "South Side Hitmen."

Capone, a frequent visitor to Wrigley Field, was well known as a baseball fan. On September 9, 1931, while seated with his entourage in the front row at the Friendly Confines, he summoned Cubs catcher Gabby Hartnett to sign an autograph for twelve-year-old Al Capone Jr. When Hartnett obliged, a photographer snapped a picture: the two Capones, resplendent in suits and ties and pocket squares, nearly nose to nose with the catcher. When Commissioner

Kenesaw Mountain Landis saw the photo in the next day's papers, he wired Hartnett, ordering him to cease signing baseballs for crime bosses. Hartnett reportedly wired back, "Fine, but *you* tell him."

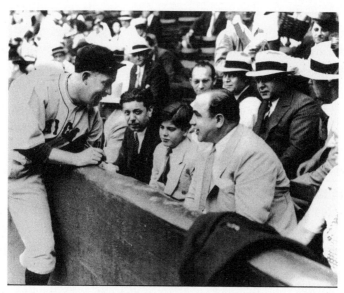

Gabby Hartnett, Al Capone, and Sonny Capone, September 9, 1931, Wrigley Field. *(National Baseball Hall of Fame Library, Cooperstown, NY)*

In the end, the edict proved moot: Thirty-eight days after Hartnett signed for his son, Capone was sentenced to eleven years in prison for tax evasion.

Twelve months later at Wrigley, in the fifth inning of Game 3 of the World Series, Ruth hit his—and to that point, perhaps all of baseball history's—most famous home run. It would go down as his "called shot." (It would be nineteen years, almost to the day, before Bobby Thomson would eclipse Ruth with his still-more-famous Shot Heard 'Round the World.) In the overheated prose of the day, home runs were shots or blasts or bombs. But then, by World War II, baseball bats and firearms shared more than the mere language of ballistics.

During the war, the Hillerich & Bradsby production line in Louisville also turned out M1 carbine gunstocks for American GIs. As the army was developing the baseball grenade, its soldiers were carrying rifles produced at the Louisville Slugger plant—carrying them around the world, in the manner (if not entirely in the spirit) of Albert Goodwill Spalding.

Although ash remained abundant, other woods suffered wartime shortages. Among its many military uses, wood was employed in airplane ribbing, which is why Howard Hughes's amphibious airplane—though primarily ribbed with birch, and officially christened the H-4 Hercules—was ridiculed in newspapers as the "Spruce Goose."

The basketball court at the Boston Garden grew, if you will, from the wartime wood scarcity. Celtics owner Walter Brown, in need of a floor in 1946, went with short boards of surplus Tennessee oak rather than the more traditional but expensive long boards of maple. The short boards were grouped together in five-foot-by-five-foot squares and arranged in a parquet mosaic not because the pattern was attractive but because it was cheap.

From the beginning, Hillerich & Bradsby, like other bat manufacturers, had tried heavy hickory and easily shattered maple before settling on northern white ash as the best wood for a baseball bat. *Fraxinus americana,* specifically that grown on either side of the border between New York and Pennsylvania, is lighter than hickory but exceedingly hard, which is why tool handles and oars were—and still are—made of it.

Bats were made harder still by players rubbing them with a cow femur, or a soda bottle, or a metal rod. Players thought doing so "tightened the grain," making the bat denser. In the 1930s, Hillerich & Bradsby began stamping the phrases "Bone Rubbed" and "Hand

Bone Rubbed" on the barrels of their bats—accompanied by a hand-and-bone symbol that looked a bit like the hand of Zeus throwing a lightning bolt. The lightning bolt itself was already on the Slugger barrel, serving as the letter *Z* in "Powerized," another word coined by Hillerich & Bradsby for a process to harden the barrel of a baseball bat. The company had a genius for this adjectival poetry, sometimes using the lyrical—and accurate—phrases "Oil Tempered" and "Weather Seasoned" to create a desire among children and baseball stars alike for a Powerized, Bone Rubbed, Oil Tempered, or Weather Seasoned magic wand.

All of these rituals served as a riposte to the bat as a symbol of violence. The level of love and care accorded them was ludicrous and often poignant. Players rubbed bats with oils and other unguents. They literally salivated over their bats, tobacco juice serving as a popular hardening agent. Bats were taken to bed, to dinner, even to the doctor. Jim Fregosi had his injected with cortisone during a slump. In short, bats have always been loved. Not loved platonically, mind you, but loved romantically, and imbued with all the rituals of mid-century courtship.

After hitting his Shot Heard 'Round the World, Bobby Thomson was photographed late on the afternoon of October 3, 1951, evidently attempting to eat his bat, as if it were an ear of corn. A closer look revealed Thomson to be kissing it, label out, in a ritual that served two purposes: It fulfilled the request of wire-service snappers, clamoring for him to smooch the lumber. And it perpetuated the Pete Browning notion that this length of wood—long after it was felled in a forest—was a still-living organism, deserving of gratitude, appreciative of affection.

Thomson's bat was a thirty-four-ounce model—number 302—manufactured by Adirondack. That company was started in 1946 by a Dolgeville, New York, woodworker named Edwin McLaughlin, who found himself surrounded by white ash, in the way that Michelangelo was surrounded by Carrara marble. And so McLaughlin set to carving. That first year, he hired newly retired Giants pitcher Hal Schumacher to introduce the bats to his former teammates, one of whom—Thomson—had just completed his rookie season. By 1951, Yankees stars Johnny Mize and Phil Rizzuto—the reigning American League Most Valuable Player—were also using Adirondacks. Above that company's brand, in script, were the words "Northern White Ash," and just below it, "Dolgeville, New York." Thomson made sure to display that label for the cameras as he kissed the most famous bat in baseball history. From its birth to its long and comfortable retirement, that bat made a journey of just seventeen miles—if you subtract its lively detour to the Polo Grounds—from Dolgeville to Cooperstown, where it resides to this day.

Bobby Thomson kissing his Adirondack 302 on October 3, 1951. *(National Baseball Hall of Fame Library, Cooperstown, NY)*

A year before Thomson's famous home run, Joe DiMaggio gently leaned forward in the bowels of Yankee Stadium and held his bat as if he were dipping a dance partner. At the request of photographer Herb Scharfman, DiMaggio softly kissed the barrel of the bat that had hit the game-winning homer the night before, in the tenth inning of Game 2 of the 1950 World Series. Of the two principals in the photograph—DiMaggio and his D29 Louisville Slugger—the former looks the much more wooden.

"The Yankee Clipper seldom gets this affectionate with a bat," read the original caption in the archive of International News Photos, "and even more rarely poses for an unusual picture like this."

The picture was anything but unusual—not for DiMaggio, nor for anyone else in baseball. The very next day Yankees infielder Jerry Coleman was photographed giving a pregame kiss to his "lucky bat." It was very nearly compulsory, after an important hit, to plant one on the bat responsible. After his historic season of 1941, in which he hit safely in fifty-six consecutive games, DiMaggio was captured on film wearing an impeccable suit, seated in a leather chair, in a business office lined with leather-bound books, gently kissing his D29, as if it were a secretary with whom he was having an affair.

DiMaggio, after all, doted on his favorite D29, which he called "Betsy Ann." He was her jealous guardian, and had reason to be. She had been bat-napped in the middle of the Streak that summer. On June 29, between games of a doubleheader at Griffith Stadium in Washington, Joe D's Betsy Ann was stolen from the Yankees dugout.

He had just tied, in Game 1, George Sisler's American League record forty-one-game hitting streak and had to use, for the next week, a D29 he had loaned to teammate Tommy Henrich. It was after DiMaggio broke Willie Keeler's major-league record of forty-four games that Betsy Ann was anonymously returned, in good health and a plain brown wrapper, by private courier to Yankee

Stadium. DiMaggio, with Betsy Ann restored to his warm embrace, kicked the Henrich bat to the curb: He signed it and donated the bat to the USO, which raffled it off at a San Francisco Seals minor-league game. Tickets cost $0.25 and the raffle raised $1,678. The great man's parents, Giuseppe and Rosalie DiMaggio, personally handed it to the winner, whose name was Jim Osborne. As Richard Ben Cramer put it in his biography of DiMaggio: "The treatment of Joe's relics was the surest sign of his new saintly status." He was can-onized on July 17 of that summer, when he hit safely in his fifty-sixth consecutive game, a record that has since only grown in stature and mystique.

Ted Williams, DiMaggio's great rival that summer, played his final game of the '41 season on September 28, finishing the year with a .406 batting average, a milestone he celebrated by unbuttoning his jersey to the waist in the Red Sox clubhouse at Fenway Park before planting one — nose turned a shade to the right, in near-perfect parody of a mat-inee screen kiss — on *his* Louisville Slugger.

Williams didn't have to feign passion. He made annual spring visits to the Louisville Slugger plant. "He would hardly break stride saying hello to executives in the office, but once with 'his boys' in the factory, he called them by name and greeted them as old friends. Williams would soon be out of his coat and on a ladder, hand-picking timber for his bats."

Williams, like a possessive newlywed eyeing his wife's waist, once complained to the company that an order of bats was too thick in the handle. Or possibly too thin. In any event, it didn't feel right. Hillerich & Bradsby took the bats back and discovered Williams was right: They deviated from his other bats by five thousandths of an inch.

All of which is to say that while many of those bat-kissing photo-graphs were staged, their sentiments were almost always genuine.

It is now impossible to read the original captions in the archives of the Bettmann/CORBIS photo agency without affecting the run-on voice of a newsreel narrator: "Yankee Johnny Mize places an affectionate smack on the bat he used to crash a fourth-inning homer off Dodger pitcher Joe Black at the Stadium in the fourth World Series game of 1952." In that photo, Mize is seated at his locker, lips glued to bat barrel, menacing eyes glued to camera lens, as if a hired gumshoe has caught him red-handed in a private moment of seduction.

Players never stopped kissing their bats. Bill Mazeroski of the Pirates did it when his home run won Game 7 of the 1960 World Series. George Brett was photographed kissing his Louisville Slugger in the 1980s. In the '90s, Mark McGwire was caught on camera kissing the crown of his Rawlings Big Stick, a photo far more innocuous than the phrase suggests.

The tradition dates to at least the 1920s, when the photographs began appearing: Babe Ruth, in slacks and dress shirt, photographed at his locker in Yankee Stadium before the 1926 World Series, his legs splayed, six bats leaning against his crotch, and a seventh—which he's kissing—cradled in his hands. "This is the Lucky One," read the original cutline. "Bronx, New York: Babe Ruth, Battering Bambino of the New York Yankees as he appeared kissing his favorite home run bat with which he expects to do much damage to the St. Louis Cardinals pitchers."

The notches Ruth carved into his R43 the next season—those notches on the gunslinger's belt—might also have been notches on a bedpost. When it came to showing affection to their bats, players didn't stop at first base, as it were. Richie Ashburn of the Phillies slept with his bats. Wily Mo Peña sniffed, kissed, and nibbled his bats. As a New York Met, Kevin Elster took a hot bat to bed one night, and then to lunch the next day. ("The bat picked up the check," he insisted.)

Babe Ruth smooching a
Louisville Slugger in the
Yankees' clubhouse
before the 1926 World
Series. *(© Bettmann/
CORBIS)*

After all this courting and foreplay, it was perhaps inevitable that
a player would want to do the honorable thing and put a ring on the
baseball bat. And so eventually Elston Howard did just that.

The weighted batting doughnut was invented by a construction
worker from Bergenfield, New Jersey, named Frank Hamilton, who
showed up at the doorstep of Elston Howard's home one evening
and asked the Yankees catcher, "How'd you like to make a million
dollars?" This was in 1967, when such a question could still excite a
Yankees star. And so Howard invited Hamilton into his basement.

Hamilton, in a sense, really had reinvented the wheel. His creation was little more than a cast-iron ring, weighing five or ten
pounds, coated in plastic. Yet it allowed players to stop swinging
three bats simultaneously in the on-deck circle, a strange and

cumbersome ritual that ended almost the instant Howard — in partnership with Hamilton — handed out the "On Deck Batting Doughnuts" to Mickey Mantle in New York, Roger Maris in St. Louis, and Willie Mays in San Francisco.

"The batting doughnut sold by the thousands, retailing at three to five dollars," Howard's widow, Arlene, recalls in her memoir, *Elston and Me.* "Little League, high school and college teams were buying them up. By the end of the 1968 season, every major league team was using the weighted batting doughnut."

Alas, when one flew off a bat in Minnesota, striking a softball umpire, the umpire sued Howard's company, and in the two years it took Howard and Hamilton and a third partner to acquire a patent, other companies began to make and market their own doughnuts. Howard made little money off the venture and was left — on the balance sheet as on the bat — one weighty doughnut.

Howard and his partners weren't the only alchemists at the time attempting to impose metal onto northern white ash. The year after Frank Hamilton produced his cast-iron doughnut, a California archery outfit manufactured its first aluminum bat, for a private label.

That company was founded by James Douglas Easton. As a fifteen-year-old in Watsonville, California, near Monterey Bay, Easton was hunting one day in 1921 when a shotgun that was leaning against a car fell over. The gun went off, shooting Easton in both legs.

During his yearlong convalescence, in 1921 and '22, Doug Easton was given a book called *Hunting with the Bow and Arrow,* which got him interested in archery. To pass the time, the boy began to make his own bows out of yew, cedar, and pine. He was a kind of Bud Hillerich of the bow and arrow, interested in craftsmanship and performance and aesthetic beauty.

As Easton lay in bed, experimenting with arrows, a man named William A. Shroyer Jr. tried to build a better baseball bat. Shroyer received United States patent 1,499,128 in 1922 for a metal baseball bat with shifting weights in its barrel. A year later, patent 1,611,858 went to one "Lloyd Middlekauff" for his bat of steel.

Easton, meanwhile, made a full recovery from his hunting injuries and went on to open his own archery shop in Los Angeles, where he met, and made bows for, Hollywood stars newly enamored of archery. By 1939, he was experimenting with a novel material for the shafts of his increasingly popular arrows. That material was aluminum, from the Latin *alum*, which means "bitter salt," as makers of wooden bats would discover three decades later, when the metallic ping of aluminum bats sounded like a death knell for their ash and hickory predecessors.

Unlike the metal bats of the 1920s, Easton's aluminum bats of the early 1970s were not prohibitively heavy, thanks in part to metal-thinning innovations that Easton had previously perfected on the company's arrows and ski poles.

Aluminum mimicked, then quickly exceeded, white ash as a driver of baseballs. Hillerich & Bradsby were slow to respond to the threat, initially dismissing aluminum as a fad. But the metal's takeover of the amateur game was astonishingly swift and comprehensive. In 1971, aluminum was approved for use in Little League Baseball, and future big leaguer Lloyd McClendon that year hit five home runs in five at bats for his Gary, Indiana, team at the Little League World Series. He was intentionally walked in each of his other five plate appearances.

In three short years, between 1971 and 1974, when the NCAA approved aluminum bats for college baseball, wood bats had become the specialist tool of professional players.

Testifying in a 1975 patent suit, Dick Groat, the retired Pirates shortstop who had won the National League batting title sixteen years earlier, could only venture that aluminum would not be used in the big leagues "in the next five or six years." Such bats, he said, would pervert the record book, allowing players to hit sixty to seventy home runs a season. It was a ridiculous figure otherwise unreachable without aluminum or—though Groat didn't say so at the time—some other performance-enhancing wonder substance.

Hillerich & Bradsby frantically played catch-up in the 1980s. By the end of that decade, half the bats the company produced were aluminum, its annual wood bat production having fallen from 7 million to 1.5 million. "I certainly see a time in the not-too-distant future when everyone will be using some alternative bat—aluminum, graphite, or some composite," Jack Hillerich, Bud's grandson, told *Sports Illustrated* that summer. "A wood bat is a financially obsolete deal.... The time will come when even the majors will use aluminum or graphite."

The cover of the magazine featured Gregg Jefferies of the Mets breaking his bat in mid-swing. The ash splintered like a shipwrecked Spanish galleon, the relic of a distant age. Above the photo ran a cover line that doubled as an epitaph: WOOD BATS ARE DOOMED.

Doug Easton didn't live to see aluminum bats, their barrels emblazoned with his name, take over baseball. On New Year's Eve of 1972—equidistant between aluminum's adoption by Little League and its approval by the NCAA—he died at age sixty-five. Still, he might have known that aluminum would come to dominate baseball, as it had done in archery, for time's arrow flies in one direction only: forward.

And yet, forty years after aluminum bats were introduced, and more than twenty years after Jack Hillerich predicted wood's demise at the major-league level, big-league bats were still hewn from trees. The premature epitaph—WOOD BATS ARE DOOMED—remained right, just not for the right reason.

By 2012, pro players' wood bats were under imminent threat not from aluminum but from an Asian monster laying waste to the landscape in the manner of Mothra, Godzilla's nemesis.

Except that this monster—an insect called the emerald ash borer—is smaller than the penny's portrait of Lincoln. With its purple abdomen and metallic-green wings, the EAB is, like so many of nature's deadliest forces, profoundly beautiful. Though no one can say for certain, the bug is believed to have arrived in North America as a stowaway in a shipping container. It was first discovered in 2002, in suburban Detroit, and its spread in the decade that followed was swift and pitiless.

This nonnative scourge—with no natural predators—swept north and east across fourteen states, killing more than fifty million ash trees and counting. Once it has infested a tree, the EAB kills it within five years—often in half that time. The U.S. Department of Agriculture urges people never to transport firewood from home to a summer campsite or cottage. The ash borer, in the words of the USDA, is "the Green Menace," its devastation potentially equal to that of chestnut blight and Dutch elm disease, two other arboreal epidemics that essentially wiped those trees from the American landscape, their only trace the countless Chestnut and Elm Streets where once their namesakes stood.

The fungus that became known as chestnut blight was discovered in 1904. Four billion chestnut trees were abruptly felled, a quarter of the entire tree canopy of the eastern United States. By the time Mel Tormé and Bob Wells wrote of "chestnuts roasting on an open fire," in 1944, chestnuts were very nearly extinct.

In the pantheon of endangered American icons, the ash baseball bat appears headed for the same fate as the roasting chestnut. The year the emerald ash borer was discovered, in 2002, ash was coming under attack on two fronts, the second being the rapid spread of maple bats around Major League Baseball.

That year, Barry Bonds was coming off a record seventy-three-home-run season for the San Francisco Giants. Each of those home runs was hit with a maple bat made by Canadian craftsman Sam Holman, who was building sets at the National Arts Centre in Ottawa in the mid-1990s when a friend—a baseball scout named Bill MacKenzie—challenged him, over beers at the Mayflower Bar, to make a longer-lasting wooden bat. Holman made his first bat in the shed next to his house, using a length of maple left over from a stair rail he'd built.

Holman took his first batch of bats to Toronto, where he persuaded Blue Jays star Joe Carter to use them in batting practice. Carter liked how hard the bats were, as did several teammates, and soon Sam Holman's Sam Bats were catching on in the big leagues, most famously with Bonds, whose colossal success had hitters pining, as it were, for maple.

By the end of the first decade of the twenty-first century, nearly half the bats in the big leagues were maple. Thirty companies were manufacturing them, including Hillerich & Bradsby, whose founder—125 years earlier—had done precisely what Sam Holman did, and turned his stairs into baseball bats.

On a summer day in 1999, while on assignment for *Sports Illustrated,* I pulled my rental car into a driveway in Hertford, North Carolina, and was greeted by the homeowner, Jim (Catfish) Hunter. I reached to shake his hand, but Hunter's famous right arm, with which he'd won 224 games, remained limp at his side, stilled by ALS (also known as Lou Gehrig's disease, after its most famous victim, the Hall of Fame player for the New York Yankees).

Inside, Hunter pointed me toward an upstairs room, a kind of attic in which he kept the memorabilia of fifteen seasons in the big leagues. As I climbed the stairs, I couldn't help notice that each of the seventy-eight balusters was made from a Louisville Slugger. Each Slugger, Hunter said, had been game-used by a Hall of Famer, some of whom—Harmon Killebrew, Carl Yastrzemski—had taken him deep.

When he could still climb those stairs, the winner of the 1974 Cy Young Award leaned on the bats for support, much as his fellow Yankee Babe Ruth had done on June 13, 1948, when the team retired his number 3 during a twenty-fifth anniversary celebration of Yankee Stadium. Ruth, dying of throat cancer, walked from the dugout to the third-base line with the aid of a bat belonging to visiting pitcher Bob Feller. The Babe would die two months later, and the photo of him, taken from behind, leaning on Feller's bat, would win a Pulitzer Prize for the *New York Herald-Tribune* photographer Nat Fein.

The bat was a companion in old age, familiar in the hand, literally a crutch to lean on.

In 1954, while attending an Indians game in Cleveland, eighty-seven-year-old Cy Young was photographed leaning on—and gesticulating with—a cane made from a baseball bat. The bat was given to him fifty-seven years earlier by Cleveland fans, in 1896, when Young was twenty-nine years old and in the prime of his career, and in no need of a walking stick.

Eighty-seven-year-old Cy Young gesturing with his baseball-bat cane at a Cleveland Indians game on April 17, 1954, fifty years after his second no-hitter. (© *Bettmann/CORBIS*)

There was, of course, irony in these two great pitchers—Cy Young and Cy Young–winner Catfish Hunter—bedeviled by bats in their physical prime, using them for comfort and support in their infirmity. And yet the sight of Hunter on his way up the stairs would have moved Johann Frederich Hillerich. His name was on all of those bats, which comprised—at long last, if perhaps a century too late—the product he originally intended to put his name on: a glorious balustrade in a respectable home.

Chapter 3

THE LOST CITY OF
FRANCISCO GRANDE

On April 11, 2000, the Giants opened their new ballpark at 24 Willie Mays Plaza in San Francisco. There, on a concourse above the left center field bleachers, the team had installed the world's largest baseball glove.

It's a four-fingered model from 1927, an exact replica—but thirty-six times larger—of a glove owned by the father of Giants general counsel Jack Bair. The glove is twenty-six feet tall and thirty-two feet wide, and should a batter ever reach it with a 501-foot shot—Marlins slugger Mike Stanton came closest, in batting practice in 2011—the ball could very well get lost in its pocket, which is twelve feet deep. In the park's first seasons, the Giants offered a $1 million bounty—payable to a randomly selected fan—if any hitter reached the glove in a game. When it became clear that nobody would do so, the Giants dropped the prize, and its $40,000 annual insurance premium, none of which made the glove any less alluring. On the contrary: In addition to the twenty thousand pounds of steel and fiberglass, its marine-grade rope, and its authentic brass grommets, the glove has been insulated over the years with "delicate garments" thrown by "female revelers" hoping to leave not just their hearts but their underwear in San Francisco.

It is difficult to tell, at a glance, which is the greater summer icon: the Giants' giant glove or the eighty-foot sculpture next to it, of Coca-Cola's contoured bottle, designed by Earl R. Dean in 1915. Suffice it to say that baseball's objects have long inspired art and architecture on a grand scale. When Yankee Stadium reopened after its renovation in 1976, the boiler stack outside Gate 4 was disguised as a bat, 138 feet tall and branded with the Louisville Slugger logo. It served as a beacon for a generation of lost fans. When Louisville Slugger opened its new museum in 1996, the company built an even larger Slugger outside—a Babe Ruth model branded with Bud Hillerich's signature—and leaned it against the building. The bat was 120 feet tall and weighed 34 tons, not ounces.

For South Korean sailors returning to port in Busan—home to a baseball academy that produced Cleveland Indians star Shin-Soo Choo, among others—the baseball bat lighthouse there is literally a beacon. It commemorates South Korea's baseball gold medal in the 2008 Olympics and is oriented, like Oldenburg's *Batcolumn* sculpture in Chicago, with the knob on the ground and the barrel in the air.

Oldenburg, the Swedish-born son of a diplomat, also created a large glove sculpture, 12 feet tall and weighing 5,800 pounds, fashioned after a first baseman's model he bought at a dime store. "Cezanne painted apples," he said. "I make mitts."

More broadly, Oldenburg rendered everyday objects—clothespins, tablespoons, rubber stamps—larger than life, as if viewed from the perspective of a child. "It's something I don't deny," he said of that childlike viewpoint. "It's something I believe in."

Which explains the appeal of the leather chair made to look like a giant fielder's mitt, positioned in a shaft of sunlight in the children's section of my hometown library: Nestling into it, like a lazy pop foul, to read about baseball, a child felt literally held in the hand of God, or at least in the hands of *a* god, a Willie Mays or a Mickey Mantle.

I was hardly the first person to imagine himself living in a piece of baseball equipment. In 1961, three years after he moved his team from Harlem to San Francisco, Giants owner Horace Stoneham opened "the finest baseball training facility and one of the most attractive resort complexes in the land." Francisco Grande was—in accounts of the day—a "diamond palace," "the most lavish, unique and fabulous baseball camp in the world," and "well on its way to becoming one of the wonders of the West."

"Welcome to Franceesco Granday," Stoneham told a crowd of local citizens and baseball officials gathered in the restaurant of the hotel he'd built on 1,150 acres of Arizona scrubland. "The bar is open all night."

If he sounded a bit like Mr. Roarke, welcoming visitors to Fantasy Island—well, in a sense he was doing just that. The village of Casa Grande, Arizona, was fifty miles south of Phoenix, seventy miles north of Tucson, and—as newspapers loved to point out, to emphasize its obscurity—fifty miles east of Gila Bend. But in that no-man's-land, Stoneham built a $4.5 million spring training complex to house, feed, and entertain his players and their families in a kind of opulent isolation.

Like William Randolph Hearst's San Simeon, Stoneham's Francisco Grande—a portmanteau of San Francisco and Casa Grande—had its own airstrip, 4,600 feet long, to accommodate private jets and commercial aircraft. It also had an eighteen-hole golf course and five baseball diamonds, one of which was in a modern stadium, with 10,000 square feet of clubhouses, a press box, and seating for 3,000 spectators drawn to Casa Grande by the team's brace of famous Willies, Mays and McCovey.

The centerpiece of the complex was a nine-story hotel, where

Giants slept in custom-made beds of Mexican mesquite, in orange-shuttered rooms — each one "air-cooled" and TV-equipped — that gave onto flower-scented verandas. In the social hall, players shot pool, watched TV, grooved to the Shirelles in the hi-fi room, or — three nights a week in spring training — viewed a movie in current release in the Francisco Grande theater.

Buses idled out front each evening, prepared to convey the Giants five miles into Casa Grande (population 8,500), but the town's pleasures could not compete with Francisco Grande's.

So the Giants lived in hermetic solitude at Francisco Grande for the first ten days of every camp before moving north to Phoenix, where they played the bulk of their exhibition games. But the whiff of cologne left behind by the famous ballplayers, Stoneham hoped, would be enough to lure vacationers and conventioneers to Francisco Grande for the rest of the year. That first spring, the hotel booked several conventions, and soon, among those making a regular pilgrimage was the original Pilgrim, John Wayne, who frequently filmed in Arizona.

Francisco Grande was to be a destination, with Interstates 10 and 8 — then still on the drawing board — expected to meet just south of Casa Grande. On 3,100 acres contiguous to Stoneham's resort, singer Pat Boone and lumberman Ben Cheney — a minority owner of the Giants — planned the Desert Carmel subdevelopment of "several thousand homes," whose property values would benefit from a happy proximity to this baseball paradise. "It's like a box seat back of home plate where you are in view of all the action," read the ads that ran in newspapers across the American North, offering lots at $2,295, with just $25 down. "The San Francisco Giants are your springtime neighbors!"

Next door, the gates to Francisco Grande were marked by a giant two-dimensional baseball, atop a Rat Pack–worthy marquee, so that Willie Mays could read, as he sharked by in his pink Cadillac with the SAY HEY plates:

San Francisco
GIANTS
OPERATING
FRANCISCO
GRANDE
COCKTAIL LOUNGE
DINING ROOM

Beyond that giant baseball was the finest example ever wrought of what we might call Midcentury Mickey Mantle–ism, an architectural style—and interior decor ethos—inspired by baseball's objects.

The hotel's hundred-thousand-gallon swimming pool was shaped like a baseball bat, permanently poised to strike the round whirlpool, the pair sitting side by side like St. Kitts and Nevis. When viewed from the Desert Sky Lounge on the ninth floor of the hotel, the concrete pool deck revealed itself to be a baseball diamond.

The flower beds were shaped like bats and balls. The exterior stairwells on the south side of the hotel exactly mimicked those on a baseball stadium, so that a man returning to his room with a bucket of ice might briefly believe himself to be ascending to the second deck of Candlestick Park.

A concrete patio overhang protruded from the ninth floor, making the entire hotel—by design—appear to be wearing a baseball cap. The parking lot was laid out like a baseball diamond, fanning out from the home plate of the hotel entrance, where the arrival of Mays, in asparagus-green pants and matching cardigan, could scarcely be missed, except when he stood camouflaged against the asparagus carpet of the lobby. "The rates are reasonable," read a newspaper display ad, "and you'll enjoy the grandeur and informal 'baseball' air." Interested parties were urged to contact Francisco Grande's general manager, Mr. Rosy Ryan, who—older guests might have recalled—pitched in three consecutive World Series for the Giants from 1922 to 1924.

It was Stoneham, with Dodgers owner Walter O'Malley, who realized baseball's manifest destiny in the American West. And here, from the second level of a two-story observation tower on the grounds of Francisco Grande, he could—like Alexander the Great astride Bucephalus—survey the world he had tamed: those five lush baseball diamonds blooming in the sand. Seven, if he counted the parking lot and pool deck.

Francisco Grande wasn't baseball's first themed city. In 1948, O'Malley built a sixty-seven-acre village, a Levittown of leather and ash, on an abandoned naval base in Vero Beach, Florida. Like the Vatican in Rome, Dodgertown was a theocratic community contained entirely within a secular city. The Dodgertown streetlamps were topped by white globes painted with red stitches, and shone their light onto avenues named for Dodgers legends. Children in Vero Beach still attend Dodgertown Elementary School, though the Dodgers themselves left for Arizona in 2008. That year, to meet the ongoing demand of people wanting to live in a 1950s baseball Elysium, Ebbets Field Estates opened in Edwardsville, Illinois. It is a subdivision of suburban homes where the streets—as in Dodgertown—are named for Dodgers immortals: Koufax Court is one, Lasorda Lane another.

The Dodgers franchise had a long-standing affection for baseball objects as architectural filigrees. The cramped rotunda at Ebbets Field, designed by Clarence Van Buskirk in 1913, was eighty feet in diameter and ringed by fourteen ticket windows. At the center of its marble floor was an enormous baseball made of white mosaic tiles and "marked with the circular stitching peculiar to baseballs." The domed ceiling, twenty-seven feet high, was decorated with stars and clouds. Descending from that false sky was a chandelier that looked from a distance like a twelve-legged spider suspended from silk. In fact, each of the chandelier's twelve arms was a baseball bat. To the end of each bat was fixed a glass-globed baseball, lit from within.

In its fixtures, the Ebbets Field rotunda would have owed a debt to the Third Base Saloon in Boston. It was called Third Base by spectators leaving the Huntington Avenue Baseball Grounds, and with good reason. For many of those fans of the Boston Americans—the team would change its name to the Red Sox in 1908—it was the last stop before home. Foremost among those fans was Michael T. McGreevy, the saloon's proprietor. Renowned as "Nuf Ced" McGreevy, he was the arbiter of all barroom arguments, and "Grand Exalted Ruler of Rooter Row." As president of Boston's Royal Rooters, the fan club of the Boston Americans, Nuf Ced ruled a congregation that included John "Honey Fitz" Fitzgerald, to become better known in his posthumous role as grandfather to President John Fitzgerald Kennedy.

But almost as lasting as that association was McGreevy's status as a seminal American sports bar. Opened in 1894, his saloon was lit by frosted globes seamed and stitched like baseballs, and suspended from bats used by Napoleon Lajoie, Cy Young, and others. A manual scoreboard on the sidewalk out front brought news to passersby (and to passers-out, of which there were many). Portraits of athletes gazed down on their corporeal counterparts—Babe Ruth drank there, as did John L. Sullivan, passing the time as a grandfather clock ticked away the seconds, its pendulum a baseball bat, weighted by the gong of a baseball.

Francisco Grande was McGreevy's Third Base Saloon—and the Ebbets Field rotunda—writ large, the closest man has ever come to a baseball theme park. Its only rival in this regard was not Dodgertown—which retained, with its naval barracks, a military feel—but another milestone of Midcentury Mantle–ism. In 1957, Mantle's business partner, Harold Youngman, opened Mickey Mantle's Holiday Inn in Joplin, Missouri, where tabletops in the Dugout

Lounge—and scratch pads on the guest-room nightstands—were shaped and seamed like baseballs.

Images of bats and balls and caps and gloves and home plates and number 7 jerseys repeated throughout the carpet of the Dugout Lounge, in the way that mouse ears repeat in the carpet and wallpaper of the Disney resorts, those temples to that other famous American Mickey.

All of it was imbued with the essence of Mickey Mantle, perhaps fatally so. "We were doing pretty good there, and Mr. Youngman said, 'You know, you're half of this thing, why don't you do something for it,'" Mantle recalled at his Hall of Fame induction speech in 1974. "So we had real good chicken there and I made up a slogan. Merlyn doesn't want me to tell this, but I'm going to tell it anyway. I made up the slogan for our chicken and I said, 'To get a better piece of chicken, you'd have to be a rooster.' And I don't know if that's what closed up our Holiday Inn or not, but we didn't do too good after that."

Indeed, Mickey Mantle's Holiday Inn eventually made way for the Lowe's home improvement store that served Joplin after the tornadoes that killed more than 160 residents in 2011. As for Casa Grande, the interstates did come but the holiday hordes and Hollywood A-listers did not. The Giants remained temporarily in residence each spring at Francisco Grande until 1981, when the California Angels moved in for three dispiriting springs. The neighborhood next door, Desert Carmel, only built a few dozen homes, its parceled lots mostly empty and inert, save for the skittering of gila monsters.

Horace Stoneham, whose father had signed my grandfather in 1926, died in 1990 in a nursing home in Scottsdale, Arizona, where he spent the last thirteen years of his life in retirement near the Giants' permanent spring training facility.

Ten years later, the Giants opened their new ballpark, with its enormous glove. Francisco Grande closed in 2003 for an $8 million renovation that preserved some of its period touches. Removed from its original context, the patio overhang just manages to look like the bill of a ball cap, while the swimming pool lost its tapering and now resembles a rolling-pin bat of the late 1800s. And while a portrait of the Duke hangs in the bar—called Duke's—the ghost of John Wayne has relocated twenty-three miles to the west in Maricopa, to the John Wayne RV Ranch on the John Wayne Parkway.

The observation tower from which Giants manager Alvin Dark shouted instructions to Orlando Cepeda and Gaylord Perry remains standing at Francisco Grande. But there are no more diamonds to survey. Imagination is required, as when touring Roman ruins, to see what was once both an exemplar of the architecture of baseball and the supreme worship of its objects, which continues to this day.

When he retired from the New York Rangers, Wayne Gretzky was given a gift by his teammates. The greatest hockey player of all time received a leather sofa shaped not like a stick or puck or an ice skate, but rather a baseball glove. To a child of the twentieth century, nothing was more evocative of North American boyhood. When a thirteen-year-old entrepreneur in Ohio began to market "man candles"—candles with masculine scents—among the first he created was Baseball Mitt, for a baseball mitt was instantly evocative of masculinity.

To think it was once exactly the opposite.

The baseball glove was born in 1870, the year the *New York Times* first called baseball the "national" pastime. "In summer there is an endless variety of out-door amusements and exercises which all can engage in more or less," the paper reported, "the most prominent of which is the national game of base-ball for men and boys, and that of croquet for girls and women."

Crucially, baseball was the national game *for men*. And man was not a fully evolved creature in 1870, any more than he is now. Charles Darwin spent the whole of 1870 writing *The Descent of Man,* in which he stated, "There is no fundamental difference between man and the higher animals in their mental faculties," a sentiment especially true of baseball catchers. They stood, stooped, several feet behind home plate—"Man still bears in his bodily frame the indelible stamp of his lowly origin"—to catch the ball barehanded on the bounce. That ball was thrown from only fifty feet away, to catchers who wore no hand protection of any kind.

The first written evidence of a player having the sense to don gloves came on June 29 of that summer, in the *Cincinnati Daily Commercial*'s report of the previous day's Red Stockings game: "Allison caught to-day in a pair of buckskin mittens, to protect his hands."

If Doug Allison, the Cincinnati catcher, used gloves the next day, there is no record of it. There is, rather, a graphic record of the time he'd spent not having done so. As a baseball retiree, Allison had his hands photographed for pathological posterity at least twice—in 1889, and again in 1908. In both photos, the fingers meander at every joint. The palms are discolored and wizened. Allison's looked like the gnarled and grasping hands of the malevolent trees in *The Wizard of Oz,* and there is little wonder why. "To shake hands with a catcher," it was said at the time, "feels like grabbing a handful of walnuts."

As a nineteenth-century male, Allison—a marble cutter by trade—knew that pain was to be concealed. He was one of thirty-two thousand casualties in the Civil War Battle of Spotsylvania in May 1864. Exploding ordnance had rendered him partially deaf, which is why—years later—he'd occasionally get to third from first on foul fly balls, oblivious to teammates and fans screaming at him to return before he was doubled up. "Allison was a gunner in Fort Sumpter [*sic*] during the late war, and is the only survivor of three batches of gunners of six men in each batch," the *Boston Globe* noted in 1876. "His service during the war accounts for his impaired hearing."

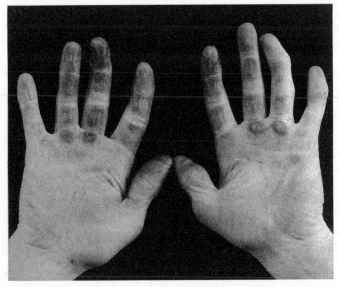

Palms of Doug Allison's hands, 1889. *(National Museum of Health and Medicine, Armed Forces Institutes of Pathology)*

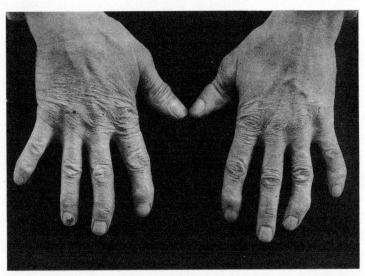

Backs of Doug Allison's hands, 1889. *(National Museum of Health and Medicine, Armed Forces Institutes of Pathology)*

Another combatant at Spotsylvania, Robert E. Lee—who died four months after Allison wore those buckskin mittens—wrote: "A man may manifest and communicate his joy, but he should conceal and smother his grief as much as possible."

And so Allison set about doing that after the war, when he joined the first professional baseball team, the Cincinnati Red Stockings, for $15 a week. He had been discovered by a team executive named John Joyce, who went for a long walk in Philadelphia one day and wound up watching a sandlot game in Manayunk, Pennsylvania. After the game—in which Allison had hit a long home run to center field—Joyce took the boy by carriage back to the Continental Hotel. There, Joyce summoned Cincinnati president Alfred T. Goshorn from his room.

"Allison was sitting there in the carriage, a tanned and freckled country boy whose boots and clothes were covered with brickyard clay," according to a contemporary account, typewritten on stained paper and filed away at the Baseball Hall of Fame Library. "On his head was a 25-cent straw hat with half the rim gone. Joyce & Goshorn bought him a suit and made him get a haircut and took him on the train back to Cincinnati."

These were the men who invented the modern game. "When I started in to catch, gloves were unknown and a team which carried ten men was well supplied with material," Allison said in 1908, when he was sixty-one. "So there was no laying off for slight injuries. The ball we used then contained an ounce and a half of rubber and would fly through the infield when it was hit."

Compared to a whistling cannonball, that flying baseball was a trifle, and wearing gloves to catch it made one a sissy. "We know that if we fearlessly grasp a nettle, it is harmless," wrote John Brookes in his book *Manliness,* published in 1875, which turned out to be the baseball glove's annus mirabilis. "Touch it timorously, and it stings."

Barehanded players continued fearlessly grasping the nettle until that very year, 1875, when Charlie Waitt of the St. Louis Brown Stockings had the courage to be timorous and wore a glove with the fingertips cut off to play first base at Boston.

"The glove worn by [Waitt] was flesh color, with a large, round opening in the back," recalled Albert Spalding. "Now, I had for a good while felt the need of some sort of hand protection for myself. In those days clubs did not carry an extra carload of pitchers, as now. For several years I had pitched in every game played by the Boston team, and had developed severe bruises on the inside of my left hand. When it is recalled that every ball pitched had to be returned, and that every swift one coming my way, from infielders, outfielders or hot from the bat, must be caught or stopped, some idea may be gained of the punishment received."

Spalding asked Waitt about his homemade glove. "He confessed that he was a bit ashamed to wear it," Spalding wrote, "but had it on to save his hand. He also admitted he had chosen a color as inconspicuous as possible, because he didn't care to attract attention. He added that the opening on the back was for purpose of ventilation.

"Meanwhile, my own hand continued to take its medicine with utmost regularity, occasionally being bored with a warm twister that hurt excruciatingly. Still, it was not until 1877 that I overcame my scruples against joining the 'kid-glove aristocracy' by donning a glove. When I did at last decide to do so, I did not select a flesh-colored glove, but got a black one, and cut out as much of the back as possible to let the air in."

Here was a watershed in baseball: one of the game's greatest stars, near the end of a glorious career, adopting conspicuous protection for his hands. "Happily, in my case, the presence of a glove did not call out the ridicule that had greeted Waite [sic]," wrote Spalding. "I had been playing so long and had become so well known that the innovation seemed rather to evoke sympathy than hilarity. I found that the glove, thin as it was, helped considerably, and inserted one pad after another until a good deal of relief was afforded. If anyone wore a padded glove before this date I do not know it. The 'pillow mitt' was a later innovation."

Spalding wore that single black glove in 1877, the year after he opened his sporting-goods store in Chicago. By removing the stigma from gloves, he could sell them to a new and burgeoning market, which he promptly did. Not everyone adopted them—some players thought gloves a hindrance to good fielding, no more appropriate to playing shortstop than to playing the piano. And even those who did wear them were hardly out of danger. While fielding a ball in 1882, shortstop Mike Moynahan broke a finger on his throwing hand and had to have it amputated at the first joint. An inconvenience, to be sure, but Moynahan did hit .310 the next year for the Philadelphia Athletics, and his 268 assists ranked second in the league—and first among men with nine fingertips.

In short, baseballs were dangerous weapons. Gloves protected players, and soon players grew protective of gloves, treating them almost gynecologically. To this day, you never put your hands in another man's gamer. And is it any wonder why? Players are wedded to their gloves—at least one was wedded *in* his glove—and have been since at least 1884.

Cornelius McGillicuddy's baseball journey began with a single step—and a pair of mitts—in East Brookfield, Massachusetts. "When I walked out of my old home town in 1884," he wrote, "my sole worldly possessions were a pair of buckskin gloves with their fingers cut off to make catcher's mitts. I was on my way to fulfill my promise to myself. I was going to try to make the big leagues, and to make my dreams come true. For this was America, the land of opportunity." If this sounds like the start of a Horatio Alger story, well, McGillicuddy grew up twenty-five miles from Alger's hometown, at the peak of the author's popularity. And it *was* a Horatio

Alger story of sorts: McGillicuddy played or managed for sixty-six years in the big leagues, but even at the end of his life, those first buckskin gloves remained a kind of Rosebud to the man who became known as Connie Mack.

In the late 1800s, gloves were still just that: gloves, a slightly larger version of the human hand. "You had to catch the ball two-handed because the glove was so small," said Casey Stengel, who was a young boy in the 1890s, by which time gloves were advertised amid dropsy cures in baseball's bible, *Sporting Life*. "You wouldn't believe how small those gloves were. Why, when I got married I couldn't afford dress gloves, so I wore my baseball mitt to my wedding and nobody even noticed. That took care of my right hand and I was smart enough to keep my left hand in my pocket." Edna Lawson Stengel was, in more than one sense of the phrase, a good catch.

Pillow gloves, those fat-fingered (often four-fingered) gloves that look to modern eyes like the Hamburger Helper mascot, were pioneered by catchers, for whom padding was most urgent.

Like Edison with the lightbulb, Albert Bushong wasn't the sole inventor of the catcher's mitt, but he made the most famous contribution to its creation. They were contemporaries, Edison and Bushong, and both would soon have towns named after them. In the history of modern innovators, the Wizard of Menlo Park is now somewhat better remembered than the Wizard of Sportsman's Park, and Edison, New Jersey, slightly more robust than Bushong, Kansas.

But it should not be forgotten that the great St. Louis Browns catcher Albert John (Doc) Bushong was — more than any who went before him — a man who knew squat.

An 1882 alumnus of the University of Pennsylvania dental school, Bushong was the first catcher to catch one hundred games in a big-league season, in 1885, while playing for those Browns, winners of four straight American Association pennants from 1884 to 1887. So beloved were Bushong's Browns that railroad executives —

as the railways expanded west—began to name towns and stations and post offices after much of the team's roster. Or so claimed a persistent Kansas legend of the early twentieth century, abetted by credulous sportswriters. Comiskey, Kansas—population 28 in 1910—was a station on the Missouri Pacific Railroad unambiguously named for Browns manager Charles Comiskey. Latham, Kansas, on the St. Louis–San Francisco Railway, shared a name with Browns third baseman Arlie Latham. Boyle, on the Union Pacific Railroad, was inspired—according to a century-old story I have always wanted to believe—by my great-grandfather's brother Jack Boyle, who replaced Doc Bushong as catcher for the Browns and was described in *Sporting Life* as "almost a copy of Bushong." In 1887, Boyle caught in eighty-seven consecutive games, an absurdity even for that age.

In fact, the towns of Boyle and Latham appear *not* to have been named for the ballplayers but for more local—if less prominent— bearers of those surnames.

But Bushong, on the Missouri Pacific—like Comiskey, seven miles to the west—was unambiguously named for a St. Louis Brown. It literally did for Doc Bushong what the catcher's mitt had done for him. It put him on the map.

Bushong lost his job to my great-great-uncle Jack Boyle when "an inshoot jellied the fingers of good old Doc Bushong.... The disabling of the dentist gave Jack Boyle the opportunity he needed to show his stuff."

The dentist/catcher had a twofold professional interest in keeping his fingers healthy. And so Doc Bushong's most significant fillings were the sponges he put into his glove, padding it out and patching it up "until it was as soft to his hand as a pillow," according to an 1887 account in the *Brooklyn Daily Eagle*, "and it was his best friend while he was up under the bat."

Doc Bushong, both hands gloved, 1888. *(Library of Congress)*

In that same year, two brothers opened a sporting-goods store in St. Louis, with designs on manufacturing products. One of those brothers, George Rawlings, had already received a patent, two years earlier, for a baseball glove modestly padded in the palm and fingers. By comparison, Bushong's was a burlesque of a baseball glove, what *Sporting Life* called "a spring mattress on his left hand."

"The Doctor was proud of this affair, and would not allow anyone to use it," the *New York Times* recalled from a twenty-five-year remove in 1915. "Out of Bushong's idea grew the idea of the mitt."

While a catcher's mitt afforded a measure of comfort, Bushong believed in a far more powerful piece of equipment, one that would also become ubiquitous in baseball: the mustache. According to Brian McKenna, Bushong's biographer for the Society for American Baseball Research, Bushong believed that a mustache improved one's eyesight: "When I shave my upper lip it always makes my eyes discharge more or less water and a man can't see in such a condition. The day that I had my finger broken in Louisville by a pitched ball I had no moustache. It had been taken off the day before, and I truly believe that this alone was the cause of the accident. I am an advocate of hairy lips in the profession."

When you recall that Pete Browning, the original Louisville Slugger, thought bathing his eyes in buttermilk and gazing directly into the sun improved his eyesight, you're left with two visionaries — early innovators of bat and mitt — who knew nothing of actual vision.

Before they were products on many hands, gloves were the products *of* many hands. In 1889, Joe Gunson of the Kansas City Cowboys stitched the fingers of a leather glove together, rigged a wire frame around it, stuffed that frame with sheepskin, and wrapped that sheepskin in buckskin, dressing his hand like a French-Canadian fur trapper of the day, in the skins of various animals.

Gunson failed to patent his mitt, but a half century later, in 1939, at the age of seventy-six, he sent a version to the brand-new Baseball Hall of Fame, along with seven affidavits attesting to its authenticity. But Gunson wasn't the sole inventor of the catcher's mitt any more than Bushong was. Very few baseball inventions sprang fully formed from a single genius. Bill Francis, library associate at the Baseball Hall of Fame, advises caution and skepticism when declaring "firsts" in baseball: "Many times, when you read of the 'first' something, you dig a little deeper and find one that came before it." Of almost all apparent breakthroughs, it is wiser to write of the "earliest known record" of a thing.

Unlike other men in the Age of Invention that closed out the nineteenth century, Gunson never became synonymous with the catcher's mitt as Rudolf Diesel did with the internal combustion engine, or even Melville Bissell with the carpet sweeper. It was Gunson's misfortune to help invent something at a time when grander devices, of greater use to many more people, were being invented. Lightbulbs were appearing—literally and figuratively—over countless heads. Everyone was an Edison, not just Edison. Telephones, motion pictures, roller coasters, escalators, and zippers were among the manifold novelties making American life easier. The glove, more than any other invention in baseball, allowed players the luxury of—in the words of the age's greatest chronicler, Mark Twain—"doing your duty without pain."

In that era, the catcher's duty *was* pain: ignoring it, managing it, absorbing and delivering it. These last two were often done in rapid succession, as happened on December 15, 1891, when two catchers were drinking in a Cincinnati saloon, as ballplayers were inclined to do on a winter Tuesday.

One of the catchers, Jack Boyle of the New York Giants, was nursing a sprained ankle suffered in an off-season football game. The other catcher, thirty-two-year-old Jim Keenan—newly retired from the Cincinnati Reds—thought it would be amusing, in an idle moment, to "playfully" kick Boyle in his injured ankle.

To men who'd become nearly insensate to physical pain, such casual violence was meant to be "hilarious," in the word of one contemporary account of the incident. But Boyle didn't take it as such. "Boyle is fond of a joke," the *Toronto Daily Mail* noted, "but this was going a little too far." Boyle, an amateur boxer, hit Keenan with a right jab, knocking him to the ground and blackening his eye, after which—per the custom of future baseball fights—onlookers jumped in and prevented further fisticuffs.

Which isn't to say that Honest Jack Boyle didn't have a vertiginously high pain threshold. On the contrary. One December evening, in 1898, Boyle was walking home at midnight—from another

Cincinnati saloon, we're left to presume—when a stranger jumped him from behind. There is no record of the catcher having been robbed, nor was the assailant ever apprehended, but the mugger did plunge a knife deep into Boyle's left (or catching) shoulder, "making an ugly wound."

By then, Boyle was a member of the Philadelphia Phillies. His left shoulder bothered him into the spring of 1899, at which time he consulted a physician, who made "a startling discovery," as the wires put it. "Dr. Walker, in probing the left shoulder of the ball player, found imbedded in the flesh near the bone the broken blade of a knife." The business end of the blade had snapped off when it hit bone, and Boyle evidently hadn't bothered to have the shoulder carefully examined. And so he set about training with a dagger blade in his shoulder. Needless to say, this somewhat impeded his preparation for the 1899 season, which was perhaps the whole point of the stabbing. For reasons lost to history, many of Boyle's friends believed that the man who jumped him intended to end his playing career.

If so, he succeeded. After thirteen seasons—after 1,087 big-league games and 4,232 at bats—Boyle never again played in the majors. As the last summer of the nineteenth century arrived, he made plans to open a saloon on Seventh Street in Cincinnati, setting them up and knocking them back with a pair of hands burled and knotted like driftwood.

As the twentieth century dawned, gloves, bats, and baseballs were becoming household items, sold by mail order, a business that began in 1872 when Aaron Montgomery Ward of Chicago sent out a single-sheet catalog offering 163 items. By 1904, Montgomery Ward had three million customers, and "sporting goods"—like dry goods and canned goods, the phrase is a vestige of the nineteenth century—were burgeoning.

Spalding alone produced a million bats in 1900. Those bats were driving baseballs into streets and neighboring yards, where children were helpless to chase them. Men like Spalding, the Rawlings brothers, J. A. Hillerich, former Philadelphia A's player A. J. Reach, and George Wright (member of the 1869 Cincinnati Red Stockings) and his partner, Henry Ditson, were all making (or remaking) names and sometimes fortunes during the greatest economic expansion in American history, what Twain called "the Gilded Age."

These men were selling the newly invented objects of the game and even inventing the game's inventor. In 1905, Spalding set up a committee to investigate the origins of baseball, specifically to suppress the growing heresy that it evolved from the British game of rounders. The commission featured A. J. Reach and George Wright and was headed by Abraham Mills, who succeeded William Hulbert as president of the National League when Hulbert was buried beneath that giant baseball in Chicago.

In 1907, after two years of dithering, the Mills Commission abruptly declared Civil War general Abner Doubleday the game's inventor. Their evidence was a letter from an elderly mining engineer in Denver named Abner Graves, who claimed to have witnessed Doubleday whip up the sport in Cooperstown, New York, in 1839. It didn't bother Americans that Doubleday was in fact a cadet at the United States Military Academy that year, confined to West Point, nor that Graves would eventually die in a Colorado insane asylum.

No, by 1935, when a farmer in Fly Creek, New York, found an ancient baseball in a trunk, it looked like something Doubleday might have used, had he ever played or expressed an interest in baseball. The ball was chocolate brown, split at the seams, like a bulb from which something is straining to grow. It was the serpent's apple required by baseball's creationists to disprove the countervailing theory of evolution. Dubbed the "Doubleday Baseball," it became a centerpiece of the Hall of Fame when it opened in 1939, the hundredth anniversary of Doubleday's fictitious invention. In its glass case there now, it looks like a detonated baseball grenade.

In the new century, gloves were ubiquitously advertised amid dropsy tonics and other curatives and—once outfielders became the last to succumb—adopted at every position on the field.

Not everyone was smitten. By 1908, as Cait Murphy points out in her chronicle of that season, *Crazy '08*, writers were calling for the abolition of outfielders' gloves: "The big mitt has made the ball-player," *Sporting Life* editorialized. "We have no desire to revert to the glove-less game, but there is a wide margin between no gloves and the present huge mitts which enable the veriest dub to face a cannon shot."

But such nostalgia was by then already twenty years old, appearing as early as the 1880s, when George Ellard wrote a poem about Doug Allison's Red Stockings team called "The Reds of Sixty-Nine," in which he lamented:

We wore no mattress on our hands,
No cage upon our face;
We stood right up and caught the ball,
With courage and with grace.

That the glove completely changed baseball is evident elsewhere in Ellard's poem, the part that never gets quoted, in his now-comical ode to the good old days, when a baseball was all but impossible to catch consistently:

The game you see them play to-day
Is tame as it can be;
You never hear of scores like ours—
A hundred and nine to three.

The irony, of course, is that barehanded big leaguers invented the baseball glove precisely so they wouldn't have to play barehanded any longer. Those hands would be needed for other toil that would provide for them when their baseball skills had faded.

When that happened to him, Doug Allison went to work for the U.S. Post Office in Washington, D.C., where he'd sit in the lobby of the Reds' team hotel whenever they were in town. It was in Washington on January 20, 1914, that Allison placed a pen in the claw hammer of his right hand and wrote a letter to Cincinnati Reds owner August (Garry) Herrmann, imploring him to help another of the original Red Stockings.

"Dear Sir," Allison wrote,

I have just received a sad letter from Cal McVey, telling me he's down and out through a mine accident. His playing in the old "Cincinnati Red Stockings" helped to put base ball on the map of today, and [he] was one of the greatest players of his day. Cannot the National League put him on the retired list say at $40 or $50 per month. He also tells me if he could put himself under a good doctor he might be able to do some work. Also told me that Pres. Lynch and Pres. Johnson was notified of his trouble but up to the present time heard nothing from them, which I am very sorry to hear. I see by the papers where the National Association was willing to pension Capt. Anson but he said he did not need it. Now, Mr. Herrmann, please do what you can in his behalf. By doing so you will greatly oblige me of his many friends. Hoping to hear from you soon in regard to same. I remain, Yours Respectfully, Doug Allison.

Then Allison appended a postscript, squeezed into the lower left-hand corner of the page: "McVey's Address is Eddie Graney's Billiard Parlor, Market Street, San Francisco."

McVey survived another dozen years. But Allison died less than two years after writing that letter, at the age of seventy, at ten forty-five in the morning, on his way to clock in at the post office.

Allison's colleague and contemporary Charlie Waitt, whose glove so impressed Albert Spalding, had preceded him in death by four years. "A more honest and harder-working professional player it would be difficult to find," the *New York Clipper* had said of Waitt in his playing days. "[He] has long enjoyed the reputation of being one of the finest outfielders in the profession." But that was 1882. By 1912, when Waitt died in San Francisco, reportedly from a fall while washing windows, he was remembered—when remembered at all—for having worn a glove, at the risk of great ridicule, thirty-seven years earlier.

The man to whom Waitt confessed his unease at wearing a glove—Albert Spalding—died in 1915, in Point Loma, California, a titan of commerce seated atop a double-stitched globe. And though he left a fortune estimated at $600,000 (nearly $14 million today), Spalding—like Waitt and Allison—died at heart a manual laborer, in the truest sense of the phrase, which grows from a Latin root, *manualis:* "belonging to the hand."

For its first three decades, the glove was primarily a protective device and often prevented the wearer from catching anything at all. (How apt that it would become a synonym for *condom,* spawning the phrase "No glove, no love.") Pocketless, fat-fingered, and inflexible, baseball gloves were not specifically designed for catching baseballs. This seemed strange to pitcher Bill Doak, who—as a spitball specialist for the Cardinals—was always in pursuit of a competitive advantage.

In 1920, Doak conceived a revolutionary accessory to what was by then a five-fingered glove. He had Rawlings loop two horizontal leather laces between the thumb and forefinger, creating a rudimentary web, ideal for snaring a baseball, for concealing a pitcher's grip, for cursing into without causing offense, and for countless other uses as yet unimagined in 1920.

Without Doak's innovation, we wouldn't have Tommie Agee's snow-cone catch in Game 3 of the 1969 World Series, no "Web Gems" on *Baseball Tonight,* nor any way for an idle Little Leaguer to wear his glove on his face as a mosquito shield. Doak's webbed glove was instantly successful and so popular that Rawlings offered it for sale for the next thirty-three years, earning Doak as much as $25,000 in royalties in a single season and ushering in an escalating arms race for the human hand.

First basemen in particular wanted more-capacious gloves, great catchment basins for collecting baseballs. Hank Greenberg was their Rube Goldberg, dreaming up bigger and more complicated gloves every season. "Last year, Hank had a glove made which looked like a mattress for a Singer midget," Bud Shaver wrote in the *Detroit Times* in 1935, name-checking a troupe of diminutive vaudevillians. "This year he has a bigger one. It is a half-inch larger in diameter and it looks somewhat like a lobster trap....It has a thumb as long as Jimmy Durante's schnozzle. Between the thumb and the rest of the mitt, Hank has something which looks like a fishnet."

By 1939, when the Singer Midgets were employed as Munchkins in *The Wizard of Oz,* Greenberg's latest mitt contained, in its bottomless depths, "three lengths of barbed wire, four corners, two side pockets, a fish net, rod and trowel, a small sled, a library of classics, a compact anti-aircraft gun, a change of clothes and a pocket comb."

Indeed, when Greenberg moved from first base to the outfield in 1940, Boston Braves first baseman turned outfielder Buddy Hassett warned: "There's a whale of a difference between a mitt and a glove. This is especially true these days, with first basemen wearing mitts that look like fish nets, mitts that snare tosses so easily that some first basemen don't even know they've got the ball in those nets."

On the other hand, as it were, Lou Gehrig's mitt was a modest thing, "the smallest glove of any first baseman I know," as he told John Kieran of the *New York Times*. The last glove he ever wore, when his undiagnosed disease made it difficult to bend over in the spring of 1939, was also his largest, but even that was little more than a leather oven mitt, with athletic tape braided around the worn webbing as reinforcement.

X-rays taken in 1938 revealed seventeen fractures in Gehrig's hands, at least one on every finger, injuries through which he famously played for 2,130 consecutive games. Gehrig's iron-man streak was aided by two other men: One was Albert Spalding, whose surname was branded above the palm of his glove, a palm in which Gehrig assiduously avoided catching the ball whenever he could help it. Teammate Bill Werber, late in life, remembered Gehrig "trying to catch the ball in the webbing of the glove when the infielders threw it to him," a small blessing for which Gehrig could thank the other man who abetted his streak: Bill Doak.

What became of that final glove is not entirely clear. In a 1979 interview with the *Sporting News,* Babe Dahlgren, Gehrig's replacement at first base, recalled returning to Yankee Stadium after spring training in 1940 to find Lou — diagnosed with ALS the previous June — cleaning out his locker. "He took his glove and threw it over to Pete Sheehy, the clubhouse man," Dahlgren told Bill Madden. "I remember him saying, 'I won't be needing this anymore, Pete.'" Dahlgren asked Sheehy for the glove, even though he was right-handed and Gehrig was left-handed.

"Lou had worn the glove so much he had Ed Rainey, of Spalding, reface and reline the glove," Dahlgren wrote in a letter. "I never knew any other player who did this."

The letter was to Barry Halper, owner of the largest private collection of baseball memorabilia in the world. Halper bought the Gehrig glove from Dahlgren and eventually made it lot 2421 in a

Sotheby's auction of the Barry Halper Collection in 1999. It was purchased, for $387,500, by an anonymous buyer widely reported to be the actress and director Penny Marshall.

Trouble is, the Baseball Hall of Fame also had, in its possession, Gehrig's last glove, a gift from the Gehrig estate. With that revelation, Marshall denied ever having purchased the other glove. But the fact is *someone* bought it, for nearly $400,000, reflecting a deep desire to shake the hand that shook the hand of Lou Gehrig, whose glove had been, in the words of biographer Jonathan Eig, "an extension of his own skin."

In the Halper auction, the actor and comedian Billy Crystal purchased one of Mickey Mantle's Rawlings XPG3 gamers for $239,000, and in doing so became a baseball-fan version of Adam, on the ceiling of the Sistine Chapel, straining to touch the hand of God.

"What makes the human hand unique?" visitors to the American Museum of Natural History were asked in an exhibit on primates. Answer: "The human hand can grip with strength and fine control, so it can throw a baseball or sign a name on the dotted line." Those without sufficient skill to throw a baseball, but with sufficient wealth to sign a check, have made vintage baseball gloves a valuable commodity, and one of the most intoxicating inhalants known to man.

As an official Rawlings model, the Bill Doak glove was discontinued in 1953. And so, a year later, was Bill Doak, swiftly following his mitt into eternity the way surviving spouses often do. He died in a warm bath, over the Thanksgiving holiday, in Bradenton, Florida, where he'd lived for the previous twenty-nine years, coaching youth baseball and running a candy store called Bill Doak's Sweet Shop. "Almost every youngster here is an acquaintance of Bill Doak," the *Sarasota Herald-Tribune* noted the year before he died. "They love to chew candy and talk baseball with a fellow who really loved and loves the American pastime."

Doak's was, by all appearances, an exceedingly pleasant and Cleaveresque existence, despite his having lost his first fortune in the crash of '29. Doak taught Sunday school in Sarasota, Florida, became a golf pro, and managed a bowling alley before settling into his role as bespectacled proprietor of a candy store. "One must lead a *whole* life to succeed in any walk of life," Doak liked to say. He was duly eulogized as both inventor and confectioner — part Wilbur Wright, part Willy Wonka. His influence is still felt every time a glove is sold, when the buyer secures the webbing over nose and mouth, like an airplane oxygen mask, and takes a deep drag of its leathery essence.

Nineteen fifty-four marked not just the passing of Doak, but also the passing of a glorious glove tradition. Baseball adopted Rule 3.16, forbidding players to leave their gloves on the field when going to bat. Prior to 1954, many did just that, dropping their gloves on or near the diamond, sometimes in foul territory, sometimes in fair, but always in ankle-breaking proximity to their position. "They might as well leave tombstones out there," the *Hartford Courant* editorialized when the rule was under consideration.

Not everyone agreed. Lugging one's glove all the way back to the dugout was considered by many to be a waste of time. "It would be foolish," Red Sox scout Ted McGrew said. "If the player made the third out at second base, he would then have to run clear to the bench to get his glove before taking his place in the field." That a teammate could just run it out to him evidently didn't occur to anyone.

With one's glove unattended on the field, there was always a danger of having infield dirt or a dead mouse inserted into its fingers by opponents. And disembodied gloves occasionally affected a game's outcome, to say nothing of at least one pennant race. Philadelphia beat the White Sox on September 28, 1905, when Harry Davis of the A's singled to left and the ball struck the unattended glove of teammate Topsy Hartsel, who promptly scored from second. (The A's would go on to win the American League pennant by two games over the White Sox.)

The Sox got that game back forty-five years later, on August 4, 1950, when Nellie Fox hit a bloop to shallow center field at Comiskey that caromed off his *own* glove and went for a double. Had Fox left his glove palm up, and had the ball landed in it, he would have had the distinction of being the first big leaguer to fly out to himself.

While pursuing a ball two seasons later, White Sox shortstop Sam Dente stepped on a glove in a game at Washington, allowing a run to score. He was charged with an error, and the Sox lost 2–1, and talk was renewed about banning the practice of abandoning gloves in the field. Rule 3.16 was approved in November 1953 thanks to the strong advocacy of an ex-player on the Official Playing Rules Committee. "Aside from the possibility of hindering play," he said, "gloves on the field look sloppy." That former player, who found gloves so aesthetically displeasing, was retired first baseman Hank Greenberg, whose own mitt, two decades earlier, had resembled Durante's schnozzle.

Of course, this was the dawn of the decade when baseball was becoming art and architecture, yielding Francisco Grande and Mickey Mantle's Dugout Lounge and an almost mystical attachment to the game's objects never equaled before or since. The era's most famous literary protagonist—Holden Caulfield in *The Catcher in the Rye*—mentioned that his kid brother, Allie, scrawled poems on his left-handed fielder's glove "so that he'd have something to read when he was in the field and nobody was up at bat."

Catcher was published in 1951, at a time when baseball gloves were being manufactured and poetry came standard on them, factory-installed. Allie Caulfield's poetry was superfluous. Rawlings had a musical genius for naming its patented innovations: the Trap-Eze, for instance, and the Edge-U-Cated Heel. Baseball has always loved the hyphen and the intentional misspelling, particularly in combination with each other. Witness the Twi-Nite doubleheader, the Snow-Cone catch, the outfield billboards for GEM CLOG-PRUF RAZORS WITH SINGLEDGE BLADES. The year of *Catcher*'s publication, one of baseball's most popular gloves was the Nokona Ristankor, which consisted of *three* deliberate misspellings: not just "wrist" and "anchor," but also Nokona, a brand based in Nocona—with a *c*—Texas.

The '51 Nokona, bearing the signature of White Sox shortstop Chico Carrasquel, had an adjustable wrist strap that GRIPS THE WRIST—CAN'T FALL OFF—CAN'T BE KNOCKED OFF. This, of course, was the titular Ristankor. Baseball gloves in the 1950s were like automobiles of the 1950s—beautifully styled, lovingly named, with a range of models ubiquitously advertised. As the tagline of the Carrasquel campaign said: "Ask your dealer to show you the new Nokona line."

The pin had been pulled from the baseball grenade, and the explosion would reverberate for the rest of the '50s, a decade in which it was not unusual for a man or boy to have a baseball glove *dealer.* The year after *Catcher* came out, Bernard Malamud published *The Natural,* a baseball retelling of the Arthurian legend, with a homemade bat in place of Excalibur. Wonderboy was hewn by Roy Hobbs from a tree split by lightning. When a fastball left the bat likewise split in two, "the Knights' batboy nervously collected both the pieces and thrust a Louisville Slugger into Roy's limp hand." Stripped of his power, the mighty Hobbs struck out.

The fielder had no such equivalent Excalibur until 1957, when American ingenuity produced—in the year that Mantle opened his Holiday Inn—the Excalibur of baseball gloves. Power-giving and protective, the Wilson A2000 was the glove's great leap forward, the exemplar of the art, suitably armored with hyphenates like Grip-Rite Pocket and Twin-Split Web. The latter had two parallel vertical laces, giving fielders "the flexibility to 'close' on the ball faster." The A2000 was not just the progenitor of the modern glove — it *is* the modern glove. Its genius, in the words of Noah Liberman, author of the engaging *Glove Affairs,* is that "the A2000 doesn't look like the human hand. It took almost 90 years for ballplayers and glove makers to shake off the belief — or was it instinct? — that the glove must look like the hand."

In hindsight, the A2000 made all of its predecessors look like the Hamburger Helper glove. It resembled — for the first time — a baseball glove, or what we now think of as a baseball glove: The thumb is as long as the fingers. The fingers (joined together by laces) are flattened and curved, not thickly pillowed. Liberman quotes Tigers outfielder Al Kaline — featured in A2000 ads of the 1960s — telling a reporter: "The A2000 gave you so much confidence, especially when you had to catch the ball with one hand. The glove seemed to automatically collapse around it."

Instead of a hand-mattress that cushioned the blow of a baseball, the A2000 was designed for catching. The glove premiered the year the Giants moved west, toward Francisco Grande, and was still going strong a decade beyond 2000, that far-off, far-out, sci-fi date that it was intended to evoke in 1957, the year of *Sputnik*'s launch.

Many have tried, but it's nearly impossible to overstate what an object of beauty the A2000 is, with its near-perfect symmetry and a golden-brown glaze that makes many models resemble a Thanksgiving turkey, fresh from the oven. "It's not just a baseball glove," *Esquire* declared fifty years after the A2K's introduction, "it's the single greatest piece of sporting equipment ever built." To sportswriter Dave Kindred, who kept an A2000 on his desktop computer as a muse, "the Wilson A2000 is a masterpiece of man's creative urge."

In 1960, Horace Stoneham paid a $110,000 signing bonus to Randy Hundley, a seventeen-year-old catcher just graduated from Bassett

High School in Madison, Virginia. Hundley's father, Cecil, was a semi-pro catcher whose throwing hand had been broken in twelve places by a baseball. As a result, Cecil Hundley taught his son to catch one-handed, with a flexible, hinged catcher's mitt. The skeptical Giants watched him catch six games that way before abandoning the experiment and dealing him to the Cubs before the 1966 season, at which time he single-handedly—the pun is very much intended—changed forever the way catchers caught.

In 1967, Hundley's second season in Chicago, he made only four errors and won the Gold Glove. With the stiff catcher's mitt, the catcher had to clap his free hand over the ball, like a trumpet mute on a trumpet bell. But catching one-handed, with a hinged mitt, Hundley could keep his bare hand at his side, or behind his back, out of harm's way, where it remained: In 1968, when he made five errors, Hundley caught in 160 games—a record still.

One of Hundley's distant predecessors behind the plate at Wrigley, Jimmy Archer, had his meat hand photographed by *Baseball Magazine* in 1917, his last year catching for the Cubs. "The first and fourth fingers look like the wreck of the Hesperus," the magazine pointed out. "The little finger curves like a barrel hoop." Archer had broken every finger on that right hand, which was nevertheless an aesthetic improvement on his right arm, twice broken and once burned to the bone after he fell into "a vat of scalding tanners' liquid."

For Hundley, never taking a foul tip off his meat hand had another salutary effect. It helped him keep a promise to his mother never to swear, though he did develop, in fourteen years in the big leagues, an extensive vocabulary of anodyne expletives like *shucks* and *blooming*.

More significantly, the hinged mitt helped Hundley honor his father. He promised Cecil half the $110,000 signing bonus he'd received from Stoneham, compensation contested by the IRS in 1967. In the landmark case *Hundley v. Commissioner of Internal*

Revenue, the U.S. Tax Court decided that the payment was indeed a genuine business expense, Cecil Hundley having performed a unique and invaluable service for his son. "A few years before Cecil retired from active participation in baseball as a player, he developed a one-handed method of catching which was unique and unorthodox," the ruling stated. "This technique was beneficial because injuries to the catcher's throwing hand were avoided."

The ruling vouchsafed one-handed catching in the American tax code. But Hundley had not entirely done so on the baseball field—despite his simultaneous Summer of Love victories of court case and Gold Glove. In fact, that first Gold Glove would be Hundley's last, for the following season, 1968, a more prodigiously talented catcher—also the son of a semi-pro player—would win it, and do so without pause for the next decade.

Johnny Bench was a two-handed catcher on July 31, 1966, when he broke his thumb in the very first inning of his very first game for the Buffalo Bisons. In sitting out the rest of the season, he had time to witness Hundley's ascension in Chicago, and to contemplate catching one-handed, which he was doing, rather adeptly, by 1968, when he was named the National League Rookie of the Year.

In winning the National League Most Valuable Player Award in 1970, Bench—like Spalding with his black glove—had the bona fides to change the way all his colleagues caught the baseball. And it was neat that he did so in Cincinnati, one hundred years after that other Cincinnati catcher, Doug Allison, first caught in buckskin mittens.

The year Hundley moved to the Cubs and Bench broke his thumb in Buffalo, a ten-year-old in Seattle, the son of an attorney, drew up an ironclad contract with his sister: For $10, he would get unlimited use of her baseball glove, whenever and wherever he wanted. The contract is often cited as early evidence of the budding business sense of Bill Gates, who—like Hundley—would also prove revolutionary.

*　　*　　*

By its centennial, 1970, the catcher's mitt was so firmly fixed in American culture that a key American outpost in the Vietnam War was called just that. The "Catcher's Mitt"—formed by prominent bends in the Song Be River north of Saigon—would become a late line of defense for the capital against the advancing Vietcong.

"To get to Bien Hoa and Saigon, the enemy has to come through the Catcher's Mitt," Don C. Hall, recalling a superior officer's briefing, wrote in his memoir, *I Served*. "If you will, men, it's the sword pointed at Saigon, which the enemy has as his major objective."

American boys were throwing baseball grenades in an effort to defend the Catcher's Mitt and, by extension, democracy itself. This object that didn't exist a century earlier—the catcher's mitt—was now a cartographical fixture: on the Song Be River in Vietnam, but also in the Wasatch Mountains of Utah—you can ski the Catcher's Mitt, a white-filled concavity on the east side of Kessler Peak—and of course in Bushong, Kansas, namesake of old Doc Bushong, a town as devoted to baseball in its own way as the lost city of Francisco Grande.

The baseball glove had come so far, and seen so many innovations—stuffed, hinged, webbed, dyed—that it took some reminding: It remained, in essence, a mattress for the hand, or any other part of the human anatomy requiring protection. Whether purchased at auction to admire, or at a sporting-goods store to wear, the glove—be it writer's muse or candle scent—was above all meant to comfort.

That comfort came in World War II. Stanley Pisk fought in the 38th Field Artillery of the Second Infantry Division, which spent 320 consecutive days in European combat. Pisk stormed Omaha Beach at Normandy on D-Day and fought, six months later, at the Battle of the Bulge in Belgium. He and his comrades were moving off Eisenborn Ridge there when his attention was seized by something in the snow. Pisk uncovered a partially buried catcher's mitt, a

1941 Wilson model that moved him unexpectedly, filling him with an intense desire to make it home to his wife, Kaye, in New Britain, Connecticut, and to play ball there someday with his newborn son, Ted.

"I think this caused an immediate transformation in his outlook, a life-changing experience," his son, Ted Pisk, told their hometown newspaper sixty-five years later. "It reminded him that there was another life out there. After months of fighting and trying to stay alive, this glove jogged his memory of home, of his son, his wife, of baseball and all the good things that would await him if he could make it."

Stanley Pisk carried that glove in his backpack to combat's end in Pilsen, Czechoslovakia, and back to the United States, where it very slowly made its way, in 2009, to Cooperstown. There, its story will give comfort to many more, in a way that only catcher's mitts can.

There are other ways, of course. Former Orioles and Rangers catcher Johnny Oates, afflicted with hemorrhoids in his retirement, found relief from his pain by sitting on his old gamer.

Chapter 4

THE MEN IN THE GRAY FLANNEL SUITS

A s June turned to July in 1901, New York City succumbed to five straight days of record heat. On July 2, at 2:15 in the afternoon, it was ninety-nine degrees in Manhattan and office workers abandoned their stifling buildings to ride the Staten Island ferry, packed with people desperate for a breeze. "Tunnel workers crawled from the depths," the *New York Times* reported, "complaining of a heat that humans could not stand." Families spent nights sleeping in parks or on fire escapes. The dying were carried away in horse-drawn ambulances, until the horses, too, dropped dead in the streets.

In Brooklyn, in the twenty-four hours from July 1 to 2, 198 burial certificates were issued. Among the dead in that borough was Barney Morris. Born in Ireland in 1792, survivor of 109 years touching three centuries, Morris finally yielded not to war or famine or disease but "to the terrible weapon of death" that was—in an age before air-conditioning—the urban heat wave.

The *Brooklyn Daily Eagle* ran an editorial cartoon that week in which Satan, sweltering beneath a parasol, said: "I'll be darned if this place doesn't remind me of home, sweet home." Clutched in the devil's cloven hand was an electric fan, like the ones being flogged down on Pearl Street by the Edison Electric Illuminating Company, whose slogan — "You Can Be Comfortable In The Hottest Weather" — was not entirely true.

We've forgotten how hot the world was not so very long ago, how inhospitable life could be in places incapable of cooling. In those days, comfort was often forbidden by conventional modes of dress. In Ronkonkoma, on Long Island, villagers were scandalized that some people — in a week when many were driven to insanity by the weather — wore their bathing suits on the streets, in the train station, and even to the post office.

And so, on that fifth straight day of heat, while all about them man and horse were dropping, and brazen suburbanites were posting letters in their swimsuits, the National League champion Brooklyn Superbas hosted the St. Louis Cardinals at Washington Park, in ninety-three-degree heat, in flannel uniforms.

Three years earlier, for its personnel stationed in Cuba, Puerto Rico, and the Philippines, the United States Army had abandoned its smothering flannel in favor of lighter-weight canvas. In the theater of baseball, no such comforts were afforded. Players could only hope that the heat would break during the game, which would go on as scheduled despite that terrible weapon of death all around them.

The game began in the suffocating nineties, but the temperature dropped twelve degrees in two hours, thanks to an Old Testament litany of meteorological phenomena, best summed up in the headline above the *Eagle*'s game story: BROILING SUN, WIND, RAIN AND HAIL SERVED UP AT WASHINGTON PARK. A hot wind, like a dog's breath, descended on the diamond, stirring the dust that clung to flannel fibers like an early version of Velcro. The dust storm was followed by torrential rain that delayed the game. Hail — its metaphorical size went unrecorded, alas — followed rain, "which deluged the ground and precluded any further proceedings." The Cardinals were declared winners, 4–2, but fans and players alike remained in the ballpark to watch nearby St. Agnes Church — struck by lightning during the game — go up in flames. The players could not stay long, however: Like so many men in gray flannel suits in the years to come, they had a train to catch. The Superbas were traveling overnight to Chicago, on a hot train fired by coal, to a still hotter hotel advertised — as so many were in that day — as ABSOLUTELY FIREPROOF.

In the scorching summers at the turn of the last century, man needed reassurance that all about him things weren't going to spontaneously combust. The Superbas, and their twenty-nine-year-old second baseman, Willie Keeler, would have been grateful as they left Brooklyn by train, windows open, the coal cinders sucked into their compartments a small price to pay for the sensation of moving air. A horse had expired on Myrtle Avenue in Brooklyn thirty-six hours earlier but was never removed and "the stench in the neighborhood since that time," the *Eagle* reported, "has been something almost unbearable." The players were exposed to all of this — to deadly heat, welcome rain, pelting hail, the smoke of a church fire, the aroma of dead horse, the dust stirred by urban siroccos — in a single afternoon, in wet flannel. That players of the era often went straight to the station in uniform to catch a scheduled train almost beggars belief.

"When I played for Toledo around 1908 or 1909," Yankees manager Joe McCarthy said in 1957, "we'd pile into a Pullman right after a home game and head for Milwaukee. Our clothes would be dirty and soaking wet, and the first thing we'd do would be to change and hang everything to dry. When we ran out of places to hang clothes, we'd raise the windows and drape the wet shirts out in the breeze. You should have seen how some of the passengers would lose their appetites when they passed through our car en route to the diner."

In all the films and photographs, the radio accounts and interviews from baseball's first half century, what doesn't survive are the smells. But they were powerful, and most powerfully absorbed by wool flannel.

It was still hotter than the Fourth of July when the Superbas played their first game of that western swing to Chicago—*on* the Fourth of July, as it happened. Brooklyn manager Ned Hanlon had a chore for idle pitcher Jay Hughes that torrid afternoon. "I asked Hughes to come up from the dressing room to coach," an irate Hanlon said after the game, "but he disappeared in the shade somewhere and came out at the end of the game cool as a lily."

Superbas infielder Tom Daly squared to bunt in that game in Chicago and popped the ball into one of his eyes, which promptly swelled shut, after which leeches were applied, with little positive effect. But leeches weren't a daily torture in the summer heat. Flannel was.

The Superbas left Chicago for St. Louis, where, on another very hot day, Brooklyn beat the Cardinals on a disputed call at home plate, where umpire Hank O'Day ruled Cardinals left fielder Jesse Burkett out. A crowd of several hundred spectators descended on O'Day as he passed the Cardinals dugout, shouting "Robber!" at him, like the baying mob had done to Barabbas at Gethsemane. Some of the St. Louis players kicked O'Day, then an arm in the mob reached out and punched O'Day in the jaw, and the ump responded with a flurry of blows, at which time he was pummeled beneath a cartoon cloud of flying fists.

And yet, while getting punched, O'Day was dressed as if going to the theater, in flat cap, wool jacket, and a tie knotted at the throat. Surely some of the madness of the day had to do with the heavy clothing of spectators and umpires, to say nothing of the players, sprinting beneath a broiling sun in their flannel pants, shirts, and caps—often collapsing beneath that wool flannel, which weighed eight ounces to the yard, even before it was soaked in sweat.

There was one small consolation: This was lighter than what players had once worn. "Owing to the heavy weight flannels used in our Nos. 0 and 1 Uniforms, we have found it desirable after many years of experience, to use a little lighter weight material for the shirts," read an 1896 ad for uniforms manufactured by the A. G. Spalding & Brothers Company. "This makes them more comfortable, much cooler, and wear just as well as the heavy weight."

The heat literally made people crazy. When Brooklyn made its road swing through St. Louis and Chicago in 1901, some players recalled the same trip in 1897, made in the same insufferable heat. In Chicago, on July 9, 1897, the eighty-eight degrees at eight o'clock in the morning was the highest temperature ever recorded at that hour. The weather filled the papers with its terrible toll: "Charles Benson committed suicide while insane, caused by the extreme heat. John Eaton shot himself while suffering from the heat.... Henry Hazemann, found dead hanging near Park Ridge, [was] driven to the deed by heat.... The night was terrible. There was comfort to be found nowhere." One hundred horses fell dead in the street.

On that road swing in 1897, the Brooklyn players wouldn't visit Chicago for another forty-eight hours, stuck instead in stifling St. Louis, where seven people died on the twelfth consecutive day of the heat wave. Two of the seven that day—"one a New Orleans negress"—were driven insane by the heat. Among the "numerous prostrations" were two who couldn't remain upright during their exertions in that afternoon's baseball game. They were St. Louis first baseman Mike Grady and Brooklyn catcher Aleck Smith, who afterward was said to be unconscious and in serious condition.

Prostration — rendering one prostrate, horizontal in the merciless sun — was a baseball buzzword in that age before night games. Heat was a malevolent force made doubly dangerous by baseball's inexplicable attire. Broadway Aleck Smith would survive the prostration of July 9 — he died twenty-two years later to the very day, of what was poignantly called an "athletic heart" — but it remains a wonder how he and any other catchers so often remained upright.

As for Mike Grady, he too survived, so that he could be photographed in 1905, at the West Side Grounds in Chicago, wearing his St. Louis uniform of long flannel sleeves, a broad collar like a pair of pterodactyl wings turned up at his neck, a wide belt cinched around his waist, high and tight like a fastball. Grady's cap was pulled low to throw half his face in shadow, but otherwise, the only concession to the midday sun was the feeble hole cut in the back of the leather-clad pillow of a glove that must have made his left hand, in the heat of July, feel like a grilling steak.

Grady's opposite number at first base that day in 1905 was Chicago's Frank Chance, who would become the Cubs' player-manager. On July 3, 1911, Chance was overseeing the team's workout "under a hot sun" in Cincinnati when he returned to the bench and collapsed. Players carried him to the clubhouse, where he was examined by the Reds' physician, Dr. H. H. Hines, who declared Chance unfit to continue. "Excitement or physical effort," the next day's paper reported, "might prove fatal at any time."

And while Chance had developed a blood clot in his brain from manifold beanballs, he wasn't done any favors by the Cubs' uniform of the day. In 1911, the team wore a flannel pullover with four buttons up the front, as on a nightshirt. Above the flannel, over Chance's heart, was a large felt *C* all but encircling that gorgeous bear-and-bat logo. To make matters significantly worse, the road uniforms — pants and shirt conjoined at the waist by a cinched leather belt — were a deep midnight blue, the better to absorb and retain the Cincinnati sun.

Frank Chance in the Cubs' stifling road uniform. *(National Baseball Hall of Fame Library, Cooperstown, NY)*

At least one of Chance's jerseys survives from that potentially fatal 1911 season. It is a home shirt, with Albert Spalding's label beneath the collar. In 2009, it sold at auction for $62,213, for let us not forget: These instruments of torture were also among the most beautiful and evocative garments that ever graced the earth, and young men were dying to put them on, not take them off.

And death was a potential side effect of those uniforms, for reasons having nothing whatsoever to do with heat. When the Brooklyn Superbas hosted St. Louis in the subtropical conditions of July 2, 1901, before catching that train west to still hotter miseries, they did so without starting catcher Duke Farrell, who was blood poisoned after one of his shins was torn open by the spikes of Cincinnati player Harry Steinfeldt.

To understand why this would have been terrifying to Farrell's teammates, we have to go back to the very beginning of professional baseball in 1869, when the Cincinnati team identified itself by the vivid socks of its players. By 1870, the Red Stockings were joined by the Chicago White Stockings (who would become the Cubs), and in 1880 by the Worcester Ruby Legs (a lovely nickname that unaccountably fell into disuse), and in 1896 by the Detroit Wolverines (whose yellow-striped socks prompted people to call them the Tigers).

The Chicago White Sox arrived in 1901, the deliberate misspelling in preemptive obeisance to headline writers, who would shorten it anyway. By December 18, 1907, when the Boston Americans changed their name to the Red Sox, baseball had a long history of colorful hosiery.

Long before baseball caps were accepted as appropriate attire in civilian life, bright socks were the one piece of the uniform players tried to replicate in their civilian dress. "One of Hornsby's great features as a dresser is his socks," one writer noted. "They cry to heaven. They can be seen at night." When Casey Stengel left boisterous Brooklyn to manage the Boston Bees in 1938, his ankles were tamed for the trip north. "Honestly, you wouldn't recognize old Casey this spring," a wire-service reporter cabled from St. Petersburg. "His shoes are shined, his nails manicured and his socks of sober hue like those of a modest bank president."

To men already predisposed to blinding fashions, baseball's uniform socks were bewitching. The trouble was, colorfast dyes did not exist for professional baseball's first several decades, and when a player like Duke Farrell of the Superbas was spiked in the shin in 1901 — the blood of his open wound commingling with the running dye of his socks — he risked getting blood poisoning. Or so people believed.

Blood poisoning was a grave illness, and seemed to afflict ballplayers disproportionately. Napoleon Lajoie, the great Cleveland infielder who abandoned his double-knobbed bat for a Louisville Slugger, was felled by blood poisoning after being spiked in 1905. As the *Boston Globe* reported, "The scratch is on the inside and not bigger than a fingernail, but it is thought some of the dye in his stocking got into the wound and affected it."

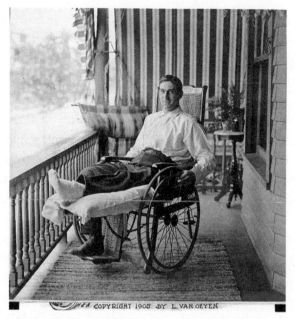

Nap Lajoie convalescing on his porch, 1905. *(Library of Congress)*

To prevent this, teams began to wear a second pair of dye-free socks beneath their vivid uniform hose. These plain white "sanitary socks" were every bit as uncomfortable as they sound. Imagine, on a hot summer day, stuffing a second pair of socks into your baking leather shoes. To ventilate that heat, arched openings were cut in the front and back of the uniform socks, exposing great white moons of the "sanitary sock," a phrase that now sounds oxymoronic to most of the world but is perfectly familiar to anyone who played baseball in the twentieth century.

For the next eighty years, long after the introduction of colorfast dyes, players would wear these "sanis" beneath their vestigial uniform socks—or stirrups—as an unnecessary and obsolete hedge against turn-of-the-century blood poisoning.

Which isn't to say that blood poisoning wasn't a real menace. It would have seemed especially so among baseball people. After Lajoie missed most of the 1905 season with blood poisoning, big-league veteran Frank Bonner—then on his descent with Kansas City of the American Association—died of blood poisoning. The next season, the Senators' rookie first baseman, Jerry Freeman, was blood poisoned and nearly lost a finger on his throwing hand. The season after that, while playing for the Providence Grays, former Cardinals shortstop Forrest Crawford died of it, quite suddenly, which came as "a great shock" to his manager, Hugh Duffy, "who had no inkling he was sick."

That's how abrupt and insidious blood poisoning was. It would kill both the owner of the St. Louis Cardinals (Stanley Robinson) and the owner of the St. Louis Browns (the gloriously named Phil De Catesby Ball). As ailments go, it had an extraordinarily high profile, the phrase frequently attaching itself to obituaries and news bulletins. Blood poisoning was the official cause of death of Yankees manager Miller Huggins and before that—when her appendix burst—of Mary McGraw, wife of future Giants manager John McGraw, then with Baltimore.

Blood poisoning rang the curtain down on one of baseball's most baroque lives, that of Rube Waddell, the great southpaw (and alcoholic "sousepaw") whose manifold eccentricities included having the attention span of a carpenter ant. (Waddell was known to leave the mound to pursue, on foot, any passing fire truck.)

In 1913, while playing for Minneapolis in the Northern League, on the treacherous down slope of a Hall of Fame career, Waddell bruised one of his thighs and was promptly hospitalized in serious condition with blood poisoning. As was often the case in such situations, amputation of the leg was mooted and—though that option was rejected—Waddell died anyway, a year later, of what proved to be tuberculosis. He was an old man of thirty-seven.

Players lived dog years. "In 11 years, I've changed uniforms some 23 times, broken my left leg three times and suffered such little things as blood poisoning, infected fingers and a brain concussion," the pitcher Bobo Newsom said in 1938, when he was thirty-one and well into a pitching career—the *only* pitching career—that would span both Babe Ruth and Mickey Mantle.

That socks might serve as a magical shield against the malady was not entirely wishful thinking in that age before antibiotics. By far the most famous victim of blood poisoning was Calvin Coolidge Jr., sixteen-year-old son of the president. On June 30, 1924, while playing tennis on the White House lawn against his older brother, John, young Calvin developed a blister on his toe. It became infected, the infection spread swiftly, and the boy died a week later, in Walter Reed Hospital, in the arms of the bereft president, who shouted that he would soon join the boy in the great beyond. "When he went," Coolidge wrote, "the power and the glory of the presidency went with him."

Calvin Coolidge Jr. *(Library of Congress)*

A rumor quickly spread—in malign imitation of the infection that killed him—that Calvin Jr. had worn black socks in his fatal tennis match, and that toxic dye had seeped into the wound. In fact, something like the opposite was true: Young Calvin hadn't worn socks at all that day, when doing so might have prevented the blister that killed him.

It wasn't the first time that fear of blood poisoning abruptly led to rumor and in turn to public hysteria. In the top of the ninth inning of Game 3 of the 1911 World Series, Philadelphia Athletics third baseman Frank Baker—who had already won Game 2 with a home run—hit another bomb, this one off Giants ace Christy Mathewson, to tie the game 1–1. In the bottom of the tenth, while getting thrown out at third at the Polo Grounds, Giants center fielder Fred Snodgrass spiked Baker in the leg. The slugger was "cut and bruised severely," and when the Series moved to Philadelphia for Game 4, the Giants' train was met at the station by a mob of fans calling Snodgrass "Spiker!" and "Dirty!" and doubtless more colorful epithets unfit for newspapers of that or any other day.

Teammates hustled Snodgrass into a taxi, which whisked him off to the Majestic Hotel, a twelve-story jewel on Broad Street in the theater district of north Philadelphia with a grand tradition of hosting ball clubs. The five-foot-five Rabbit Maranville once entered a twelfth-floor room at the Majestic by way of the narrow cornice that ran beneath the windows on the hotel's exterior, his teammates having locked him out of a card game.

As torrential rains fell on Philadelphia, Game 4 of the 1911 World Series was twice postponed. (A week would pass before it was played.) In the meantime, and with little else to do, a crowd of Philadelphians gathered outside the Majestic. They "hooted and hissed" whenever Snodgrass passed, and an A's fan jostled with Arthur Fletcher, claiming that the Giants shortstop had hit him with a newspaper. The fan vowed to return that night and exact vengeance.

In such an atmosphere, in those idle days between games, rumors (and wounds) were likely to fester.

And they did. A report quickly circulated that Baker had been hospitalized with blood poisoning, a result of the spiking. Snodgrass wisely holed up in his room at the Majestic, his absence on the street leading to reports that he'd been shot by an A's fan. Several Giants players had to be pulled from a nearby theater to deny the rumor to the baying mob, but such mobs are seldom quelled easily. And so McGraw finally sent Snodgrass back to New York to wait out the rain, at once proving that his defiant center fielder was very much alive and neutralizing the bloodthirsty crowd on the sidewalk.

A's fans had tried to get his goat, but as Snodgrass memorably put it: "My goat is not for sale." A line in the next day's *New York Times,* beneath the headline SNODGRASS HOOTED OUT OF PHILADELPHIA, drily understated the tenor—then as now—of that city's sports fans: "Partisan feeling here is very strong."

Baker, meanwhile, was not in a hospital with poisoned blood but at home, resting comfortably, in advance of what would be a two-for-three performance in Game 4. His winning shots in Games 2 and 3 had already earned him a brand-new nickname—Home Run Baker—that would last the rest of his life and beyond, inscribed as it is on his Cooperstown plaque.

History was less kind to Snodgrass. After losing to Philadelphia in 1911, he and the Giants would return to the World Series in 1912, in Boston's brand-new Fenway Park, where they led the Red Sox 2–1 in the decisive game. The home team opened the bottom of the tenth inning with an easy fly ball to center field that "fell from the pouch of the padded glove" of Snodgrass, beginning a game- and Series-winning rally for which Snodgrass would forever be held responsible. A father of two who played nine seasons in the big leagues, Snodgrass became the mayor of Oxnard, California, and died—a grandfather of five—on April 5, 1974, in his native

Ventura, California. And what was the headline in the next day's *New York Times*? FRED SNODGRASS, 86, DEAD; BALL PLAYER MUFFED 1912 FLY.

The Giants would lose a third consecutive World Series in 1913, again facing the A's, an experience so dispiriting to McGraw that he was said to have committed suicide in his Philadelphia hotel room. The desk clerk at the Majestic received so many inquiries from the press that he "finally went up to McGraw's room to reassure the New York papers and was informed via the keyhole that 'the report was greatly exaggerated.'"

But then man's worst fears and darkest thoughts came to life in the absence of facts. Which goes a long way toward explaining how stirrups and sanitary socks came to be, but not how they continued to thrive long after dyes were rendered nontoxic, and blood poisoning (or sepsis, as it has come to be known) was treated with antibiotics, a phrase coined by a Ukrainian microbiologist named Selman Waksman, who discovered many of the bacteria-fighting agents used today. Waksman won the Nobel for medicine in 1952 for his discovery of streptomycin, which fights tuberculosis, albeit too late to help mad Rube Waddell.

In the age of antibiotics, after stirrups and sanis lost whatever function they were intended to serve, they were simply accepted as part of the proper costume of a ballplayer. A century after the Cincinnati Red Stockings started big-league baseball, big-league teams—Cincinnati among them—were still wearing stirrups. But not happily so. The Reds of the 1970s were ordered by management to wear their stirrups so low that only a small arc of sanitary-white showed beneath, like the white crescent moon at the base of your fingernail.

The players ridiculed these stirrups as "ankle-chokers," better suited to Midwestern winters than to Cincinnati summers, a fact not lost on Johnny Bench, who wore them while duck hunting. "You could go out any morning, no matter how cold," he said, "and stay warm as toast."

On an August day in 1939, the sportswriter Henry McLemore stood in the Yankees' clubhouse, in a sodden seersucker suit, and watched the "poor players" get dressed for battle at the stadium: "First a layer of heavy underwear. Then two pairs of socks. Then a layer of sliding pads. Then a heavy sweat shirt, and finally, their Yankee uniforms, made of the hottest, thickest, most luxuriously smothering flannel that can be bought." Catcher Bill Dickey, before donning a mask, chest protector, and shin guards that day, put on "leg warmers" beneath his pants. And while the airless clubhouse was "boiling hot," it was an oasis compared to the playing field that summoned them at the last possible moment. "Out the Yankees went," wrote McLemore, "to suffer under the Congo sun." It was, he noted, 102 degrees.

The baseball uniform was a study in masochism but also its near anagram — machismo. The photograph of my grandfather that hung in the house I grew up in — and now greets my children daily in the hallway of our home — is a portrait of quiet suffering. Jimmy Boyle is in his catcher's crouch at the Polo Grounds, wool Giants cap pulled low over his forehead, its blunt bill providing the only shade, his arms covered in long sleeves of thick flannel, his collar high and tight against his neck, a leather mattress on his left hand as he stares implacably at the camera. "To Mother & Dad," reads his inscription, in a neat Palmer script. "7/29/26. New York Giants. Lovingly, Jim."

Of course, the umpire standing behind the catcher had it worse, in his cap, blazer, dress shirt, and necktie, his slacks and polished shoes attempting to exude the authority of a prosecutor. When umpire Red Ormsby suffered heat prostration during a doubleheader in St. Louis in 1935, White Sox reserve center fielder Jocko Conlan filled in for him and — just like that — switched careers. Conlan would work as a National League ump for twenty-five years, officiate in six World Series and as many All-Star Games, and be inducted, in 1974, into the Baseball Hall of Fame. But in his speech at Cooperstown, all he could talk about was the heat that at once gave him a career and made baseball life so exceedingly uncomfortable.

Trains and train stations were a special misery. "When you think you had to carry two fifty pound bags [of equipment] and those [porters] would run away from you at 116 degrees," he said. "I wish after reading the papers these days that these 20- and 30-year-old guys playing get tired, if they had to ride the train from St. Louis to Boston with a screen on the window, [and] thank God the screen was there....I think they'd change their story. We just didn't know any different." Then he thanked former National League president Warren Giles for his unsung contribution to the game: arranging to have umpires' bags airfreighted from one city to another at the conclusion of a series.

As if it weren't hot and heavy enough on its own, the flannel uniform doubled its weight with perspiration. It was almost medieval. At the Battle of Agincourt in 1415, the French outnumbered the English five to one. But each suit of steel-plate armor worn by French knights weighed as much as 110 pounds. A study by biomechanic scientists in 2011 concluded that those knights moved at half the speed while expending twice the energy of their more lightly clad English counterparts.

The flannel uniform wasn't just heavy, though. It was as itchy as a medieval hair shirt. The outfielder Andy Pafko likened it to wearing burlap. "The uniforms were so uncomfortable," Yankees first baseman Moose Skowron once said. "Maybe that's why our games lasted two hours. Because we wanted to go take a shower instead of scratch."

Scratching is what the young Mets outfielder Ken Singleton did throughout spring training of 1972. That April he was traded to Montreal, where he became even itchier, and developed hives from neck to knee. "It looks like he stepped out of a shower of mustard gas" was manager Gene Mauch's description of this mystery ailment, which puzzled allergists, who asked Singleton to keep a daily diary of his diet.

Alas, Singleton's hives only intensified. He was having the worst kind of breakout season. Singleton's hives became so bad he was sent home from a series in Cincinnati, after which the hives mysteriously disappeared. But when he returned to play, so did they, driving Singleton to such great distraction that he couldn't even remain on the bench.

Mercifully, the Expos, suspecting it was the flannel, had ordered a single sample that spring of a new double-knit polyester uniform, and they had Singleton wear that in the clubhouse during one game. But only the shirt. The pants didn't fit. He spent four blissful hours, hive-free, but still had to petition the league to wear it in a game, as a team's uniforms were required to be just that: uniform.

The mystery was solved and Singleton—allowed to dress in double-knits—hit .274 in 142 games that season. As Expos general manager Jim Fanning said, "The knits are more comfortable, harder to tear, easier to clean and cost almost half as much." Singleton was freed from the tyranny (but also the beauty) of flannel. And soon, so was all of baseball.

Moose Skowron, who retired in 1967 and never knew the joy of double-knits, said, "These lightweight uniforms are like pajamas compared to what we had."

Like women's shoes, or the bearskin hats worn by Buckingham Palace guards, those flannel uniforms were at once ridiculously uncomfortable and—lest we forget—profoundly beautiful. What was on them was often more appealing than what was in them.

In February 1921, Cardinals manager Branch Rickey was scheduled to speak at a lunch at the First Presbyterian Church in Ferguson,

Missouri. The young lady in charge of table decorations, Allie May Schmidt, saw two birds alight on a sprig outside her window. Inspired, she cut out a series of paper redbirds and strung them together with yarn. The vivid birds captivated Rickey, and the following season, for the first time, across every Cardinal's chest sat a pair of redbirds, perched on a bat.

That birds-on-a-bat logo would become one of the sport's most evocative icons, for years embroidered on St. Louis uniform tops by a woman named Eulah Street, maestro of a technique called chain stitching, an ancient art that produces the beautifully curved lines of the script "Cardinals."

Angled script is quintessentially baseball, and was first worn in the professional ranks, according to the Hall of Fame, in 1902, by both Oakland and San Francisco of the California League. Its most famous manifestation was the scripted "Dodgers" that first appeared in Brooklyn in 1938, that rich blue against the crisp white, as if God had signed it there with a Sharpie. In 1952, the team added red numbers on the left rib cage. Against that blinding white, the red popped like lipstick on a starched collar.

In 1910, the Spalding company offered six different styles of lettering on its baseball uniforms, among them the "Block," the "Fancy," and the "Old English." They sound a bit like offerings at a turn-of-the-century brothel, but in fact had become baseball's typefaces. From this limited font menu, the Detroit Tigers in 1904 went with Old English, whose Gothic capital *D* became, over the next century, a proud symbol of a beleaguered city, tattooed on the right forearms of Detroit natives Eminem and Kid Rock, so that it became a kind of global export, a worthy rival in baseball's alphabet to the interlocking *NY* of the Yankees.

These were not accidental fashions. Teams devoted great effort to trendsetting, often without success. In 1916, the Giants wore uniforms of purple plaid. The black-and-white photography of the time has given those uniforms historical cover, but they were hideous to behold, and were abandoned after one season. That same summer, across town, the Brooklyn Robins wore blue checks. But as ever, baseball and windowpanes didn't mix well.

Also in 1916, for the first time, a big-league baseball team wore numbers on their uniforms, a practice the Indians abandoned after one season. At the National League's annual meeting at the Waldorf-Astoria in 1923, Dodgers president Charles Ebbets suggested the league adopt numbers, either on both sleeves or the peak of the cap, the latter evidently as an aid to migrating birds. Ebbets had begun his life in baseball selling scorecards, but a scorecard bereft of uniform numbers.

In the end, only the Cardinals chose to wear numbers in '23 — on the left sleeve — and even then only briefly. In his online exhibit on uniform evolution, "Dressed to the Nines," Hall of Fame curator Tom Shieber quotes Branch Rickey lamenting the results thirty-nine years later. "Ridicule followed throughout the country, presswise and otherwise," Rickey said. "More particularly, the players were subjected to field criticism from the stand and especially from opposing players.... The effect upon the team was bad and 'busted up' the team morale or spirit completely. They really didn't want to show themselves on the field. Because of the continuing embarrassment to the players, the numbers were removed."

Uniform numbers wouldn't take hold until 1929. The summer before in England, Arsenal and Sheffield Wednesday wore numbered shirts for the first time in association football, on August 25, 1928. Each number corresponded to the player's position, beginning with the respective goalkeepers, who wore number 1.

The following spring, the Indians and Yankees opened the season doing something similar, except their numbers corresponded to the batting order, famously accounting for Babe Ruth's number 3 and Lou Gehrig's number 4.

In a game beholden to superstition, numbers quickly took on magical, sometimes diabolical, properties. In April 1951, Ralph Branca was photographed on Friday the thirteenth displaying the number 13 on the back of his Dodgers jersey. On his left shoulder was a black cat. It was a rare kind of provocation for baseball, and after Bobby Thomson homered off Branca that October, robbing the Dodgers of the pennant and bringing lifelong fame to both men, Branca briefly switched to number 12.

Branca's future son-in-law, Bobby Valentine, born May 13, 1950, wore the number 13 until he was ravaged by injuries, then he too switched numbers. Carlos May became the only big leaguer to wear his birthday on his back: MAY 17. When he owned the Braves, Ted Turner gave pitcher Andy Messersmith the number 17 but with CHANNEL instead of MESSERSMITH above it, because Turner owned Channel 17 in Atlanta. Playing for Fargo-Moorhead in the Northern League in 1951, Johnny Neves wore a backward 7 (read NEVES backward), two decades before Red Sox pitcher Bill Lee would request the number 337 (look at the number upside down).

It was White Sox owner Bill Veeck who first put player names on the back of big-league uniforms, in 1960, black letters four inches high sewn onto their road uniforms only. "The fans in Chicago are thoroughly familiar with their players," Sox PR man Ed Short told reporters. As ever, players did not entirely embrace the innovation. "We look like semi-pros," Nellie Fox complained in spring training. Another thought it an invasion of privacy, and asked why the team didn't just print their home phone numbers on the uniforms.

But fans and writers were immediately won over by a small revolution that only cost, as Veeck boasted, $200. Of course, he got what he paid for. The letters were poorly spaced — Nellie Fox's three-letter surname managed to take up most of his back — and the names sometimes randomly spelled. When the team played in New York in

May, slugger Ted Kluszewski strode to the plate with KLUSƷEWSXI on his back. The *Z* had been sewn on backward. Even so, Big Klu expressed gratitude for his broad back, so that his name — however badly butchered — had ample room for display, and didn't exile the *K* and the *I* to either armpit.

Ted Kluszewski's name misspelled on the back of his White Sox jersey, 1960. (© *Bettmann/CORBIS*)

Klu's armpits were frequently exposed by the sleeveless uniforms he'd worn in Cincinnati and Pittsburgh. Before double-knits, the flannel vest was about the only way to avoid heatstroke. Another was Orlon. In 1941, DuPont created this acrylic polymer, which was an improvement over nylon in that it decomposed, rather than melted. But Orlon didn't find a market until the middle 1950s, when it became an essential component in the tight women's sweaters of the era. By 1960, the material was everywhere. "Orlon," as DuPont noted in its own history of the wonder substance, "had become a 19-year-old overnight sensation."

Lightweight, space-age, comfortable, Orlon was married with wool and introduced into baseball uniforms that decade. The blend became—in the words of uniform historian Marc Okkonen—"the 'ultimate' material for baseball flannels" at the time. Those flannel uniforms were lighter than my grandfather's, and also tighter, the pants tapering, a watershed often credited to Willie Mays, whose tailored pants more closely reflected the civilian style of the day.

Of course, tapered pants weren't Mays's only sartorial affectation: He remains more famous for his too-small cap, which flew off his head like a champagne cork when he sprinted after fly balls.

Casey Stengel of the Pirates walked to the plate at Ebbets Field on a Sunday afternoon in 1919 expecting to be booed. It was the first year Sunday baseball was allowed in New York, and Dodgers fans enjoyed the novelty—the illicit pleasure—of booing Stengel loudly on the Lord's day. Stengel acknowledged the boos by doffing his cap, at which time—and to great cheers—a sparrow flew out.

A year later, at the Baker Bowl in Philadelphia, Stengel trapped another sparrow beneath his cap on the outfield grass, donned his cap with the bird underneath, and promptly caught a fly ball. He then doffed his cap, loosing the bird on delighted spectators.

Hats have been donned (a contraction of "do on") and doffed ("do off") since at least the 1500s, when milliners—literally, merchants from Milan—were becoming renowned for their women's hats. Doffing one's hat is an unwitting homage to military history. Medieval knights raised the visors of their helmets to reveal their faces and, by extension, their peaceful intentions. From this gesture we get the modern military salute, which reveals a right hand free of weaponry, but also serves as a token doffing of a hat when real hat-doffing is impossible or impractical. Removing one's hat in the presence of a lady—or to a cheering crowd at a baseball park—is part of this code of chivalry, though the fact is likely now lost on the modern player making a curtain call.

There was much history, then, bound up in hats by the time Stengel doffed his in 1920, in the middle of a golden age of headwear, when no respectable scalp went uncovered. That year, German-born Ehrhardt Koch borrowed $5,000 from an aunt and opened the E. Koch Cap Company at the corner of Genesee and Bailey Streets in Buffalo, where he began to make "newsboy" caps—eight-paneled wool flat caps of the sort worn by kids shouting, "Extra! Extra! Read all about it!" while waving newspapers full of ads for felt trilbies and straw boaters.

That first year, Koch made five thousand dozen caps for men, and in 1922, reflecting this heady age of hat-wearing, he changed the name of his burgeoning operation to the New Era Cap Company.

There was little market then for baseball caps, which were worn only by baseball players, who were profoundly grateful to have them. On a diamond, baseball caps provided marginal shade (an 1895 cap with a transparent green bill, like a poker player's eyeshade, never caught on) and protection from the rain. But beneath the bill, or on the crown, a spitballer could store all manner of foreign substances, or simply use it as his briefcase. In the deciding game of the 1925 World Series, Washington pitcher Walter Johnson asked the home plate umpire for sawdust to scatter around the wet pitcher's mound. When the ump obliged, Johnson filled his cap with it, and carried it back to his position like a busker begging for change.

So the cap had all manner of uses. It was awning, birdcage, and wheelbarrow. It was also a potent symbol, doffed and held over the heart during the national anthem. It was a thing of beauty, too: adorned with Detroit's Gothic *D*, or the linked *St* and *L* of the Cardinals, or the big *S* that coiled around the smaller *O* and *X* on the White Sox cap, like a snake protecting its eggs.

Baseball caps represented a growing alphabet of American iconography. They were integral to baseball's many superstitions. Giants coach Clarence Mitchell "wore his cap inside out at the Polo Grounds on Sunday, hoping it would bring victory"—an early citation, in the *New York Times* in 1932, of what would come to be known as the rally cap.

That year, Ehrhardt Koch was persuaded by his American-born son Harold to design a baseball cap. There were echoes here of American-born Bud Hillerich persuading his German immigrant father, Johann Frederich, to manufacture baseball bats half a century earlier. Within two years, New Era had struck a deal to supply the caps of the nearest major-league team, the Cleveland Indians, and was making caps for minor-league and amateur teams, while also making private-label caps for Wilson and Spalding, who would sew on logos and sell them on to teams.

By the 1950s—when New Era was directly supplying the Indians, Tigers, Dodgers, and Reds, and indirectly supplying other teams through Spalding and Wilson—the public was becoming covetous of these game-worn caps. Some teams offered replica caps for a dollar, in any of three sizes: Boys' Small, Boys' Medium, or Boys' Large. But what of the grown man who wanted one? After Phillies pitcher Curt Simmons beat the Giants at the Polo Grounds on September 23, 1956, a fan ran onto the field and stole his hat. Simmons ran after him, intent on retrieving the cap, quite possibly with the head still in it. In 1957, after the final out of the World Series, Braves pitcher Lew Burdette chased down the man who stole his cap and wrestled it from his grasp.

What was the appeal of a sweat-stained cap that offered little more than eye shade? That's what Soviet premier Nikita Khrushchev wondered while cooling his heels in an Indonesian rest house after delivering an anti-American speech in Indonesia in 1960. Khrushchev, aboil after touring the Buddhist temple of Borobodur, beckoned American journalist Roy Essoyan to sit next to him, in a seat just vacated by President Sukarno of Indonesia. Essoyan, the former Kremlin correspondent for the Associated Press, by now stationed in Southeast Asia, obliged, and doffed his baseball cap as he sat down. Khrushchev snatched the cap from his hands, "examined it"—in Essoyan's words—"and waved it around."

"This is the sort of thing that baffles me about the United States," Khrushchev said. "America is such a rich country and you Americans wear rags like this."

"That's no rag," Essoyan replied, standing up for his country. "It may not be very beautiful, but it's very handy at baseball games."

Khrushchev was photographed putting the cap on his head, providing a momentary thaw in the Cold War. "It must keep the sun off very well," he said, fascinated and perhaps even envious. "It looks very utilitarian."

And it was. Baseball players may have dressed like farmers a century earlier, but farmers were now dressing like baseball players, having ditched straw hats for baseball caps emblazoned with the names of feed companies. Caps were colonizing the rest of the world, and even places beyond. New Era supplied baseball caps to members of the USS *Hornet*'s Splashdown Recovery team when they fished the *Apollo 11* astronauts out of the Pacific Ocean. A few years earlier the astronauts themselves had begun wearing baseball caps adorned with the gold-braided "scrambled eggs" of navy officers, an embellishment that was offensive to at least one columnist.

The scrollwork "is pretentious and insensitive, and it is ruinous to the most democratic, functional and even lovable piece of headwear in our contemporary folklore," wrote the syndicated columnist Charles McDowell, who likened braids on a ball cap to rhinestone buttons on blue jeans or white sidewalls on a jeep. "The plain old baseball cap is something that matters in this country. Admiral Halsey wore one, plain, on the bridge of his flagship in World War II.

Service station attendants wear them. General Westmoreland wears one in Viet Nam. Football coaches and golfers and truck drivers wear them. Presidents Truman and Eisenhower have worn them. Farmers are abandoning straw hats to wear baseball caps on their tractors. Movie directors wear them. A miler from Kenya wears one to run in. Y. A. Tittle wore one to keep the sun off his bald spot at football practice." And so on.

Baseball players, it was easy to forget, also wore them. By 1974, New Era was outfitting twenty of the twenty-four major-league teams. Truckers could buy foam-crowned, mesh-backed hats equipped with plastic "snapbacks" that turned any cap into a fitted cap. But baseball fans could not easily purchase a fitted cap of the kind the players wore.

That changed in 1978, when New Era ran an ad in the *Sporting News* offering to sell fitted major-league baseball caps to anyone who sent the company $12.99, "check or money order," the kind of direct marketing Montgomery Ward pioneered in the previous century.

New Era was inundated with orders, which was a blessing, as America was already eighteen years into a *new* New Era—a hatless age, ushered in when President Kennedy went without head cover at his 1960 inauguration. Almost instantly, men stopped wearing dress hats to ball games, or anywhere else.

John Board was an usher at Crosley Field in Cincinnati in 1947, working for $1.50 a game. He escorted fans to their seats through the 1950s and '60s, through the close of Crosley in 1970 and the opening of Riverfront Stadium in 1971, through the entire thirty-three-year duration of that new stadium and into the first decade of the Great American Ball Park, where he was still ushering, for $8.50 an hour, in 2010, when he told the *Cincinnati Enquirer* that the biggest changes he had seen in his sixty-three years of ushering were the increased presence of women and the increased absence of dress sense.

"Used to be almost all men," said Board. "Lots of people [now] wearing Reds hats, jerseys, shirts. Used to be mostly men in coats and ties and dress hats. They were more polite. Now, when you have a problem, they can be a little crude."

Baseball crowds had always been exceedingly male. In 1915, the Red Sox scorecard urged fans to VOTE NO ON WOMAN SUFFRAGE FOR THE PROTECTION OF YOUR WOMEN WHO DO NOT WISH TO BE FORCED INTO POLITICS. Forty years later, the same program ran an ad that read: "Some say it's SEX, some say it's Seaforth! The Shave Lotion that gives your face a zing! A zip! A lift! And its 'Come-Heather' aroma is really a gal-getter!" To illustrate the benefits of this $0.59 unguent, a model was literally draped over a man, wrapped around his neck like a shawl.

It is strange, then, that as more women attended games, men began dressing not as if they were accompanying a date to the theater—as they had when no women at all attended—but rather as if they might be summoned, at a moment's notice, into the game itself. The rise of officially licensed caps in the 1980s saw spectators entirely made over: in hats, but also in jerseys.

In 1985, Peter Capolino, the middle-aged owner of Mitchell & Ness, an eighty-year-old sporting-goods store in Philadelphia, found, in a warehouse in that city, twelve thousand yards of wool flannel. Even to a visionary merchant doing growing business in the sale of base-ball caps, seven miles of flannel did not instantly look like a red carpet rolling out, or a revenue stream running to the horizon. That it would become both of those things—leading him to Hollywood parties and tens of millions of dollars in annual revenue—was beyond the scope of even his imagination.

Which is not to say that Capolino lacked creative spark. On the contrary, with his flannel treasure, he obtained a license to make old baseball jerseys, exacting in detail, meticulously reproduced in color, cut, fabric, and embroidery. The hot hair shirts that players couldn't wait to take off were coveted by bankers and dentists gripped by boyhood nostalgia for the Brooklyn Dodgers and New York Giants—"older, white, conservative males who have this thing [for baseball] that goes back to childhood," as Capolino put it.

At the same time, these jerseys became popular with rappers and filmmakers. A 1955 Brooklyn Dodgers jersey was the most versatile of garments, one that could say both "hip-hop" and "hip replacement," depending on who was wearing it.

Director Spike Lee was seldom photographed in anything but a blue or white Brooklyn Dodgers cap. In his 1989 film *Do the Right Thing*—set in Brooklyn on the hottest day of the summer—Lee played a pizza delivery guy named Mookie who sweltered in a Jackie Robinson jersey, much as the Dodgers' predecessors, the Superbas, had sweltered in their jerseys on Brooklyn's hottest day eighty-eight years earlier. Only now, jerseys were fraught with cultural symbolism. As racial tensions reached a boil in *Do the Right Thing*, a black character, Buggin' Out, has his new Air Jordans scuffed by a white man wearing—a deliberate provocation—the Boston Celtics jersey of Larry Bird.

The summer after *Do the Right Thing*, the Chicago White Sox—always a fashion-forward franchise—looked backward for inspiration, playing a "Turn Back the Clock" game against the Brewers in the uniforms from their last championship season. Even a Cubs fan could recognize the beauty of those 1917 Sox uniforms, especially in contrast to their uninspired contemporary double-knits.

To a large segment of the population, the retro caps and jerseys that came to be called "throwbacks" were divorced from team loyalties. They were largely about fashion. New Era became the exclusive supplier of caps to every team in Major League Baseball in 1993, and three years later Spike Lee asked the company to make him a red Yankees cap. The director promptly wore it to the World Series, at

Yankee Stadium, stirring enormous demand for alternative caps for major-league teams. Before long, New Era was making more than 120 different Yankees caps alone, and the 59Fifty cap—named for its original model number—had become a staple of American streetwear, the circular gold sizing sticker left on the brim. Deposed Libyan dictator Mu'ammar Gadhafi was executed moments after being pulled from a drainage pipe in his hometown of Sirte, where he'd been discovered by a young rebel who wore—as a new era dawned for his country—a camouflage-patterned Yankees cap.

One of the first stores to carry the Mitchell & Ness uniforms was Distant Replays in Atlanta, where the rap duo Outkast bought retro Braves and Cubs uniforms, which they wore in the photo that appeared in the liner jacket of their platinum 1998 album, *Aquemini*. When that album blew up, so did uniform sales. In 2001, Capolino hired a young African-American customer named Reuben Harley as his liaison to the music industry, and soon the two of them—Capolino and "Big Rube"—were consorting at parties and premieres with hip-hop stars like Fabolous, Big Boi, Scarface, and P. Diddy, who called the garrulous Capolino "P. Chatty."

And yet, when I asked Capolino which star he was most excited about meeting, he answered "Eulah Street," the woman who did the chain-stitching embroidery on Stan Musial's St. Louis Cardinals jerseys.

Given the beauty of those garments, it is perhaps unsurprising that Turn Back the Clock games have become a staple not only of baseball but of every sport, and a lucrative marketing scheme. By 2011, New Era was making thirty million caps a year.

Their caps are now infinitely more numerous in the stands—and on city streets around the world—than they are on the baseball field. As one example among countless, an "underground urban streetwear" emporium called 5Pointz, in Bristol, England, offers 120 varieties of New Era baseball caps, for the youngster on the southwest coast of the United Kingdom who has never heard of the Texas Rangers but remains in thrall to hip-hop fashion. The company has offices in Hong Kong, Paris, and Cologne, and New Era stores in London, Berlin, and Toronto, in addition to New York City.

In 2011, New Era opened an 1,100-square-foot store in Tokyo, in the youth-culture hothouse of Harajuku, supplying Japanese hipsters with an endless array of Major League Baseball caps but also a selection of men's dress hats—including the eight-paneled newsboy number that started it all ninety years earlier. Those caps were part of the company's EK line, named for Ehrhardt Koch, who achieved something remarkable: He literally elevated the lowly American baseball cap onto heads around the world, including in the former Soviet Union, where that utilitarian "rag"—as Khrushchev called the baseball cap—thrives long after the demise of Communism.

Twenty-five years after the fall of the Berlin Wall, those nostalgic for the Cold War could buy a baseball cap embroidered with the letters CCCP, or KGB, or simply a hammer and sickle, a development Khrushchev is unlikely to have foreseen, much less welcomed, on that blistering day at Borobodur.

As for New Era, its headquarters are still in downtown Buffalo, but no longer on the third floor of a storefront on Genesee Street. In a parting of fortunes for baseball and the American economy, New Era now occupies a venerable glass-and-steel edifice on Delaware Street, in a building once home to the United States Federal Reserve Bank.

Chapter 5

THE BEANPROOF CAP OF FOULPROOF TAYLOR

The baseball cap had briefly crossed over into the wider world of civilian fashion by 1910, when *Men's Wear* magazine devoted an item in its Hat Chatter column to an exciting innovation in headwear. Fred Clarke, the player-manager of the Pittsburgh Pirates, had designed a new cap for use in the sun field, that part of the diamond from which a fielder was forced to look directly into the sun, a position unloved by all but Pete Browning, for whom staring into the sun did wonders for the lamps.

"The cap has a long aluminum peak to which a pair of smoked glasses are fastened with a hinge," *Men's Wear* said of Clarke's creation. "There is also a strong spring arrangement, and when not in use the glasses lie up against the peak of the cap in a horizontal position. All that is necessary to make them fall over the eyes is a touch of the finger, and this is far easier than pushing an ordinary pair of glasses from the point of the nose upward."

If not quite the birth of cool, it was the birth of flip shades, the coolest fashion ever spawned by baseball. "We never heard of flip-down sunglasses," Ty Cobb wrote in his autobiography, while launching into a get-off-my-lawn litany of other luxuries enjoyed by modern players of the 1950s, including "gloves with fantastic webbed extensions," "outfield walls with cinder-track borders," and—these kids today—"finely clipped infield grass."

Cobb would have been familiar with ordinary sunglasses on the baseball field, though. As early as 1888, Paul Hines of Indianapolis "has taken to wearing smoked glasses while fielding," reported *Sporting Life*. "He does this to shield his eyes from the sun. When batting he discards them." Within a decade, more players began wearing smoked glasses, protecting their eyes in the dawn of a new century.

Casey Stengel, photographed in shades in the Brooklyn sun field in 1915, wore them. Even Cobb, who would claim to have never heard of flip shades, was photographed wearing sunglasses at the plate in 1926, after eye surgery. "No outfielder should balk at wearing sunglasses," he wrote. "In some fields they are absolutely necessary. A little practice will accustom you to the use of them."

Stengel in sunglasses. *(National Baseball Hall of Fame Library, Cooperstown, NY)*

As a twenty-two-year-old rookie with the Yankees in 1933, Dixie Walker borrowed teammate Ben Chapman's flip shades and botched a fly ball as Babe Ruth screamed at him from left field. Which was rich, as Ruth didn't care for sunglasses—he never "accustomed" himself to the use of them—and never played the sun field. Perhaps it was that ninety-seven-degree day in his National Guard uniform, attempting to catch flies dropped from an airplane, that put Ruth off fielding baseballs beneath a hot sun. But his refusal to play the sun field accounts for his frequent switch-fielding, which saw him shuttling between left and right, in opposition to the sun's transit across the sky. Bob Meusel was the cursed teammate forced to play the sun field every day, and liked to say that he was performing a kind of parlor trick: which is to say, *Meusel* wore sunglasses to protect *Ruth's* eyes.

"The Babe can't play the sun field," his manager Bill McKechnie conceded in 1935, when Ruth was with the Boston Braves for his final season as a player, creating a dilemma for his new manager. "But he's used to right field. Right field is the sun field in only a couple of American League parks. But it's the sun field in six of the eight parks in our league."

In the 1932 World Series, Ruth had played left field at Wrigley because right was in the sun. "I played the sun field for 10 years and used to be fairly good," Stengel said, "not like Babe Ruth, who they never let play those sun fields and they'd switch him with Bob Meusel, so it would not hurt his eyes."

Even way back in 1897, Jack Boyle of the Phillies was complaining that first base in Philadelphia "is the worst position to play in the league owing to the sun."

"According to Jack," confirmed a *Sporting Life* correspondent, "no other sun field is quite so bad."

In inventing flip shades, then, Fred Clarke was solving a very real problem, as he was wont to do. He had patented a pulley system for deploying the tarp more efficiently, and claimed to have invented sliding pads. When he wasn't managing the Pirates, Clarke managed a ranch in Winfield, Kansas, where he kept a mule named Honus in honor of his best player. (Clarke wired the Pirates' office one winter with the cardiac-arresting message, "Sold Honus for $190. Particulars later.")

Indeed, Wagner, with his giant melon, would become the most famous advocate of the original flip shades, the kind that were literally bolted to the brim of the cap. A version he wore as a Pirates coach in 1940 is enshrined in Cooperstown, the smoked glasses secured by three long spindles that protrude through the top of the brim a good two inches. It looks less like the handiwork of Fred Clarke than of an acupuncturist or voodoo priest.

To avoid having spindles in his brim, Red Sox right fielder Harry Hooper secured his smoked glasses by means of a string looped through two holes punched in the bill of his cap. By 1951, when rookie Mickey Mantle lost a fly ball while wearing flips in spring training, the lenses were hinged to empty eyeglass frames. "You got to find the ball before you flip down the glasses," teammate Hank Bauer told the Mick.

"Casey didn't tell me that," Mantle replied.

DiMaggio wore them. Cool Papa Bell wore them. As with everything else, Willie Mays wore the hell out of them, so much so that he signed a $3,000 endorsement deal with Foster Grant in 1954. A pair of flip shades he wore in the 1960s—with green lenses on black frames and MAYS spelled in black punch tape on the left arm—sold at auction in 2002 for $7,589. While artfully running out from under his cap, Mays made sure the flip shades stayed on by means of a wide rubber band athletic-taped to the earpieces.

Fred Clarke lived to see Mays rock the flip shades. Three months before Clarke's death, in 1960, a writer visited the eighty-seven-year-old at his ranch in Winfield. During the interview, Clarke sipped a bourbon highball—his doctor allowed him two a day—and lamented that the mementos of his baseball life had vanished in a fire years earlier. He had no flip shades to show the reporter, though one of his two daughters, Muriel Sullivan of Newkirk, Oklahoma, "has carefully guarded the records which show that her father patented the method of handling the canvas used to protect the playing field, the flip-down eye glasses used by outfielders on sunny days and sliding pads." If Clarke made any money from any of these inventions, the fact was hardly worth mentioning. Oil had been discovered beneath his ranch forty-three years previously, making him in 1917 an instant millionaire. Fred Clarke died an enormously wealthy man, the embodiment of the phrase "made in the shade."

Sunglasses that didn't flip up and down had been used as—and at—sporting spectacles since at least the time of ancient Rome, when Nero viewed the gladiators through an emerald.

By 1911, they were already making baseball too easy. "Smoked glasses of late years have been of immense advantage in these sun parlors," the *New York Times* reported that spring, "as the player can see the ball even when it is on the edge of the sun."

Those who chose to play without them were, like Icarus, punished by the sun for their hubris. When Tris Speaker couldn't field a Joe Dugan popup, he saw it in the next day's papers: "Speaker, scorning the aid of smoked glasses, lost Dugan's fly in the sun, the ball dropping out of his hands for a technical two-bagger."

But even Nero never wore shades to such fearsome effect as Ryne Duren, the Yankees reliever of the late 1950s whose terrible eyesight—20/70 in his right eye, 20/200 in his left—required him to pitch in sunglasses thick as bottle bottoms.

On the advice of eye doctors, Duren wore a pair with gold lenses for afternoon games and pink lenses for night games, with earpieces that wrapped all the way around the ears and were mummified in trainer's tape so as not to fly off his face during his flame-throwing exertions. Summoned from the bullpen, Duren would sometimes throw his first hundred-mile-an-hour warm-up pitch over the catcher's head to the backstop, after which he might theatrically clean his lenses with a handkerchief. When Duren couldn't read the signs from his catcher, manager Casey Stengel had Elston Howard's fingers painted red with Mercurochrome. Duren's eyesight was so bad that Gus Triandos of the Orioles came to the plate one night while Duren was on his knees, running his hands over the pitcher's mound to repair a hole left by the opposing pitcher.

"What's he doing?" Triandos asked, to which Yankees catcher Yogi Berra replied, "Trying to find the rubber."

In all, Duren owned seven pairs of sunglasses. His gold "twilight" sunglasses were sold in the Sotheby's auction of Barry Halper's collection, but Duren wrote to the collector that "I have kept the rose-tinted glasses for myself." As well he should. Having overcome alcohol abuse, and lobbied for beer-free sections in ballparks, Duren was entitled to view the world through those rose-tinted glasses. When he died in Lake Wales, Florida, in 2011, aged eighty-one, he left a happy memoir called *I Can See Clearly Now,* a title that was metaphorically, if not ophthalmologically, accurate.

"He had several pair of glasses," Berra said at the time of Duren's passing. "But it didn't seem like he saw good in any of them."

Flip shades didn't make Willie Mays cool—it was the other way around—but flip-down sunglasses remain tied, sometimes literally, to the coolest players of the 1960s and '70s. On his 1980 Topps card, Ralph Garr of the White Sox memorably wore his flipped up, like the raised visor of Sir Galahad's helmet. On his own cards, behind the limousine windows of his flip shades, Garr's teammate Chet Lemon maintained a rakish panache even while enduring that team's short-lived short pants. But then flip shades, like so many of baseball's accessories, were as much fashion as function. Reds infielder Bip Roberts was uncannily photographed in action for a succession of baseball cards in the 1990s while gazing at a summer sky, waiting for an infield fly to descend, his shades always defiantly flipped up, useless except as a fashion accessory.

Pete Rose wore flips, up, on his 1976 Topps card. When Rose was chasing Ty Cobb's all-time hits record in 1985, collector Barry Halper gave him an eighty-pound bronze bust of the Georgia Peach, who became part of the Reds' traveling party that summer. Home or away, equipment manager Bernie Stowe would set Cobb out in the clubhouse, and the players would dress him in cap and flip shades, causing Cobb—one can only presume—to slowly rotate in his marbled vault at Rose Hill Cemetery in Royston, Georgia.

By the time Rose passed Cobb in '85, flip shades were falling from their preeminent place of cool. They were probably finished as a phenomenon in 1987, when they became the wardrobe signature of sitcom character Dwayne Wayne, on *The Cosby Show* spin-off *A Different World*. Their decline was hastened by a Southern Californian named Jim Jannard, who in 1975 invented, in his garage, a motorcycle grip that paradoxically grew stickier with sweat. He sold these grips from the trunk of his car, along with other motorcycle parts, eventually designing athletic sunglasses for the company he named after his English setter, Oakley Anne.

In 1986, wearing Oakley sunglasses, cyclist Greg LeMond became the first American to win the Tour de France, and wraparound "Oakleys" quickly became the sunglass fixture in baseball clubhouses.

Ray Lankford still wore flips on his 1993 Fleer card, but he wore them up, like an arc welder at rest. The flip shades were largely a statement. For sun protection, Lankford—like Mays before him—wore his shades with the underscoring of eye black.

Eye black has underscored the lamps of football players since at least World War II. The earliest photographic evidence of it yet discovered is a 1942 picture of Washington Redskins running back Andy Far-kas. The Skins' flamboyant owner, George Preston Marshall, had asked players to dress as Native Americans for a pregame publicity photo. Farkas burned cork and rubbed it beneath his eyes to mimic war paint, which he didn't bother to wash off for the day's game.

But Farkas wasn't the first athlete to wear eye black. In his ency-clopedic history of baseball, *A Game of Inches,* Peter Morris notes that veteran outfielder Patsy Dougherty was wearing it thirty-eight years before Farkas. "Pat Dougherty rubs mud or charcoal under his eyes," *Sporting Life* reported in 1904, "after the practice of many minor league ball players, who assert that it lessens the glare of the sun on a bright day."

When Dougherty was traded from Boston to the New York Highlanders that season, the *Boston Herald* headline — DOUGHERTY AS A YANKEE — is the earliest print citation of that nickname for the Bronx ball club. We can trace a direct line, then, from Dougherty (first Yankee, first in eye black) to Don Mattingly (raccoon-eyed Yankee of eight decades later) with a single black stripe of paraffin.

Dougherty quit his final team, the White Sox, in February 1912 with a letter to owner Charles Comiskey. "Dougherty declares his reason for retiring is that he has all the money he needs and does not care to play ball any longer," according to the next day's *New York Times*. And he was awash in cash every day. Dougherty worked for the next twenty-eight years at the State Bank of Bolivar, in his native Bolivar, New York, where he died at age sixty-three, of a heart attack, having attained the position of assistant cashier.

Bank cashier was an unlikely position for a pioneer of eye black, for those early wearers in baseball would have resembled bandits, the greasepaint often encircling their eyes entirely, in the manner of the McDonald's Hamburglar. Peter Morris cites another seminal refer-ence, from *Sporting Life* in 1905: "Sandow Mertes tried that new sun field wrinkle here [Chicago] the other day — that trick of painting black circles round the eyes instead of wearing smoked glasses. It made Sandow look like an Apache on the warpath, and the only perceptible result was, that Sandow misjudged a long fly and let in the winning run."

Mertes had a beloved dog that ran around the outfield with him during Giants practices, a bull terrier like Spuds MacKenzie, the Bud Light mascot with a black ring around his eye. In applying eye black, Mertes may have simply begun to resemble his dog, as do many pets and their owners. In retirement, he ran a newsstand in San Francisco, where he died, in 1945, just as eye black was becoming popular in football.

Football players invested eye black with an ability — never proven by science — to reduce glare from sun- and floodlights. Eye black had the quality of snake oil, and may even have contained some, given the cauldron of ingredients comprising it — beeswax and paraffin and carbon, if not eye of newt.

It wasn't until 2003 that a scientific study, by two researchers at the Yale School of Medicine, set out to determine if eye black had anything other than a placebo effect on athletes. Ophthalmologists Brian M. DeBroff, M.D., and Patricia J. Pahk, M.D., concluded that daubed-on eye black was indeed effective at reducing glare, though less so in the form of the adhesive decals that had by then come to predominate in football, replete with Bible verses, area codes, and other encrypted messages.

In baseball, eye black became a permanent feature of several top players, among them Mattingly and Will Clark, and of former college football player Kirk Gibson. After signing as a free agent with the Dodgers in 1988, Gibson found, in his first exhibition game at Dodgertown, that the band of his cap had been coated in eye black. (When he removed the cap to wipe his forehead with his forearm, he found both covered in black grease.) Before relief pitcher Jesse Orosco was fingered as the prankster, Gibson left the park in a rage, his head circled by a black halo.

Gibson was ahead of his time. Twenty years later, the misapplication of eye black was intentional. Bryce Harper, the number one pick in the 2010 draft, liked to smear it halfway down his cheek, Alice Cooper–style. It looked like his mascara had run in the rain.

At the start of a six-game home stand in 2010, Bobby Crosby of the Pirates challenged everyone on the team to grow a mustache. Fellow infielder Ronny Cedeño couldn't raise sufficient facial hair, so went out in the Sunday matinee with a magnificent Fu Manchu mustache eye-blacked onto his upper lip. It was thin and neat and shone in the sun as he stood at the plate, where Cedeño looked like the unholy offspring of Prince and Prince Fielder.

With two outs in the ninth that afternoon against the Giants, he hit a single to end an 0-for-20 slump. And still Cedeño shaved off his mustache with a hand towel afterward. "It's for one day," he said of the 'stache. "I sweat too much."

Their five World Series titles notwithstanding, the Pittsburgh Pirates' greatest contributions to baseball history have been sartorial flourishes from the chin up, among them Fred Clarke's flip shades, Ronny Cedeño's nose black, and the century-old pillbox caps—with horizontal piping—that the Bucs brought back, without so much as a murmur of popular demand, in 1979. For reasons that defy explication, the franchise has had a flair for cranial adornment unmatched in baseball. But the most important of these innovations, by far, was the batting helmet.

Over the better part of a century, baseball players, loath to be called sissies, began wrapping their hands in leather, wore sliding pads beneath their pants, and even protected their arms from undue abuse. In the 1930s, Lena Feller made a sleeve that resembled a snug pants leg to warm the pitching arm of her son, Bob. Crucially, all these implements were—or began as—*hidden* protection. Batting helmets were no different.

The earliest known batting helmet was inflatable. Invented by Frank Pierce Mogridge in 1905 and patented by the A. J. Reach Company, it was so ridiculously conspicuous, and conspicuously ridiculous, that it fairly demanded a new adjective: *conspiculous?* When flaccid, the device looked like an empty backpack. But placed on the head of an unfortunate player, and inflated by an unlucky teammate blowing into a hose, it became — officially — the Pneumatic Head Protector. The *Toledo Blade,* in 1902, called a similar device — also billed as a Pneumatic Head Protector — "a practical idea for the use of firemen and policemen" when inflated and worn beneath their existing helmets, which were then made of a single layer of felt.

Baseball players would not allow themselves even that thin membrane of protection. In Cincinnati on June 18, 1907, Reds pitcher Andy Coakley hit Giants catcher Roger Bresnahan with a fastball behind the left ear. Bresnahan fell unconscious for a full ten minutes, was briefly revived, then lost consciousness again. He was taken to Seton Hospital, and a week later to his home in Toledo, where he convalesced for a month before returning to the lineup. Bresnahan had a rare quality for his age — the courage of self-preservation — and had heretically worn cricketers' shin guards on Opening Day of that season, to great protest. When he returned from the Coakley beaning, he sought the temporary comfort of the Pneumatic Head Protector, though he quickly abandoned it, and there's little wonder why.

To look at the army-green contraption, which lacks any aesthetic consideration whatsoever, is to feel a vague sense of unease. It doesn't quite inspire the revulsion of some of the more medieval medical implements, but neither does it have the attraction of most vintage baseball equipment of that era. In 2001, one of six extant Pneumatic Head Protectors sold at auction for $675, an infinitesimal sum for a historic baseball item that has otherwise passed into obscurity. For more than a century now, inflating a player's head has been—as it ought to be—the exclusive redoubt of fans, agents, and sportswriters.

Bresnahan played eight more seasons without head protection and went on to the Hall of Fame. Andy Coakley, who beaned him, did not. But he did spend thirty-six remarkable seasons as head baseball coach at Columbia University, where he had a young first baseman named Lou Gehrig in the early 1920s, when afternoon baseball—in the slanting shadows of upper Manhattan—was rife with perils.

In the late-afternoon shadows of the Polo Grounds on August 16, 1920, the enormously popular Indians shortstop Ray Chapman stood in close to the plate to face Giants right-hander Carl Mays, never flinching when a ball up-and-in caught him in the left temple with such force that it returned, with a loud report, to Mays, who thought it had struck the barrel of the bat.

Mays fielded the ball and threw to first, unaware that Chapman's skull had been fractured and his brain lacerated. The twenty-nine-year-old died in St. Lawrence Hospital at four thirty the next morning.

"Headgear for ballplayers, to use while batting, is being considered by club owners and players as a result of the unfortunate accident which resulted in the death of Ray Chapman this week," the *New York Times* reported three days later. "It will not be surprising if batsmen of the future go to the plate with a covering on that side of the head that is nearest to the opposing pitcher."

Mays, the son of a Methodist minister, voluntarily appeared in the district attorney's office, where he was immediately exonerated of any wrongdoing, but the real crime in this terrible accident would take longer to play out: Batting helmets were not mandated in major-league baseball for another fifty-one years, despite the exhaustive efforts of an eccentric inventor who arrived in America as James Philip Leo Taylor but quickly came to be known as Foulproof.

A year after his arrival—from his native England, aboard the *Carmania,* as a twenty-year-old in 1907—Taylor saw his first baseball game. He paid $0.50 to enter the Polo Grounds and see the Dodgers beat the Giants 1–0 in thirteen innings. The Englishman didn't understand what he was witnessing. After eleven innings, with as many zeros hung top and bottom from hooks on the scoreboard, Taylor asked the man next to him what would happen when the remaining five hooks "were hung with naughts."

The man spit out tobacco juice and replied, as if to an imbecile: "They're gonna knock the grandstand down and build a skating rink."

By the time of the Chapman tragedy, a dozen years later, Taylor had become an athlete of sorts, and a student of American sports. He stood only five six and weighed 125 pounds, but those dimensions worked to his advantage in 1918, when he set the world record in the sack race by hopping a ninth of a mile in thirty-two seconds in a burlap sack in front of 65,000 spectators at the Calgary rodeo. Sack racing was sufficiently popular that Spalding had manufactured Taylor's official sack-racing sack, three feet by five feet and roped at the neck. Sporting goods, it seemed, offered inexhaustible possibilities for products and riches to those willing to pay attention.

Taylor took notice on the night of November 16, 1926. He was working for a telegraph company and moonlighting as a second tenor in the Metropolitan Opera chorus when he appeared at the Met in the American debut of Puccini's *Turandot*. At the end of the first act, a spear-carrier hurrying off the stage accidentally kneed Taylor in the groin, changing his life and—briefly—his register. "I went from second tenor to baritone [*sic*] to boy soprano with the yelp I let out," Taylor recalled years later.

Young Foulproof Taylor, sack-racing world champion.
(*Courtesy of Diane Taylor*)

The day after he was kneed, Taylor purchased a sheet of aluminum, and then a supply of rubber cigars from a novelty shop on the Bowery, and fashioned—in his basement workshop in Brooklyn—a protective aluminum cup, which he wore to that night's performance of *Turandot.*

"Kick me," he told the spear-carrier.

"With pleasure," the spear-carrier replied.

Taylor's groin, ensconced in this new contraption, proved unassailable. He had no way of knowing, in that moment, that he'd "invented" something that already existed. His cup, he was certain, was about to runneth over.

Man has been protecting his nethers literally from the beginning, if we're to go by Genesis, in which Adam covers his nakedness with a fig leaf. All manner of devices followed: loincloths, codpieces, chain mail. But it was the invention of the bicycle that spurred the great leap forward in groin safety.

The first bicycles—the word was coined in 1867—were called boneshakers, and for good reason. They had wooden wheels and seats and, for two decades before the invention of the pneumatic tire, were excruciating to ride on the cobblestoned streets of urban America.

Those boneshakers were shaking more than bones. In 1874, a cyclist and inventor named Charles F. Bennett invented the "bike web" to give comfort and support to male "bicycle jockeys," for whom the undergarment became known as a "jockey strap." The Bike Web jockey strap—as it was eventually branded—was quickly adopted by other athletes. When boxer George Dixon knocked out Eddie Pierce in Brooklyn in 1893, the victor "wore nothing but a white jockey strap and brown shoes." A year later, Gentleman Jim Corbett vanquished Charley Mitchell in Jacksonville, Florida, in "nothing but a jockstrap and a tri-color belt of ribbons."

Alas, as those fighters well knew, the jockey strap offered comfort without protection. In Paris in 1899, the British navy boxing champion Jerry Driscoll fought the French champion Charlemont in a bout refereed by Charlemont's father. Driscoll was dominating the fight in the eighth round when the Frenchman "landed an upward kick on Driscoll's groin." Driscoll, it almost goes without saying, "doubled up in agony and was carried out of the ring"— while the crowd, somewhat uncharitably, shouted, *"Vive la France!"*

Baseball players were even more vulnerable than boxers, catchers especially so. Their pain was easily imagined from the undignified injury reports published in newspapers. "Berger, the Poly catcher, will not be able to play against Browne's Business College at Prospect Park to-day, owing to having been hit in the groin in the High School-Poly game," the *Brooklyn Daily Eagle* reported in 1901. "Berger is liable to be out of the game for some time."

No other human endeavor has employed the word "groin" as frequently—or as euphemistically—as baseball has. And none has had so many reasons to do so, as medical textbooks and journals of the late nineteenth and early twentieth centuries attest. "The testicle being an exquisitely sensitive organ, the pain and shock produced by its injury are very pronounced," wrote George Frank Lydston, M.D., in his groundbreaking—one hesitates to call it seminal—textbook, *The Surgical Diseases of the Genito-Urinary Tract,* published in 1900. "The author recalls one severe case produced by a blow with a baseball."

That chapter, "Traumatisms of the Testis," could have shared its title with any number of baseball memoirs. One can spend a leg-crossing afternoon reading tales of testicular trauma from the baseball diamond in nineteenth-century medical literature, dating nearly to the dawn of professional baseball. "Mr. D., single, aged twenty-eight years, had enlarged left testicle for about ten years," begins one harrowing tale of amputation in an 1893 issue of *Medical Review.* "This had dated back to a blow by a baseball."

Catchers had no groin protection, and umpires relied on catchers as *their* form of groin protection. In the eighth inning of an Eastern League game between the Baltimore Orioles and Buffalo Bisons in 1907, umpire Brick Owens took a pitched ball to the groin that felled him like a tree. "It was several minutes," the *Baltimore Sun* noted drily, "before he was revived."

The following spring, "Iron Man" Joe McGinnity was confined to his hotel room in Dallas during the Giants' exhibition tour of the American South, unable even to visit the dining hall while "suffering from severe pains in the groin" after an unspecified trauma in a team workout.

Something needed to be done. Enter Claude Berry, born on Valentine's Day of 1880 in Losantville, Indiana, the state to which he returned every baseball off-season, to his Berry Brothers grain and coal dealership in Lynn. After three seasons in the big leagues with the White Sox and A's, the diminutive Berry spent five seasons with the San Francisco Seals of the Pacific Coast League, catching an unfathomable 167 games in 1908, and 166 more in 1909. For five straight years in San Francisco, he would catch at least 151 games a season. To say that he did so unflinchingly may not be an exaggeration. As one writer put it: "In moments of stress the little catcher was as imperturbable as if he had been discussing the price of corn with a farmer back in Indiana."

By 1915, Berry was back in the bigs with the Pittsburgh Rebels, of the Federal League, the short-lived, breakaway, third major league, where he continued to catch with uncommon composure and self-assurance, qualities enhanced by the piece of molded steel in his pants, which necessitated a separate kind of jockey strap, pocketed to hold this new device.

Berry was wearing, in 1915, the first known protective cup. It was steel, with ten ventilating holes in a bowling-pin pattern, and resembled—in shape, construction, and ability to induce dread in those who view it—the muzzle worn by Hannibal Lecter. The protective cup, embossed PATENT PENDING and vouchsafed now at the Baseball Hall of Fame, had a distinct advantage over gloves and helmets: It was hidden from view. Wearing one wasn't emasculating. Not wearing one very well could have been.

The Washington Senators were hoping to force a seventh game as they clung to a 2–1 lead in Game 6 of the 1924 World Series. From a buntinged box at Griffith Stadium, President and Mrs. Coolidge looked on, three months after the blood-poisoning death of Calvin Jr. The president hadn't intended to go, but the first lady prevailed upon him at the last minute. And so they saw, with one out and a runner on first in the top of the ninth inning, Giants left fielder Irish Meusel hit a hot grounder to Senators shortstop Roger Peckinpaugh, who fielded the ball, threw to second baseman Bucky Harris, and promptly fell to the ground, having reinjured the strained left thigh muscle that kept him out of Games 4 and 5.

Harris caught the ball at second and stepped on the bag for the inning's second out, but his throw to first baseman Joe Judge for the double play was in the dirt. With the home team's shortstop already in agony in the infield, and the World Series on the line, the first baseman was hit in the testicles by a baseball thrown with great urgency. "There was a fresh cry of alarm from the stands," wrote a witness from a wire service, "when Joe Judge was hit in the groin by Harris's low throw and fell to the ground in pain."

Peckinpaugh was stretchered from the field as the president and first lady stood to applaud him. But Judge stayed in the game for one more batter—Giants slugger Hack Wilson, who struck out to end the game. The Senators won the World Series the following day, in twelve innings, to the obvious delight of Mrs. Coolidge, who had earlier called the series "the greatest thrill of her life." The grieving president openly rooted for the Senators and said he "had never seen such exciting games." The Senators' twelve-year-old ball boy, Calvin Griffith, wept when the supply of baseballs he was supposed to be guarding was stolen by celebrating fans.

After being speared in the groin at the Metropolitan Opera, Foulproof Taylor set aside his protective cup for two years, not fully realizing its potential until he found himself gazing at the stage in another New York City cultural institution, Madison Square Garden.

That night, on a full card of boxing, two bouts had ended prematurely on below-the-belt punches, enraging the crowd. In the 1920s, when a fight ended in a foul, all bets were declared void. "The Prohibition gangsters sat at ringside and had thousands of dollars going," Foulproof said in 1961. "If their boy was losing, they'd just yell to him to foul the other guy. He wouldn't even feint it, he'd just sock the other guy. Down he'd go, moaning, and the fight would be off. So would the bets."

And so Taylor began to wear his cup to prizefights, local gyms, and the offices of the New York State Athletic Commission, chaired by James Farley. Everywhere he went, Taylor implored boxers, fight promoters, and sportswriters to kick him as hard as they could in the testicles. "Kick me here" became Taylor's catchphrase, and many fighters — which is to say most — happily obliged.

He called the device his "Foulproof Cup," and he quickly became familiar in New York boxing circles as "Foulproof Taylor." It would remain his preferred form of address for the rest of his life. One evening at Madame Bey's, a training camp for champion prizefighters run by a Turkish woman in Chatham Township, New Jersey, Foulproof asked Hype Igoe, boxing writer for the Hearst newspaper chain, to hit him in the groin with a baseball bat. Igoe graciously obliged. He swung from his heels, and the resulting collision — of Bud Hillerich's bat and Foulproof Taylor's cup, a meeting of two great American inventions — nearly knocked the inventor through a wall, leaving a man-shaped hole in the plaster. A plaque was hastily commissioned to cover the hole. It read:

Hypus Igoe Through This Wall
Knocked Foulproof Taylor, Cup and All.

Alas, such intrepid salesmanship went mostly in vain until the night of June 12, 1930, when Max Schmeling of Germany fought Jack Sharkey of Boston for the heavyweight championship of the world, a title vacated by the retirement two years earlier of Gene Tunney.

A few days before the fight at Yankee Stadium, the boxing writer for the *New York Evening Graphic* wrote, "Chairman Farley could save himself many gray hairs by ordering Sharkey and Schmeling to wear Taylor Foulproof cups." (That particular boxing writer—Ed Sullivan—had a soft spot for the world's eccentrics, as he would demonstrate decades later on his own television show.)

In any event, Farley didn't mandate Foulproof Cups for the title bout. And so Sharkey was leading the fight with four seconds left in the fourth round, in front of eighty thousand baying spectators at Yankee Stadium, when his left hook caught Schmeling flush on the groin and felled the German. Referee Jimmy Crowley began counting Schmeling out, oblivious to the foul, but when a lone judge alerted him to the low blow, Crowley had no choice but to declare Schmeling the winner and new world champion.

The Schmeling–Sharkey fight was the first heavyweight championship to be awarded on a foul, and Farley and the rest of the New York State Athletic Commission wanted to make sure it was also the last.

On July 1, three weeks after the bout, Farley and the State Athletic Commission made cups mandatory. The device profoundly changed the fight game, and did the same for New York's boxing commissioner. Hailed as the man who saved boxing, Farley was also Franklin Roosevelt's campaign manager in that year's New York gubernatorial race. Two years later, he would serve the same role in the 1932 presidential campaign. Farley swept Roosevelt into the White House, but left Foulproof Taylor at the curb, forlorn and forgotten, befitting a man whose mantra was "Kick me here."

Foulproof's Foulproof Cup failed to become the industry standard because—he would claim for decades to come, in court and out—Farley steered boxing to the cast-iron cup of Jacob Golomb, Foulproof's archnemesis.

As a child, Golomb had left Riga, Latvia, for the Lower East Side of Manhattan, where—in 1910, aged seventeen, with $5 and a sewing machine borrowed from his father—he began to manufacture swimsuits that would last for more than a year. A swimmer himself, Golomb also boxed briefly as a ninety-pound flyweight at a time when fighters' gloves were little more than leather skins, and a heavy bag was a sailor's duffel stuffed with sawdust. Without mouth guards, headgear, and soft gloves, the heavyweight champion Jack Dempsey toughened his hands and face by soaking them in slaughterhouse brine.

Like flannel baseball pants, boxing trunks were held up by leather belts, until Golomb made an elasticized waistband for the trunks of Jack Dempsey. In 1927, Farley mandated that all fighters in New York wear Golomb's trunks, an order he rescinded only after receiving heavy criticism. It didn't matter. Golomb's wonderful trunks appeared soon enough on boxers everywhere. Their waistbands, glove cuffs, and jockstraps, their punching bags and sparring headgear, were all emblazoned with his ubiquitous brand name: EVERLAST.

In boxing, as in baseball, "the trouble at first was in getting them to use 'em," Golomb said of the cups. "Many oldtime fighters thought they were sissy."

But the cup, hidden from view, caused an athlete no embarrassment, and Foulproof—undaunted in his pursuit of sales—managed to sell some prominent heavyweights on his version.

Primo Carnera was intrigued when Foulproof approached the six-foot-seven, 270-pound Italian with a proposition. "I told Carnera to place his huge paws on my shoulders and then whang me in the groin full-strength with his knee." The Italian obliged Foulproof, who required extra aluminum and a greater quantity of rubber cigars when making the heavyweight's cups. "Carnera was hung like a horse," Foulproof said.

When Carnera was knocked out by Joe Louis at Yankee Stadium in 1935, both fighters wore Foulproofs. Four years later, as he stood over the fallen Two Ton Tony Galento, Louis allowed Foulproof's name to peek above his trunks, visible on the waistband of his jock-strap, an honor Taylor recorded in his autobiography, which set a new high-water mark in jock-sniffing memoirs.

Despite these successes, Foulproof felt that Farley had sold him out to Everlast, whom he would sue unsuccessfully for patent infringement. But at the same time, he took a perverse personal pride in the rising star of the former boxing commissioner, seeing Farley's success as his own.

"Farley saved boxing by okaying my protector and passing the no-foul rule," Foulproof wrote in 1945 in his self-published auto-biography, *Prizefight Government*. "This made Farley a big man. He got too big to be wasting his time in boxing—right? So he got hold of Roosevelt and managed him into the White House. If Sharkey hadn't fouled Schmeling and if I hadn't invented my gadget, this would never have happened—right? I guess you can call me a President-maker as well as a boxing-saver. I'm the guy who did the whole thing but I don't seem to get any credit for it. They kick me around and it's a good thing I wear my own invention."

Not everybody did. Baseball never mandated cups, and countless examples of agony could not persuade everyone to wear one. Pepper Martin never wore a cup despite his role as the St. Louis Cardinals' third baseman, a position that placed his groin in terrifying proximity to line drives. Miraculously, in thirteen seasons in the big leagues, Martin suffered no catastrophic groin injuries, prompting Leo Durocher to say of him: "God watches over drunks and third basemen."

Durocher played with Martin for five seasons in the Gashouse Gang infield and noted that the Wild Horse of the Osage invited catastrophe and discomfort. He wore his flannel Cardinals uniform directly over his skin as a hair shirt while going unencumbered by a cup at the hot corner. "He was just a lucky man, I guess," Durocher said. "But that's the way Pepper was—never wore a cup, an undershirt, or sanitary socks, neither—just his cap, jersey, pants, stirrups, and shoes. I suppose he was comfortable that way."

But even Pepper got religion. In 1943, in Rochester, New York, he managed a young second baseman named Red Schoendienst. As the future Cardinal dressed before a game in Newark, the former Cardinal asked Schoendienst if he was wearing a cup. Schoendienst was not. He didn't find them comfortable, he said. Martin summoned a cup from a clubhouse attendant and Schoendienst wore it in that day's game. As a result, when a powerful hitter named Ed Levy smashed a ground ball to second, and it caught the edge of the infield grass and shot into Schoendienst's groin, it was only the cup that was halved like a walnut shell. "I saved you," said Martin.

By then the jockstrap—the simple athletic supporter, not the device that held a protective cup—was advertised as a safety device: "No coach is interested in part-time protection for his athletes. Full protection every playing moment is essential." Or so went a 1943 ad for the Bike supporter, made with "Lastex, the miracle yarn," from the Bike Web Manufacturing Company, whose logo remained—to the bafflement of many—a spoked bicycle wheel. Of course, the "Bike Web jockey strap" had long since been pruned in popular parlance to "jockstrap," and further whittled to "jock," which became by the late 1950s a synonym for the kind of athlete standing in the batter's box, adjusting his cup at home plate.

The sportswriters who covered those jocks were frequently derided as "jock sniffers," an epithet that wasn't always wrong. Two days after he beat Jack Dempsey in their second heavyweight title fight, in 1927, Gene Tunney "exhibited" for reporters "a black and blue spot in his groin five inches in diameter where, he said, Dempsey landed low left hooks."

Dempsey appeared on the cover of *Prizefight Government,*

whacking Foulproof over the head, which was protected by a new-fangled helmet—a protective headgear for fighters—that was also the handiwork of Foulproof Taylor. He had set about creating other fortified devices in the laboratory of his Brooklyn basement, seeking a sport more receptive (and less corrupt) than boxing.

Among his other products were football headgear and shoulder pads. In 1932, Foulproof and a film crew from Pathé visited the Fordham University campus to demonstrate his new Shockproof Helmet before one of the nation's most famous football teams. The helmet was constructed of cane reed, steamed and shaped and embedded in foam rubber. In this hat, Foulproof ran headlong into an exterior wall of the Fordham gymnasium. The wall was made of granite blocks, each a yard thick. Foulproof repeated his stunt for the camera fourteen consecutive times.

Insufficiently impressed, Fordham football officials invited Foulproof back the following season. Again a film crew accompanied him. This time Foulproof wore a lighter helmet—only fifteen ounces—and began by butting heads with Rameses, the live ram mascot of the Fordham Rams. That the inventor did so while wearing a dress shirt was the least absurd feature of the tableau.

Next, a Fordham back named Bill Curran was handed a black Louisville Slugger and asked to smash Foulproof over the head with it. Curran reluctantly complied. "All I felt was a jar, followed by a momentary flash of light in the eyes at the moment of impact," said Foulproof. "I was normal immediately after."

A still frame of the film recorded the instant when bat met head: The half-inch circular vent holes in the helmet appear as slots three inches long. Foulproof's nose, in the frame, stretches from ear to ear. And while he said he emerged from this encounter as lucid as any man with a history of running headlong into granite walls could be, Taylor could not close the deal with Fordham.

"Foulproof, we can't let our boys run onto the field with homemade looking gear," coach Jim Crowley told him. "Give it a factory finish and we'll use them." But Foulproof couldn't finance a factory finish on his salary with the French Cable Company, where some of his colleagues had given him a second nickname: Brass Nuts.

And so it was that three decades after he first set foot in the Polo Grounds for that Giants–Dodgers extra-innings game—and nearly twenty years after Ray Chapman was killed in the same stadium—Foulproof Taylor set out to save baseball with his greatest invention yet: the Beanproof Cap.

He tested this batting helmet as diligently as he had the Shockproof Helmet and the Foulproof Cup, and in much the same manner. Helmeted, he asked strangers to bang him over the head with a baseball bat. Toward that end, Foulproof wangled his way into the Giants' clubhouse at the Polo Grounds, where he left prototypes for Carl Hubbell and trainer Bill Schaeffer, without reply. If he was to find an early adopter, Foulproof needed another galvanic moment, a baseball equivalent of the Schmeling–Sharkey fight.

It came on May 25, 1937, in the fifth inning of a game in the Bronx, when Tigers catcher-manager Mickey Cochrane was struck in the left temple by a pitch from Yankees right-hander Irving (Bump) Hadley. The beanball was an accident: Hadley was pitching with a full count, and he immediately rushed to the side of the supine Cochrane, whose skull was fractured in three places.

He was thought to be near death. As the catcher fought for his life at St. Elizabeth's Hospital in upper Manhattan, his wife, Mary, flew to his bedside. And while Cochrane would survive, his career did not. At age thirty-four, and still in the prime of a Hall of Fame career—he was hitting .306 through the first twenty-seven games—Cochrane was finished playing.

If it could happen to one of the game's best and most famous players—Cochrane had been on the cover of *Time* magazine only two seasons earlier—imagine what lay in store for lesser men. In Class A ball, when Des Moines hosted Cedar Rapids that week, both clubs wore helmets borrowed from a local polo team. Players pronounced the devices adequate, if a little top-heavy. "I think some lighter guard can be worked out," said Cedar Rapids manager Cap Crossley. "After all, the temple facing the pitcher is all that needs protection."

In the big leagues, teams began soliciting submissions for a suitable protective cap. Foulproof turned up unbidden at the Giants' offices, on 42nd Street, but was turned away at reception. A dozen other inventors, he was told, had already come calling.

That summer, the unsinkable Foulproof Taylor attended the All-Star Game in Washington and buttonholed Senators owner Clark Griffith, imploring him to order foulproof helmets for his players.

With Cochrane still convalescing in Detroit, Griffith needed little persuading. The man who had dropped a baseball from the Washington Monument in 1894 knew the devastating effects of a speeding ball. Griffith ordered the helmets. "They arrived yesterday," Shirley Povich wrote in the August 1 edition of the *Washington Post*. "It is now Griffith vs. his ball club because the players, after taking a look at the lop-sided caps, vowed they wouldn't wear the dizzy-looking things. They'd rather get hit in the head, they said."

Taylor's helmet, while foulproof, wasn't foolproof. One flaw in particular was proving too great to overcome. The Foulproof Cup cleaned up boxing, but the Beanproof Cap risked doing the opposite for baseball. Owners feared it could make the game crooked. Griffith told Foulproof of his principal reservation. If the seventh game of the World Series was tied 3–3 with the bases loaded, a hitter only had to lean into a fastball and take one off the coconut to force in the winning run. The Beanproof Cap was, Griffith was very sorry to say, too effective for its own good.

Two years passed, and as Cochrane's injury faded from memory, so did the perceived need for a batting helmet. Undaunted, Foulproof sought an audience in 1940 with Dodgers general manager Larry MacPhail, but not before securing a letter of introduction from his friend, the *New York Daily Mirror* columnist Dan Parker. "Throgmorton Slovinsky MacPhail," Parker's letter began. "This will introduce Foulproof Taylor, the man whose boxing protector saved boxing from repeal. He has a beanproof baseball cap, which he claims will make baseball as safe as boxing for Democracy."

In the Dodgers offices at Ebbets Field, MacPhail declined to see him. Instead, he summoned third-base coach Charlie Dressen to receive Foulproof. On the inventor's instruction, Dressen took a bat to Foulproof's head like a mallet to a tent stake. Impressed with Taylor's impassivity, the former third baseman invited Foulproof to return at one o'clock, this time to the Dodgers' clubhouse, before the afternoon's game.

On Taylor's return, Dodgers outfielder Joe Medwick and manager Leo Durocher took turns tentatively tapping Foulproof on his Beanproof Cap. Only after trainer Jackie Wilson whanged him with a full swing was Foulproof satisfied that he had successfully demonstrated his handiwork. Medwick had already been hit in the head that season. He tried on the helmet, walked to the mirror, and said: "I guess we'll be wearing these soon."

Medwick was half right. He would soon be wearing protective headgear, but not the Beanproof Cap, which had its insurmountable design flaw. The Beanproof Cap could not be hidden from view. It still sat, misshapen, on top of the head. The Dodgers wouldn't wear it for the same reason the Senators wouldn't: human vanity.

"They wouldn't wear a thing that was cumbersome and so conspicuous that everybody could see it," Dodgers president Larry MacPhail explained in 1941, before a spring training game in Havana. There, in front of a contingent of traveling reporters, MacPhail revealed what he called "the biggest thing that has happened to the game since night baseball."

MacPhail's innovation—"a protector for batsmen"—wasn't

just another batting helmet. Designed by Dr. Walter E. Dandy, a brain surgeon at Johns Hopkins School of Medicine, and his colleague Dr. George Eli Bennett, this particular "protector" solved the problem of the Beanproof Cap.

What Dandy and Bennett designed was a featherweight plastic insert that fitted into a zippered pocket on the inside of Dodgers caps. They were inspired by a jockey's helmet MacPhail had received from his friend Alfred Gwynne Vanderbilt II, a great-great-grandson of Commodore Cornelius Vanderbilt. Alfred Gwynne Vanderbilt II was the innovative father of modern Thoroughbred horse racing, to which he introduced the use of the starting gate and the photo finish, among other novelties.

The "armored caps," as Dr. Dandy called them, could accommodate two inserts, one for the left side of the skull, the other for the right, so that a batter could choose to wear only one at the plate. In fact, most Dodgers would choose to wear both, and not only at the plate. Joe Medwick—who had taken up Foulproof Taylor on his offer to whack him over the head—wore it in the outfield. Dodgers pitcher Freddie Fitzsimmons wore it to throw batting practice. The day before MacPhail made his grand unveiling, Medwick and shortstop Pee Wee Reese wore them in an exhibition game against the Indians, during which the caps had passed the most important test of all: Nobody noticed them.

This was critical. Helmets had been discussed since the Chapman beaning, but—as in Washington—they were always proscribed by the boundless nature of human vanity. "The objection I heard from other club owners," MacPhail said, "was that players would never wear them." But Reese and Medwick were only too happy to do so. As a rookie the year before, Reese missed eighteen days after being beaned at Wrigley Field, where he never saw a pitch emerge from the white shirts in the center field bleachers. Three weeks later, Medwick, too, was hit in the head.

That same season, another device like a boxer's headgear was patented, but also patently ridiculous, at least to players' eyes. It was designed to be worn *over* the cap, not instead of it. As a result, the wearer always resembled someone who had just sustained a head injury, rather than someone seeking to prevent one.

But the hidden inserts of Dr. Dandy robbed the helmet of any such stigma. MacPhail predicted that all players in the big leagues would be wearing them by 1942.

That prediction was echoed at season's end by the magnificent Dr. Dandy, who reminded reporters that Dodgers star Pete Reiser had been beaned low on the cap, near the cheekbone, in late April. If not for the insert he was wearing, he'd have been sidelined for some or all of the season. Instead—his coconut cocooned in an armored cap—Reiser led the National League in both hitting *and* being hit by pitches. He was drilled six times in 1941, twice in the head, but survived to lead the Dodgers to the pennant by two and a half games over St. Louis, whose captain, center fielder Terry Moore, missed a month down the stretch after being concussed by a pitched ball in August. Had the Cards worn the armored caps and the Dodgers gone unprotected, St. Louis would likely have advanced to the World Series, Dr. Dandy asserted.

Though many still refused to wear them, seventy-eight-year-old Connie Mack thought invisible inserts were underkill, not overkill: "The man who invents a helmet that insures absolute protection will make a fortune," he said, oblivious to Foulproof Taylor's Beanproof Cap. "Some players may feel now it would reflect on their gameness to wear one but the time is coming when they will be standard equipment."

That time didn't come fast enough. Mack had underestimated human vanity. Players continued to step to the plate in a soft cap. Cardinals outfielder Harry (the Hat) Walker got his nickname for fiddling with his cap after every pitch. Dandy lived to see many players in both leagues wear his armored cap, but none was yet wearing a helmet when the good doctor died in 1946, of a coronary occlusion at age sixty.

In death, W. E. Dandy was revealed as "the greatest neurosurgeon of his time," a magician who was summoned to the deathbeds of George Gershwin and Leon Trotsky. He was a pioneer of a surgery called ventriculography—a technique for locating tumors and one of the most important developments in the history of neuroscience. And still, the subhead above his obituary in the *New York Times,* seeking to summarize his life in a few syllables, inevitably said: HE DEVISED MANY METHODS OF OPERATING—CO-DESIGNER OF BASEBALL HELMET. Such was the power of the national game.

What baseball needed, as Connie Mack recognized, was something more. The liners could prevent a rung bell, but not a fractured skull. "These protective liners made of fibroid material that are inserted inside the cap aren't the answer," White Sox general manager Frank Lane said in 1954. "They are of some benefit of course. Cass Michaels would have been killed if he hadn't worn one because it caught at least part of the blow."

On August 27, 1954, a pitch thrown by Marion Fricano of the A's fractured Michaels's skull and ended his career. The resulting sound—at once familiar and otherworldly—was peculiar to baseball beanings. As Roger Kahn wrote in *Sports Illustrated,* "This sound without echo meant—always—a solemn circle of men, busy trainers in white and finally the stretcher, borne by the victim's teammates, on whom baseball uniforms suddenly looked out of place."

And so it was that Mack's prophecy—"The man who invents a helmet…will make a fortune"—came to pass. In 1952, a Pittsburgh engineer named Ralph Davis brought a primitive prototype of a "protective cap" to the Forbes Field office of Pirates general manager Branch Rickey. It was a bulletproof, military-grade device made of fiberglass and polyester resin. Rickey ordered them for each of the teams in the Pirates system.

Rickey asked a Pirates executive named Charlie Muse to work with Davis and designer Ed Crick to refine the helmet. But the helmet they came up with could not protect the head of a player who refused to wear it. Which described most players. "It was more difficult than people think," Muse said in an interview with the Associated Press in 1989. "The players laughed at the first helmets, called them miner's helmets. They said the only players who would wear them were sissies."

A promising young farmhand on the Pirates affiliate in Brunswick, Georgia, had declined to wear the team's single helmet before he was beaned that summer of '52 by Jack Barbier, a sidearm pitcher in the A's system. "Only sissies wore helmets then," Mario Cuomo recalled years later, when he was the sitting governor of New York. He joked that the residual effect of the hematoma on his brain was what drove him into politics.

Helmets could not remain optional much longer, at least not on the Pirates. As with his signing of Jackie Robinson to the Dodgers six years earlier, Branch Rickey recognized both a moral and a financial benefit to the batting helmet. He owned a hat-making company, American Baseball Cap, Inc., which grossed $6,000 in 1953, a figure likely to increase exponentially if helmets became acceptable. That year, Rickey ordered all his Pirates to wear the new helmet, a mandate that protected the players' heads but not their dignity: Children seated behind the bullpen at Ebbets Field threw marbles at the Pirates. There is an industrial quality to those first Pirates helmets, a halo of holes drilled in each crown for ventilation, as if the players were wearing them to mine for coal or repair power lines.

But the players also saw the benefits. Like the glove, just one prominent athlete wearing the helmet made it instantly less sissified.

And so baseball's first $100,000 bonus baby, Pirates pitcher Paul Pettit, wore one as a pinch runner and was promptly hit in the head by a thrown ball. The helmet was dented but Pettit's head was not, serving as a powerful example to many of his teammates that it was possible to un-ring a bell.

That same summer, a star Dodgers farmhand—heir apparent to Pee Wee Reese as shortstop in Brooklyn—was biding his time leading the American Association in home runs and RBIs for the St. Paul Saints. In that role, Don Zimmer dug in at the plate one day in Columbus to face Red Birds right-hander Jim Kirk. Zimmer wasn't wearing a helmet, and struggled in the twilight to see the ball emerge from a backdrop of trees. The fastball he took to the temple fractured his skull, leaving Zimmer unconscious for six days. Four holes were drilled through the bone to reduce pressure on his brain, and those holes were later plugged with buttons of tantalum, a metal used in lightbulb filaments, which was apt, as lightbulbs were slowly buzzing to life above the heads of a scant few major-league hitters, if not the world at large.

That watershed year of 1953, University of Southern California professor C. F. (Red) Lombard applied to patent his new motorcycle helmet, which had a cushioned inner layer for comfort, but also an outer shell that absorbed and evenly distributed the energy of a collision. Lombard's battle would be every bit as uphill as baseball's, for his patent application coincided with the release of *The Wild One,* in which Marlon Brando played an outlaw biker whose wardrobe became iconic: black leather jacket, white T-shirt, and a pillowed service cap of the sort Ralph Kramden wore to drive his bus on *The Honeymooners.*

In baseball, as with Brando, helmets weren't cool. The Cardinals followed the Pirates in making them mandatory, but the $25 fine for noncompliance suggested that enforcement would be lax. Phil Rizzuto was the only Yankee to wear a helmet in 1954. When Zimmer made it to the majors that season, he and Don Hoak were the only two

Dodgers to wear them. Not wearing a helmet was reckless, but wearing one was hardly a guarantee of safety, for the act of facing a major-league pitcher was (and remains) an inherently perilous undertaking.

On June 23, 1956, in the fourth inning of the Dodgers game at Ebbets Field, Zimmer, wearing a helmet, was hit in the face by a ninety-mile-an-hour fastball thrown by the Reds' right-hander Hal Jeffcoat. The pitch shattered Zimmer's left cheekbone and nearly detached his left retina, yet such were the duties of the American game to the American public that Jean (Soot) Zimmer, the shortstop's wife, consented to be photographed hours later holding the hand of her inert husband, laid out on a slab in Long Island College Hospital, still in his pristine Dodgers home flannels.

When Zimmer emerged from that hospital, nearly three weeks later, in dark glasses that allowed only a pinpoint of light through either lens, his vision was blurred beyond fifty feet. For three months, he couldn't tie his shoes, pick up his children, or ride in a car. That season, Dr. Dandy's liners were made mandatory throughout the majors, but full helmets, finally, were growing in popularity, too, worn by one or more members of every major- and minor-league team. Branch Rickey's helmet concern—American Baseball Cap, Inc.—grossed more than $200,000 that year, finally fulfilling Connie Mack's prophecy.

Many others wanted a piece of those profits. In 1960, the unsinkable Foulproof Taylor received U.S. patent 2,926,356 for yet another iteration of the Beanproof Cap the Senators wouldn't wear a quarter of a century earlier. As ever, his market research involved epic bouts of self-endangerment. "In demonstrations of the cap, the inventor has been slugged or beaned repeatedly, without sustaining injury," the patent stated. "The inventor claims that his bean-proof cap frees baseball players from serious injuries by transforming the effect of a pitched baseball at one hundred miles an hour (more or less) into a mere jarring vibration, with no concussion."

But the helmet did not make Foulproof a fortune, or indeed a new name. Nor did any of his other manifold inventions, including a protective bra for lady wrestlers, the Bustproof Brassiere. His great-niece, Diane Taylor, recalled "Uncle Foulproof" persuading her mother to put one on, then "charging her in the chest" by way of demonstration. By the 1960s, Foulproof had an electroshock of white hair that fit neatly with his other eccentricities, which included several daily doses of Guinness and a predilection for pouring water on his cornflakes.

Foulproof remained known, by those who knew him at all, as a fixture at the televised *Friday Night Fights* of the 1950s and '60s. On the back of the jacket that he always wore ringside were the words I AM FOULPROOF TAYLOR. Below that was the hard-won phrase

Foulproof Taylor, late in life but still in the sack.
(Courtesy of Diane Taylor)

FOULED 30,000 TIMES. It's a wonder that he bothered to keep count of the various assaults on his nether regions, just as McDonald's still boasts of "billions and billions" of burgers served. That Taylor still answered to Foulproof, and not Beanproof or Bustproof, was testament to which of his inventions was most successful.

In the end, Foulproof Taylor's greatest invention was Foulproof Taylor. Before he went into the hospital with terminal stomach cancer in 1970, the inventor alerted the few contacts he still had in the New York newspaper trade that the great Foulproof Taylor was dying. They made little record of the fact and Taylor left no record in the form of offspring. He and his Canadian-born wife, Margaret, never had children.

As his great-niece put it: "We supposed all those years of being kicked you-know-where had taken their toll."

He did leave one legacy, however. By the time of his death, most baseball infielders considered the cup invaluable. Mark Belanger played shortstop from 1965 to 1982 without one — and without incident — but most of his colleagues weren't so brazen. The cup had become such an article of blind faith among baseball infielders that an eight-year-old second baseman in Romulus, Michigan, was banned from the local Little League in 1975 for failing to wear one, despite the fact that young Nancy Winnard was unimpeachably a girl. Her parents sought a federal injunction, and briefly seized headlines across the nation, before the league relented and the story ebbed away, a tempest in a different kind of cup altogether.

Little Leagues had good reason to be vigilant. Cups saved lives, at least of those unborn. In the big leagues, however, with ninety-five-mile-an-hour fastballs and line drives up the middle, a cup could only offer so much protection. During a spring training game in 1974, a foul tip off the bat of Joe Torre struck Red Sox catcher Carlton Fisk in the cup. Fisk was hospitalized for three days with a ruptured testicle, missed the first seventeen games of the regular season with "considerable swelling," and was replaced by his backup, Bob Montgomery.

Fisk returned to the lineup in May, and in the next six weeks took five more foul tips to the cup. The last, in Chicago in June, knocked him unconscious. Fisk had to be revived with smelling salts. "All catchers get hit between the legs," he said afterward, "but this is ridiculous."

Fisk tried new cups, altered his catching stance, and altered the standards of local journalism. "Newspapers held long, soul-searching editorial conferences to determine whether the word *testicle* might appear in print," Bud Collins wrote in the *Boston Globe* that summer, having won over his editors. "Writers were running out of euphemisms."

Collins's column appeared on June 12, 1974, forty-four years to the day since Max Schmeling won his heavyweight championship at Yankee Stadium after Jack Sharkey hit him flush in the groin, briefly elevating Foulproof Taylor's Foulproof Cup to national significance.

Forty-four years later, Fisk wore something almost as inviolable, a hockey goalie's cup likened to iron underwear. And that only dulled the pain slightly. On the night in 1989 that he broke Yogi Berra's record for most home runs by an American League catcher, Fisk felt connected to Yogi in a much deeper way: He took a foul tip to the groin at Yankee Stadium. "I didn't think I was going to make it," Fisk said afterward. "Yogi would appreciate that part of the game."

Johnny Bench broke seven cups in his career. Umpire Dave Pallone had his shattered by a ninety-four-mile-an-hour Nolan Ryan fastball. The protective cup wasn't indestructible and was sometimes an oxymoron, but players treated it as a magical talisman. "It's like my American Express," Joe Girardi said when he was catching for the Cubs. "I don't leave home without it." Mark McGwire wore his high school cup throughout his college, Olympic, minor-league, and major-league careers, spanning three decades, until the summer of 1998 when—en route to hitting seventy home runs, and at the peak of his global fame—he had it stolen from his locker. The thief was presumed to have been a craven collector, with one exceedingly strange curio cabinet.

Now, most outfielders don't wear a cup, and—seven decades after Pepper Martin saw the light—some infielders still don't. Three starting infielders on the Florida Marlins—Derrek Lee, Luis Castillo, and Alex Gonzalez—won the 2003 World Series without a cup among them. Adrian Beltre never wore a cup at third base, despite having been hit in the groin at that position. To this day, even though most who play it are suitably armored for battle, baseball is tied with lacrosse as the cause of more testicular injuries than any other sport, including cycling and horseback riding.

In almost all sports, jockstraps have begun a slow fade from existence, replaced by skintight compression shorts. Clubhouse wits find it increasingly difficult to put Bengay or a live amphibian in the jockey strap of an unsuspecting colleague, and perhaps that is progress, though try telling that to anyone who witnessed Gorman Thomas put a live frog in the jockstrap of his Brewers teammate Sal Bando.

But cups endure. Cups even overfloweth, sometimes literally so, as when the Tampa Bay Rays clinched the American League East title in 2008. After the game, in the visitors' clubhouse in Detroit, Rays outfielder Jonny Gomes—carried away on a tide of emotion—filled a protective cup with beer, then drank lustily from his plastic chalice.

It was evidence, if any were needed, that the cup still inspired fascination, to say nothing of innovation. Mark Littell pitched nine seasons in the major leagues with Kansas City and St. Louis, and spent much of his retirement building a better cup, which he called the Nutty Buddy. To demonstrate its efficacy, Littell videotaped himself squatting, legs splayed, on top of two Gatorade tubs. Ten feet away, a young lady fed a baseball into a pitching machine, which abruptly fired a ninety-mile-an-hour fastball, point-blank, directly into Littell's crotch.

Littell didn't flinch much less curl convulsively into a fetal ball, and the video—approaching half a million hits on YouTube—was replayed on television around the world. Littell would repeat the demonstration wherever the cup-buying public gathered, and the cue he frequently gave to have the ball placed in the pitching machine—"Here we go, Ramrod, let's go!"—called to mind the masochistic catchphrase of Foulproof Taylor: "Kick me here."

So Foulproof lived to see some iteration of the Foulproof Cup flourish in baseball. But the Beanproof Cap, worn on the head and not in the pants, was still met with metaphorical hardheadedness. Ray Chapman was the only big leaguer to die in a baseball game, but baseball players died every year, without fail, when struck in the head by a thrown or batted ball. Even those wearing helmets are not entirely safe. In the span of twenty-four hours in July 1963, two boys—a fourteen-year-old in Alexandria, Louisiana, and a twelve-year-old in Jackson, Mississippi—were killed in organized play. That spring, three others were killed, among them fourteen-year-old David Bremser of Omaha, struck just beneath his plastic batting helmet. The next summer, eighteen-year-old Tom Douglas, playing for Cascade College in Portland, Oregon, died after being struck near the ear on the lower part of his helmet. Less than two weeks later, a hundred miles down the road in Eugene, a sixteen-year-old boy, Joseph Ziegler, was killed after being struck in the helmet, which improved safety but couldn't guarantee it.

At the highest level of the game, helmets were still met with reluctance and occasional ridicule. In Kansas City in 1964, Jimmy Piersall walked to the plate wearing a Beatles wig where his helmet should have been. (Home plate umpire Frank Umont made him doff his hair before hitting.) Ted Williams famously declined to wear one, suggesting it impeded his progress when lighting out of the batter's box for first base.

They took some getting used to—Joe Garagiola thought his should have had a miner's lamp affixed to the front—and helmets were often scapegoated for a hitter's failure. Mickey Mantle flung his helmet into the afternoon ether in a famous 1963 picture by *Life* photographer John Dominis, the helmet suspended upright, as if on an invisible head, between the second and third decks of Yankee Stadium.

But every serious beaning left an impression, and not just metaphorically. When Dodgers rookie Lou Johnson was hit in the helmet by Astros pitcher Bob Bruce, the ball left an inch-deep valley that would have been left, in a less enlightened age, in Sweet Lou's forehead. Instead of dying, Johnson was taken to Daniel Freeman Hospital in Los Angeles for twenty-four hours of precautionary observation. There, the outfielder engaged in that cliché of sports journalism and medicine: "resting comfortably," his life saved by a $10.50 helmet from Branch Rickey's American Baseball Cap company.

That worrisome dent didn't go unnoticed by Johnson's teammates. Pitcher Don Drysdale immediately became a partner in Southern California's Daytona Helmet Company, whose mission was to manufacture an undentable baseball helmet, something it was already doing for race car drivers and motorcyclists. The Dodgers' team physician, Dr. Robert Woods, pronounced Daytona's batting helmet "much more resistant" than the one Johnson had worn, though it was more expensive, at $14.95. Drysdale, perhaps the most feared brushback pitcher of his day, began passing them out to opposing hitters, among them Willie Mays and Dick Allen. When Drysdale handed one to Gene Freese before a game, the Pirates' third baseman said nervously, "You trying to tell me something?"

Long before they put on those motorcycle helmets—before they wore the Oakleys fashioned for California motocrossers, before they grew Fu Manchu mustaches, before they wore coiled titanium choker necklaces—baseball players had embraced other aspects of motorcycle culture.

In the middle of the 1913 season, Reds pitcher Rube Benton was traveling "at a high rate of speed" when his motorcycle collided head-on with a streetcar in Cincinnati. Benton "was hurled to the street with terrific force," according to the next day's papers, whose headlines pronounced him NEAR DEATH and FATALLY HURT. Reds owner August (Garry) Herrmann—who had forbidden Benton to ride a motorcycle—obstinately declined to pay the player's hospital expenses. The player, meanwhile, obstinately declined to die. On the contrary, Benton didn't even retire, playing eleven more seasons, mostly with the Giants, and living to age forty-seven, when he died in another head-on collision, near Dothan, Alabama, this time in a car.

These were men not overly concerned with personal safety. As a four-year-old in 1944, Mickey Lolich rode his tricycle into a parked motorcycle, which fell on him, breaking his right collarbone. The effect of the collision was twofold: Lolich began throwing with his left hand, and he developed an abiding fascination with the vehicle that maimed him. As a star left-handed pitcher for Detroit, he rode one of his seven motorcycles to Tiger Stadium most days, a sixty-mile round-trip from his home in suburban Washington, Michigan. Manager Mayo Smith asked him to drive a car, but Lolich wouldn't oblige him.

But Lolich did wear a helmet. He had a healthy fear of the projectile that got him to the ballpark, and also of the projectile he faced on arrival there. "I'm afraid of motorcycles," he said in 1969, a year after he won three games in the World Series. "I wear a helmet, boots and gloves." But he acknowledged in the same conversation that a baseball could be every bit as terrifying, and every bit as lethal. "When a man can throw a baseball upwards of 90 miles per hour, a strong batter can make good contact and send it back at him at better than 150 miles per hour," he said. "I'm not gun shy, but I don't like the odds somehow."

In baseball in 1969, the one hundredth anniversary of the professional game, these were not just encouraging words but—to use a phrase that entered the culture that summer—one giant leap. After all, a ballplayer who wouldn't wear a motorcycle helmet on a motorcycle was exceedingly unlikely to wear a motorcycle helmet on a ball field.

To celebrate the century that had passed that summer since Doug Allison and the Red Stockings first took the field as professionals, players in both leagues wore sleeve patches bearing the new logo of Major League Baseball. It was created by a graphic designer named Jerry Dior, from the New York marketing firm of Sandgren & Murtha, who delivered—for a one-time fee somewhere between $10,000 and $25,000—what has come to be known as the Silhouetted Batter, which sounds like the name of an Agatha Christie novel, though in fact it was less a whodunit than a who-*is*-it. The short-sleeved batter, silhouetted in white, poised to strike a ball, was widely presumed to be Harmon Killebrew. It is not, and in fact could be just about any square-jawed hitter of the era, except for one unmistakable detail: He is wearing a batting helmet.

But many of the players who wore that logo were not wearing helmets. At the time, helmets were still regarded by some with suspicion and contempt. The White Sox were so bad in 1970 that no players complained when their names were removed from their jerseys, rolling back the club's decade-old innovation. They no longer cared to be identified. It was like filing the VIN off a stolen car. After one game in that 106-loss season, infielder Syd O'Brien threw his helmet in the tunnel after striking out. A few days later, when the Sox charged O'Brien $17.50 for a new helmet, he asked if he could have the cracked helmet back. His request was obliged. O'Brien set the helmet down gently and ritually shattered it with a bat.

More broadly, though, baseball was officially embracing helmets, and if owners wanted to mandate them, that off-season gave them the perfect cover to do so. At the 1970 winter meetings in Los Angeles, owners considered—or at least pretended to consider—Charlie Finley's proposal of colored bases. His Oakland A's had used gold bases for their home opener that season, and Finley wanted to paint first base red, second base yellow, and third base blue for all future games. The idea was the brainchild of a fifteen-year-old fan named Brian Barsamian, who had written to the A's owner, suggesting that he turn the infield into a kind of primary-colored Legoland. "Under the lights it will be beautiful," Finley said. "Simply beautiful." At the winter meetings that December, ensconced in the Beverly Hilton, Finley's fellow owners denied him—and us— that dream.

They likewise demurred at Finley's suggestion of a twenty-second clock for pitchers, and declined Pittsburgh's avant-garde offer to use colored foul lines for the season ahead. Faced with these and other terrible ideas, the nine-man rules committee—including two players, Bill Singer and Joe Torre—passed the helmet requirement with little controversy, nor even much publicity. At a stroke, helmets were made mandatory for all major-league baseball players, beginning with the 1971 season.

Or not *all* players. Those who were already in the big leagues were grandfathered in and allowed to do whatever they pleased. Some still declined to wear helmets, others subjected them to ritual abuse.

On July 9, 1971, in the nineteenth inning of a scoreless game,

Angels outfielder Tony Conigliaro stepped to the plate in Oakland, where he'd gone a dispiriting 0-for-7 against A's pitchers Vida Blue and Rollie Fingers. As a member of the Red Sox in 1967, Tony C. was the toast of Boston when he was partially blinded by a pitched ball that fractured his left cheekbone. The helmet he was wearing was unable to protect him, and Conigliaro never again felt comfortable at bat. So when A's reliever Bob Locker struck him out looking in the nineteenth in Oakland, dropping him to 0-for-8 on the night, Conigliaro was determined to hit something. He threw his helmet in the air, swung at it with his bat, and drove it sixty feet down the first-base line, at which time he was mercifully ejected from the game.

After the 1–0 loss, Conigliaro called a press conference for five o'clock the next *morning,* an hour at which sportswriters would be constitutionally incapable of attending, as he well knew. And so it was that before dawn on July 10, 1971, Tony Conigliaro announced his retirement from baseball. "I have lost my sight," he said, "and am on the edge of losing my mind." He caught the first flight home to Boston.

There, the city's newest sports hero, Bobby Orr, was playing beautiful hockey for the Bruins while unencumbered by a helmet. "This is certainly no sport for sissies," Orr said in 1971. "I'd feel unnatural in a helmet." At the same time, the Minnesota North Stars' forty-one-year-old goalie, Gump Worsley, refused to wear a *mask,* even though three years earlier, teammate Bill Masterton died after hitting his head on the ice in a game. "I'm too old to start now," Worsley said. In 1971, North Stars goal-scorer Bill Goldsworthy was one of only twenty players in the National Hockey League to voluntarily wear a helmet. "It's too hot," Goldsworthy said, "but I'll probably keep wearing it." Three times, after all, he'd been knocked unconscious.

All of which is to say that helmets were still too often a hard sell.

Bob Montgomery, the backup catcher of the Red Sox, was one of those players protected by the grandfather clause who chose not to wear a helmet. Through 1979, he continued stepping to the plate against big-league pitchers wearing only the protective liner—the armored cap of Dr. Dandy.

But there were other Dr. Dandys out there, too, men laboring to build a better helmet. In 1971, George "Doc" Lentz was serving his twenty-fifth year with the Minnesota Twins organization, having joined it as a trainer in 1946, when that franchise was still the Washington Senators. When helmets were made mandatory, Lentz announced his intention to design improved models for hitters, catchers, and umpires alike, and to reap great profits in the process. He didn't—he died of a stroke in Silver Spring, Maryland, four years later—but then he'd already left a sufficient legacy of protection. In 1946, in Lentz's second game with the Senators, third baseman Eddie Yost sprained his ankle. Lentz ran onto the field and sprayed Yost's ankle with a mixture of ice and ethyl chloride. At the time, the unguent was used to numb boils prior to lancing. Boston third-base coach Joe Cronin, looking on from his box, asked Lentz, "What the heck is *that?*"

That was the first recorded use of magic freeze spray on a field of play. "Two weeks later," Lentz said, "everyone was using it."

Alas, even magic freeze spray, with its mystical misting powers, could not work on the head of a man hit by a major-league fastball. In 1978, Bob Montgomery was still not wearing a helmet when teammate Dwight Evans was hit in the head by Seattle pitcher Mike Parrott. Evans went to the hospital instead of the morgue thanks to the $17.50 helmet he wore. "If Evans had been wearing the thing Monty wears instead of the helmet, Evans could have been dead today," said the shaken manager of both men, Red Sox skipper Don Zimmer, who knew whereof he spoke.

Montgomery retired the next year, 1979, the same year the National Hockey League mandated helmets for its players. Monty was the last man in baseball bereft of a batting helmet. It took 110 years, but lessons had been learned. And even then they weren't enough: Mike Coolbaugh, the thirty-five-year-old first-base coach of the Double-A Tulsa Drillers, was struck in the head and killed by a line drive in North Little Rock, Arkansas, in 2007. Within four months, at their annual meeting, major-league general managers decided that all base coaches in the big leagues would also wear helmets, effective immediately.

As a Yankees bench coach, Zimmer had already done so. In the fifth inning of Game 1 of the 1999 American League Division Series, while seated in the home dugout, his left jaw was bruised and his left ear bloodied by a foul off the bat of Chuck Knoblauch. The next day, an advertising executive who had attended the game purchased an authentic U.S. Army helmet at a military surplus store, affixed a Yankees logo to the front, and delivered it to Yankee Stadium, where Zimmer wore it during Game 2—and during the Yankees' subsequent World Series parade, and later on the cover of his autobiography. His much-concussed head carapaced in that army helmet was, Zimmer conceded, the most famous image of his career, literally a capstone to his life in baseball, and a worthy legacy.

By 2011, helmets were part of every hockey player's uniform and mandatory on motorcyclists in twenty-one states. But they were also required—by law or by social custom—on bicyclists, tricyclists, skateboarders, Rollerbladers, and users of nearly every other wheeled conveyance. Parents whose children didn't wear a helmet while guiding a two-wheeled scooter down a flat road risked social exile in suburbia. And all the while baseball helmets grew earflapped and ever larger. When David Wright of the Mets was concussed by a ninety-four-mile-an-hour fastball in 2009, he wore on his return an enormous Rawlings S100 helmet that drew comparisons to Marvin the Martian, bobblehead dolls, and the Flintstones character the Great Gazoo. It looked as if it were inflated, like Roger Bresnahan's Pneumatic Head Protector. "People can say what they want," Wright said, "but at the end of the day, it's about trying to protect yourself and be as safe as possible."

That same year, at the Mets' Citi Field, Jerry Dior was honored for the MLB logo he had created forty years earlier. Commissioner Bud Selig said, "The Silhouetted Batter is instantly recognized worldwide," and the helmet that batter wore had by then become blessedly and universally unremarkable.

So had protection for a hitter's hands, in the form of batting gloves, though they too were once a source of ridicule, if you are to believe the persistent creation myth attached to them.

This nativity story says that Ken "Hawk" Harrelson, a right-handed platoon hitter for the Kansas City A's, wasn't expecting to play on September 4, 1964, against the visiting Yankees, who were scheduled to throw a right-handed pitcher that night. So the Hawk played golf all afternoon and arrived at the park, left hand blistered, to see the Yankees' plans had changed, and they were now starting left-hander Whitey Ford. Harrelson, suddenly in the lineup, retrieved the red golf glove that was still in his pants and wore it during the game, inviting much bench jockeying from the visitors, who called him "Sweetheart" and "Mrs. Harrelson" while casting other aspersions on his manhood. But Harrelson hit two home runs in the game, and so wore the golf glove forever after, despite the fact that several Yankees—in a unified display of mockery—wore a single red golf glove during batting practice the next day, the clubhouse attendant having purchased twenty of them on the instruction of Mickey Mantle.

Ken Harrelson in a golf glove, circa 1966. *(National Baseball Hall of Fame Library, Cooperstown, NY)*

But in fact baseball players—Mantle among them—had been wearing gloves for a very long time before Harrelson did. Author Peter Morris, in *A Game of Inches,* cites Lefty O'Doul wearing "an ordinary street glove" to the plate in 1932. Golf gloves didn't catch on in golf until the end of the 1930s, after which they found their way into baseball clubhouses, to which players sometimes came straight from the course.

Marv Rickert divided the 1948 season among the Reds, Braves, and the minor-league Milwaukee Brewers, for whom "he wears a golfer's glove on his left hand when batting." The Yankees' own Billy Martin wore a golf glove on his right hand after rupturing a thumb muscle in 1953. Pirates catcher Hank Foiles wore one on his left hand in 1957. Orioles catcher Gus Triandos wore a gray golf glove after his right thumb was operated on in 1960. "That's to give me a feeling of compactness," he told the *Baltimore Sun* that summer. "You know, a feeling of security when I swing. It's supposed to help ease the swing some, too, but mainly it will give me more confidence in my hand's ability to take the vibration when I hit the ball."

Triandos wasn't the only Oriole who wore one that season. "To ease the bat shock when he is 'jammed' by inside fast balls," the *Sun* noted, "[outfielder Jackie] Brandt has been wearing a tight-fitting leather golf glove on his right hand."

Golf gloves weren't the exclusive affectation of injured players, either. At spring training in 1961, Kansas City's rookie shortstop, Dick Howser, wore a golf glove in batting practice. Jim Piersall did, too, but golf gloves weren't only confined to BP. The golf glove was easing its way into major-league games, adopted by bigger and bigger stars. Orioles first baseman Jim Gentile led the league in RBIs in 1961. He hit a record-tying four grand slams that summer, the last one as a pinch hitter, after he removed his golf glove in the on-deck circle because the pine tar was causing the glove to adhere to the bat.

That wasn't a problem for White Sox outfielder Minnie Miñoso, who led the American League in hits in 1960. Miñoso's bat flew from his hands and into the box seats during a game at Yankee Stadium in 1961. "This happens about once a week to Minoso," the *New York Times* reported, "even though he wears a golf glove on his right hand to get a better purchase on his bat."

These gloves would not have gone unnoticed by opposing players, to whom they were in no way a novelty by 1962, when both Yankees and Giants wore them during batting practice at the World Series. "It just feels good," Giants catcher John Orsino said of his gray glove. Mickey Mantle wore a black one in the cage, and when a reporter asked how long he'd been doing so, the Mick—"in an angry mood"—answered facetiously: "Three years, six months and two days."

That season, the National League MVP was Maurice Morning (Maury) Wills, who wore a "golfer's glove" to great notice while stealing a major-league record 104 bases. Wills's glove, like Mantle's, was black, but other colors weren't unusual. Leon Wagner of the Angels hit a two-run home run against the Yankees while wearing his green golf glove in 1962. Quite why Ken Harrelson's red golf glove, worn two years later, would have moved Mantle to the bulk purchase of golf gloves for ironic purposes is a mystery lost to history.

Except that doing so fits in perfectly with the history of other innovations, whose early adopters were ridiculed and then—after a brief but uncomfortable pause—universally copied. Nobody wore a fielder's glove—or a batting helmet, or a golf glove—until somebody did. And then, very quickly, everybody wore one.

"Though the idea will sound strange to the fans, the adoption of such a form of protection will be following the trend of the sport to bring out at intervals protective devices that lessen the tendency to injury on the part of the player" is how one paper put it. "When introduced the various devices invariably met with some ridicule on the part of players who had gone through years of service without the protecting equipment and from fans as well, but in turn each additional bit of armor has come to be accepted as an essential."

That was an unsigned editorial in the *New York Times*. It appeared on August 19, 1920, three days after Ray Chapman was killed by a thrown baseball.

Chapter 6

THE DECREPIT URINALS
OF EBBETS FIELD

At a child's birthday party in Connecticut, I found myself talking baseball with the guest of honor's grandfather, a former pressman for the *Brooklyn Daily Eagle,* exiled to exurbia from his native borough but still in thrall to Ebbets Field, whose men's rooms, he said, were reprehensible.

The celebrated ballpark of the Brooklyn Dodgers, if his memory served, had only four men's rooms. The lines for the toilets—and the toilets themselves—were always backed up. "It was terrible," he said, shifting on his feet as if he'd been holding it for six decades. "You spent half the game waiting on line." As he spoke, birthday candles were lit, and with them, a long-dark corner of history.

In history, nobody goes to the bathroom. In all the books, newsreels, and documentaries about baseball—in all those black-and-white photographs of fans in fedoras—nobody did what everyone does. And so I became interested in the decrepit conveniences of Ebbets Field, and a little investigative urinalism revealed that Walter O'Malley had become obsessed with his ballpark's toilets after he was appointed Dodgers president in 1943, at which time he made, "with unfeigned horror," his first inspection of the restrooms.

From that day forward, O'Malley framed the men's rooms at

Ebbets Field the way Poe framed the crumbling mansion in "The Fall of the House of Usher"—as not just a frightening chamber in its own right, but as symbol of a larger decay.

When a Brooklyn fan went to see a man about a horse, he felt more like the latter than the former: "like a horse going to a horse trough," as one Dodgers fan described relieving himself mid-game in the 1930s. In 1946, it would cost the Dodgers $100,000 to fix their stagnant urinals, which by then had become—in the words of O'Malley biographer Michael D'Antonio—a "matter of public health as well as convenience." But that hundred grand was only a drop in the bucket.

That Ebbets Field—which opened in 1913, a year after Fenway and a year before Wrigley—so quickly fell into lavatorial decrepitude is astonishing. But at least Ebbets fell from a great height, having contained unimaginable luxuries when Charlie Ebbets and Van Buskirk drew it up as precisely the kind of corporate-friendly stadium that we like to think, in our nostalgic delusions, is a modern-day affliction. "Public telephone booths will be distributed at various points on the stands," Ebbets promised in 1912. "Desks will be provided for the accommodation of business men and physicians who may expect sudden telephone calls, to whom messages will be delivered immediately. A room will be provided where articles may be checked free, lost articles reclaimed upon proper identification and umbrellas loaned for a small fee." Everything about the place was designed to appeal to a prosperous audience.

"In the preparation of the plans," Ebbets said, "the aim has been to provide for the comfort, convenience and safety of the base ball public and when completed Ebbets Field will be about the most modern, comfortable, perfectly appointed and conveniently located base ball park in the world."

To finance the park's $750,000 cost ($18 million today), Charlie Ebbets in 1912 sold a half interest in the Dodgers to two brothers,

Stephen and Edward McKeever, the former of whom became a plumber's apprentice at thirteen, a plumbing contractor at eighteen, and—with his younger brother—opened E. J. McKeever & Bro., specializing in sewers and water mains, but that didn't matter.

Charles Ebbets and E. J. McKeever, with McKeever's wife, Jennie, April 1913. *(Library of Congress)*

While the park opened as a "modern, comfortable, perfectly appointed" cathedral, it didn't last long. Ebbets Field seated a mere thirty-two thousand people, with parking for just seven hundred cars, which wasn't a problem in 1913 but became one by the 1950s. By then, wrote the bard of Brooklyn, Roger Kahn, "the public urinals were fetid troughs," and O'Malley "saw Ebbets Field not as a shrine but as a relic, with rotten parking and smelly urinals."

That miasma of smells had no means of egress in the architectural oddity that was Ebbets. "The fans had to put up with the stench of perennially backed-up toilets and a serious lack of ventilation that made the field and seating areas feel at least ten degrees warmer than the surrounding air," notes Marc Eliot in *Song of Brooklyn,* his oral history of the borough.

In the prosperity of postwar America, when whites began to leave Brooklyn for Long Island and other suburban outposts, *Time* magazine suggested in 1958—with what reads now like racial animus—that Brooklyn's bladders were emblematic of the borough's other ills: "Brooklyn's slums have spread alarmingly. There is a burgeoning population of Negroes and Puerto Ricans.... Ebbets Field, the cramped, musty cracker box that had been the home of the Dodgers since 1913, had been reduced to the social level of cockfights. A familiar complaint was that some customers were urinating in the aisles."

O'Malley moved the Dodgers to Los Angeles in the winter of 1957—not *because* of the Ebbets Field urinals, surely, but certainly not in spite of them. They played a critical and unsung role in baseball's westward migration. O'Malley admitted as much. In April 1958, the Dodgers' first spring in Los Angeles, he unburdened himself to *Time,* bidding good riddance to Ebbets with a lavatorial valedictory.

"Why should we treat baseball fans like cattle?" he asked. "I came to the conclusion years ago that we in baseball were losing our audience and weren't doing a damn thing about it. Why should you leave your nice, comfortable, air-conditioned home to go out and sweat in a drafty, dirty, dingy baseball park? Ballparks are almost all old. They are built in the poorer sections of the city. The toilets at most ballparks are a germ hazard that would turn a bacteriologist grey. Why, when I came to the Dodgers, I spent a quarter of a million dollars just to change the urinals, and Branch Rickey, who was the general manager, nearly had a stroke. He couldn't comprehend spending that much money on the customers when we could spend it on ballplayers."

The modern history of baseball—beginning with the manifest

destiny of the Dodgers' move west—is in part the history of quotidian objects. Ebbets Field is now preserved in our national nostalgia as an Elysium. Its seats, salvaged ahead of the wrecking ball in 1960, sell for $3,000 apiece. Prominent members of the Brooklyn diaspora—from Larry King to Doris Kearns Goodwin—were still eulogizing it fifty years after its demise.

The ballpark urinal trough has likewise retained a curious allure. Before the 2010 season, when the Chicago Cubs announced plans to renovate the bathrooms at Wrigley Field—built in Chicago in 1914, a year after Ebbets—there was a public backlash. And almost certainly a backsplash. The Cubs had to reassure their fans that they would not do away with Wrigley's much-loved troughs, where men stand shoulder to shoulder above a single receptacle in a daily parody of *e pluribus unum*.

Even politicians recognized the powerful symbolism inherent in that act. As president of the Texas Rangers, George W. Bush made a point of sitting in the main grandstand at Arlington Stadium and walking among the fans. "I want the folks to see me sitting in the same kind of seat they sit in, eating the same popcorn, peeing in the same urinal," he explained. On the power of such populist rhetoric, he went from president of the Texas Rangers to president of the United States.

The urinal was indispensable to baseball because beer was indispensable to baseball—or rather, because beer was so eminently dispensable *in* baseball, dispensed in oceanic proportions almost from the beginning of the sport, a sport that sometimes seemed to exist exclusively as a delivery system for malted beverages.

Browns owner Chris Von der Ahe, the man who traded for my great-great-uncle in 1886, had by then already opened a beer garden in right field at Sportsman's Park in St. Louis. "The beer garden was considered in play," notes J. Thomas Hetrick in his biography

Chris Von der Ahe and the St. Louis Browns. "Exactly how many baseballs plunked into beer schooners, scattered revelers, or rattled around picnic tables is conjecture."

Even from its very first decade, professional baseball was a backdrop for binge drinking. In 1925, to mark the golden anniversary of the National League, the *New York Times* recalled—from a not-terribly-distant remove of fifty years—the 1870s as beer sodden and violent. "The empty beer bottle made its appearance as a medium for expressing disapproval. The filled beer bottle was also present. A saloon near a ballpark was a safe investment."

Among the many temperance champions of the late Victorian era were Albert Spalding and William Hulbert, who would be buried beneath that enormous baseball in Chicago. Hulbert banned beer sales and Sunday baseball from the National League. Cincinnati could not abide baseball without beer, and joined other dissolute river cities—among them St. Louis, Pittsburgh, and Louisville—in the American Association, which was immediately disparaged as "the Beer and Whiskey League."

But even in the National League, a ban on beer sales did nothing to prevent fans from smuggling in their own, or becoming insensate before entering the grounds. On May 22, 1886, John L. Sullivan staggered down the steps of Recreation Park in Detroit and fell into his seat to watch the hometown Wolverines play the Washington Nationals. Occasionally loosing a "mighty roar"—the boxing champion was literally roaring drunk—he rooted for the visitors, antagonized his seatmates, and was finally shouted down with a cry of "Put him out," to which Sullivan replied: "Put me out? I'd break you in two and throw you in the sewer."

In his eyewitness account, an unnamed correspondent for the *New York Times* cabled back to the office: "Interjected at suitable places in this report can be distributed sundry blanks, for which the telegraphic vocabulary has no sign, but which indicate the interpolation of profanity and obscenity that never looks well in a newspaper and is generally represented by dashes."

Many team owners in the Beer and Whiskey League were, unsurprisingly, in the beer and/or whiskey business. St. Louis Browns owner Chris Von der Ahe was a magnificently mustached saloonkeeper who commissioned, with the proceeds of beer and baseball, an enormous statue of himself gazing into the middle distance. It was placed outside Sportsman's Park and named, by a sportswriter, "Von der Ahe Discovers Illinois."

One of his "Von der Boys"—as the four-time champion Browns of the mid-1880s were called—was my great-grandfather's brother Jack Boyle, who would make the papers in the 1890s, as the Giants catcher, for his saloon fistfight with the Reds catcher. Baseball stayed afloat on a river of alcohol.

At the time of his death, on January 7, 1913, Jack Boyle owned his own saloon, on Seventh Street in Cincinnati. "In his time he was one of the best catchers in the game," read his obituary in the baseball bible *Sporting Life,* "and was famous from one end of the world to the other."

Less than five months later, Von der Ahe succumbed to cirrhosis of the liver. He was broke and out of baseball, but received a grand memorial at Bellefontaine Cemetery in St. Louis, where visitors cannot possibly miss him, buried as he is beneath his own statue—right hand on hip, staring into the middle distance, forever discovering Illinois.

When Cornelius McGillicuddy left East Brookfield, Massachusetts, with only his mitts in 1884, he made a promise to his mother that he would never imbibe. And he never did. But he was an exception among players and spectators, and his mother was right to worry.

That very summer of '84, Albert Spalding was preaching temperance among players. "Men who have said to me point blank that they 'have not touched a drop to-day' have been proved to have drank that very day over a dozen glasses of beer beside liquor, before going to a match," he said. "I tell you, sir, the leagues have got to stop this drinking business or give up running club teams."

Spalding's complaints fell on deaf ears, literally so in the case of Louisville Slugger Pete Browning, dozing just off second base in the Beer and Whiskey League, which finally disbanded after the 1891 season. Several of its teams — Cincinnati, Pittsburgh, Brooklyn, St. Louis — were subsumed into the National League, and the American Association faded into oblivion, except for its initials, which survive as shorthand for Alcoholics Anonymous.

By the 1890s, drinking was the most popular pastime within our most popular pastime. After the cops of Brooklyn's Second Precinct played their counterparts of Manhattan's First Precinct in a game at the Polo Grounds in 1892 — losers picked up the winners' terrifying bar tab — the victorious Brooklyn pitcher, Twirler Martin, composed a poem on the spot:

We're not as big as we ought to be
Not in a thousand years;
But we're big enough, as you will see,
To win a thousand beers.

Mercifully, baseball and beer conspired to produce better poems than that one. In October 1894, a sixteen-year-old outfielder for the town team in Galesburg, Illinois, was shagging flies in a pasture when his friend hit a deep ball that required him to sprint. In doing so, the outfielder stepped on a broken beer bottle, leaving a gash on his right foot that had to be closed with four stitches. The incident — and his parents' contemptuous reaction to it — made Carl Sandburg reconsider his dream of professional baseball and go into poetry instead.

More often, to believe its purveyors, beer was not the end but the gateway to a career in baseball. Beer was marketed to Americans in the same way that Louisville Sluggers were: as a performance enhancer. Beneath the headline BALL PLAYERS USE BEER IN TRAINING, a 1909 Budweiser ad quoted Brooklyn president Charles Ebbets saying, "A simple dinner with light beer [is] our idea of a proper drink for athletes in training."

When players weren't pitching beer to fans, fans were pitching beer at players. In 1907, after several Cleveland Indians were hit by thrown bottles in Detroit, American League president Ban Johnson warned clubs about airborne concessions. Then that fall, when Detroit was playing at Sportsman's Park in St. Louis, boyish umpire Bill Evans was hit in the head and badly injured by a thrown soda bottle. He told Christy Mathewson he was grateful for it, for it seemed to focus his attention on getting his calls right. "If I had any idea who the bird was that tossed the bottle I would look him up and thank him," Evans said. "He did me a good turn."

On another occasion, after making a controversial call at first base in Chicago, Evans was showered with dozens of bottles. As they rained down on him, Evans remained at his post, enduring the barrage for a full three minutes, even after players begged him to retreat to the safety of the infield grass.

The following season, Cubs manager Frank Chance had cartilage in his neck severed by a thrown soda-water bottle at the Polo Grounds, while racing off the field to the clubhouse after clinching the 1908 pennant. "Unfortunately baseball as played uptown can never be a fashionable sport because it is as dangerous to a spectator as automobile racing on public highways," the *New York Times* sniffed. "You never can tell where the danger is coming from — an empty beer bottle, a seat cushion or a bat."

One solution to bottle throwing — banning beer altogether — was not an option worth serious contemplation. Indeed, a ball club signing a contract with its beer purveyor was cause for celebratory headlines in the winter months. "The prospect of a beer-less season at the Cincinnati baseball park was removed to-day when President August Herrmann awarded the beer contract for the coming baseball year," read a January 1911 dispatch in the *Times,* beneath the comforting headline CINCINNATI FANS TO HAVE BEER.

August (Garry) Herrmann, the Cincinnati owner, employed "an army of lads" to collect the empty bottles, or "dead soldiers," that accumulated by the hundreds beneath the grandstands and on the grass at Reds games, where vendors sold "pop," sassafras, and mineral water in bottles, replete with straw, in addition to the copious amounts of beer sold and consumed there.

And so Herrmann lobbied aggressively against Prohibition. In 1917, the Reds' program carried an ad that read, "If You Want To Enjoy a Glass of Beer, VOTE AGAINST PROHIBITION. In Any Form and At All Times. Keep Your Country a Land of Personal Liberty!"

Members of the International Union of the United Brewery Workmen, who signed the ad, were preaching to the choir. When Prohibition took effect in 1920, Reds fans—and Herrmann himself—made do. On April 25, 1925, in the middle of that dry decade, the Cincinnati Royal Red Rooters—the team's fan club, which had been following the Reds on the road since 1919—chartered several Pullman cars and took over the seventeenth floor of the Statler Hotel in St. Louis for the Reds' series with the Cardinals.

A hotel manager watched the Rooters unload their larder, like a line of ants, carrying a "travelling delicatessen" that included Triple S sausages, bologna, and crates of what were labeled as Cincinnati sauerkraut, in quantities rather excessive for a four-game series. When the feds raided the floor, they found thirteen empty beer kegs, two that were tapped, and eleven more full ones in a refrigerator. "I can't believe it," said one of the guests—Reds owner Garry Herrmann—when informed that the beer had an alcohol content of 3.5 to 4.5

percent, emphatically above the legal limit of zero. "It didn't taste like that to me." Like Captain Renault in *Casablanca*, Herrmann was shocked—*shocked*—to learn he wasn't drinking near beer.

But these weren't uncommon phenomena. In 1926, Cubs star Hack Wilson was busted in a midnight raid on a Chicago "beer parlor" while attempting to egress out the back window of a North Side row house.

Prohibition was just as hard on fans. "Since beer has departed they choose ginger ale, sarsaparilla, and near-beer," the concessionaire Harry M. Stevens said in 1924. "It is but comparatively recently that they have gotten around to taking these soft drinks with any seriousness and in any great quantities."

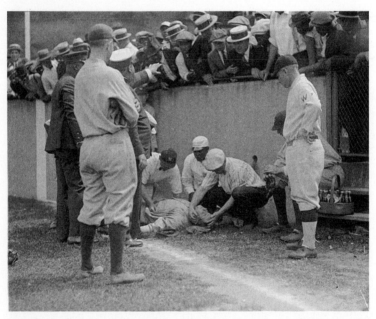

A soda vendor, his basket of bottles set down on the step, is among the first responders to Babe Ruth when the Bambino was knocked out after running into a wall in Washington's Griffith Stadium, July 6, 1924. *(Library of Congress)*

Even those fans drew the line at lemonade, to Stevens's dismay. As Stevens put it, "The fans do not hear the music of the ice clinking in the glass."

The thought of watching, owning, or playing for a major-league baseball team without the aid of alcoholic diversion was not an appealing one. Babe Ruth was sold to the Yankees on January 5, 1920, eleven days before the start of Prohibition, though Prohibition didn't prohibit Ruth from drinking anything at all. As with Herrmann at the Statler Hotel in St. Louis, beer kegs were delivered to Ruth's suite at the Ansonia Hotel on Broadway.

But the Volstead Act *did* have a material effect on many others in baseball. Boston didn't just lose Ruth when Prohibition took effect: It lost the Third Base Saloon. Nuf Ced McGreevy donated the extensive collection of baseball photographs that festooned his establishment to the Boston Public Library, which turned Third Base, in 1923, into its Roxbury Crossing branch.

Likewise bereft was Ruth's boss, the brewery scion and Yankees owner Colonel Jacob Ruppert, maker of Ruppert Knickerbocker Beer. On the very day that Ruppert bought Ruth for $100,000 from Boston owner Harry Frazee, he lost his appeal before the United States Supreme Court to legalize the manufacture and sale of beer with a reduced alcohol content of 2.75 percent.

"Maybe he will forget his disappointment over the beer decision when he sees Babe hoist a few circuit drives over the fence at the Polo Grounds," the *Boston Globe* speculated, and indeed that is exactly what got Ruppert through the 1920s.

A four-term U.S. congressman and colonel in the New York National Guard, Ruppert purportedly came to baseball as a Giants fan, though the *New York Times* columnist Arthur Daley claimed he cared little for baseball or ballplayers. "There was a Prussian formality to Ruppert," he wrote. "Everyone was on a last name basis." Twice—in 1903 and 1912—Ruppert tried and failed to buy the

Giants. Owner Charles Webb Murphy made an overture to sell Ruppert the Cubs in 1912, but the Colonel would later recall, "I wasn't interested in any thing so far from Broadway."

And so in 1914, having only seen the Yankees play twice in person, he bought the team in partnership with the memorably named Tillinghast L'Hommedieu Huston, for $425,000 apiece. Ruppert bought out Huston in 1922, and spent the rest of the decade erecting Yankee Stadium, building baseball's greatest team, and producing near beer and other soft drinks at the massive Ruppert Brewery, a Wonka-like edifice occupying three blocks of the Upper East Side of Manhattan, between 90th and 92nd and Third Avenue, a short walk from his baronial apartment on Fifth Avenue.

It almost goes without saying that near beer was not well received at American ballparks. In 1921, the second year of Prohibition, a writer at the Polo Grounds described a vendor "burdened with bottles of one-half of 1 percent, calling out: 'Here's your good, cold beer!' Undoubtedly he is a son of the man who, when his hungry baby cried for sustenance in the night time, offered it a nice milk ticket."

Ball games without beer were a perversion. "No more are empty beer bottles flung carelessly over the baseball greensward by enthusiastic fans," lamented a columnist in the *Rochester (New York) Evening Journal*. "They lent a gala aspect to opening days not found now."

He was not alone in his nostalgia for a simpler time, prior to Prohibition, when lethal projectiles lent a festive air to ball games. "The patrons of the ball yards, after standing to the bar for a few innings, drinking the rye and bourbon which were then offered for sale under official auspices, sometimes found themselves swept away on an irresistible tide of emotion, as the lady defendants say, and took to throwing all sorts of loose objects at the umpires and visiting athletes in critical moments," wrote the conservative columnist Westbrook Pegler at the time of repeal. "These objects were of great variety, being decanters, beer bottles, beer crocks, and the arms of chairs, as well as an occasional walking cane."

But Prohibition hardly prohibited the meteor shower of bottles that enlivened earlier games. For starters, the absence of ballpark beer was no barrier to drunkenness. "A slightly inebriated gentleman was out of the stand in the eighth and half way to the plate for a quiet chat with [umpire] Hank O'Day before a guard overtook him and led him to a place of refuge," went a note in the *New York Times,* of an unremarkable game at the Polo Grounds in 1924. (O'Day, you may recall, was the umpire beaten by an angry mob on that scorching-hot day in St. Louis in 1901.)

Many incidents weren't nearly as innocuous as the one at the Polo Grounds. The 1920s saw an epidemic of bottle throwing at baseball games, and an empty soda bottle proved every bit as dangerous as an empty beer bottle. Less than three weeks after Ray Chapman was killed by a pitched baseball at the Polo Grounds, New York's acting chief magistrate, J. E. McGeehan, asked for jail sentences for all bottle throwers at baseball games. "Bottle throwing, with the umpires and players as targets, has become almost a daily occurrence," he said. "A man who throws a bottle might sentence a player to six months in the hospital. I recommend that we sentence any such person to six months in jail."

The Dodgers saw their share of airborne glass, and in 1922, after a water-bottle-throwing incident at Ebbets Field, the Dodgers promised to raise grandstand ticket prices—from $0.25 and $0.50 to $0.50 and $0.75—in an effort to keep out the bottle-throwing rabble.

Later, in 1922, in the ninth inning of a crucial September game at St. Louis billed as the "Little World Series," Yankees outfielder Whitey Witt was hit between the eyes by a pop bottle, which sliced his forehead to the bone. Mounted policemen moved quickly onto the field to keep the standing-room-only crowd of Browns fans at bay while Witt lay unconscious in left center field. He would eventually be carried off by teammates. The force of the blow had knocked the bottom from the bottle, which was saved as evidence by umpire Bill Evans—the same Bill Evans, no longer boyish, brained by a bottle at the same Sportsman's Park in 1907.

Despite the presence of thirty thousand potential witnesses, and rewards totaling $2,050, the perpetrator of the "Pop Bottle Mystery" wasn't caught, and American League president Ban Johnson asked for anyone with leads to write to him. Several did—including a man claiming to have seen a ten-year-old boy throw the bottle— but no tip panned out until a witness from Evansville, Indiana, named James P. Hon wrote to Johnson. In his letter, Hon said that Witt, while sprinting across the outfield in pursuit of a fly ball, had stepped on the neck of a bottle, which cartwheeled into his forehead. Hon declined the reward money and offered to sign an affidavit swearing to his veracity. Johnson was so grateful to Hon, a salesman, for neatly—if implausibly—"solving" this mystery that he sent him a check for $1,000, round-trip transportation to New York, and tickets to every game of the World Series between Ruppert's Yankees and the team he had tried and failed to buy, the Giants.

It was in his paneled office at the brewery—with the smell of hops rising from the floor below—that Ruppert negotiated his contracts with Ruth. Prohibition had robbed even these semiannual ceremonies of their alcoholic coda. Before the historic 1927 season, Ruth hitting sixty home runs on Murderers' Row for the most celebrated team in baseball history, Ruppert signed the Babe to a three-year contract worth $70,000 a season, Ruth surpassing Ty Cobb as the game's highest-paid player. As Ruth left hastily to visit his ailing wife in the hospital, Ruppert announced to the press throng waiting outside his office what few of them wanted to hear: "Boys, let's go and refresh ourselves with a little near beer."

Perhaps because near beer was refreshing to no one, fans kept throwing soda bottles onto the field. On September 12, 1927, the *New York Times* described a Giants–Cubs game at Wrigley Field as "one-tenth baseball and nine-tenths bottle hurling." After one disputed call, it took five minutes to gather up all the bottles thrown at umpires Charley Pfirman and Glenn Harper. Players from both teams formed a cordon around Pfirman, who'd been hit in the leg, as commissioner Kenesaw Mountain Landis watched impotently from his box seat.

That year, Bill Evans recalled the early days of ballpark inebriation, beginning in 1906, when the twenty-two-year-old "Boy Umpire" became the youngest ump in major-league history, before or since. "At many of the parks there was a long bar that dispensed hard liquor and beer," Evans wrote in a first-person newspaper account. "Venders peddled half pints of whiskey through the crowd then as pop is sold now, for the small sum of two bits. Mob scenes were almost daily occurrences, riots were frequently staged."

In a game in Cleveland in 1929, Indians manager Roger Peckinpaugh argued a call, which brought jeers and a sudden shower of bottles, one of which concussed umpire Emmett T. Ormsby, who was carried off the field. Peckinpaugh was suspended five games for inciting a near riot. The crowd was only placated when an Indians executive came onto the field and appealed for order. That executive was Bill Evans, much-concussed former umpire, who had hung up his mask the year before to become the Indians' general manager.

Anyone regularly attending baseball games could have seen the folly of Prohibition. By the winter of 1932, when Ruth hoped to renew his $75,000 contract with the Yankees, he told a reporter: "Give Colonel Jake Ruppert the right to make beer again and I'll have no trouble signing any contract with the Yankees for 1933. The Colonel would be so tickled he'd never hear how much I was asking. He'd be such a soft touch for me if real beer ever comes back."

"If that's done," Ruppert said of Prohibition's repeal, "my own brewery will be ready to produce the real stuff on a minute's notice."

And so it was. When Prohibition ended five days before Opening Day of 1933—and Yankee Stadium received a license that June to sell beer—the House That Ruth Built became the single biggest market for Ruppert's product, and his Yankees de facto ambassadors for the brand. A promotional photograph from the 1930s shows Ruppert—besuited and bow-tied, hat literally in hand—posing with Yankees stars Tony Lazzeri, Joe DiMaggio, and Frank Crosetti in the bright sunshine of Yankee Stadium, above the legend KNICKERBOCKER—NEW YORK'S FAMOUS BEER. With his white mustache, dapper style, and bottomless fortune, Ruppert resembled Rich Uncle Pennybags, cartoon mascot for the Monopoly board game that was initially rejected by Parker Brothers that year.

Yankees owner Jacob Ruppert with manager Joe McCarthy and players Joe DiMaggio, Lou Gehrig, and Tony Lazzeri, in the visitors' clubhouse at the Polo Grounds, after winning the 1937 World Series. Gehrig and Lazzeri are holding Knickerbocker beer bottles. *(© Bettmann/CORBIS)*

Beer was back, in baseball as in bars, and the writer who pined a decade earlier for empty beer bottles littering the greensward didn't have to wait long until breweriana was again taking flight in American ballparks. When the Yankees played at Comiskey Park in Chicago on Saturday, July 25, 1936, plate umpire Charlie Johnston was showered with beer tins and bottles. It took seven policemen to escort him off the field after the Yankees' 5–3 win. The next day, in the second half of a doubleheader—during a full day shift of drinking by White Sox fans—home plate umpire Bill Summers was pelted with beer cans, oranges, lemons, and seat cushions. In the eighth inning, as Charlie Johnston looked on from first base, Summers was hit in the groin by a bottle thrown from the upper grandstand. The force of the blow knocked him to the ground, as you might imagine. He didn't return to the game. Witnessing this, not for the first time, from his box seat, Commissioner Landis ordered an announcement: His office would give a $5,000 reward for information leading to the arrest and conviction of the bottle thrower.

Of course, there was a simpler, less expensive solution to the menace, as the *Sporting News* illustrated in an editorial cartoon in 1935. In one panel, a player lies on the diamond holding his head, an empty bottle next to him. "A guy that would do that should be strung up," says a fan in a fedora, to which another replies, "Nobody but a rat would do it." In the cartoon's other panel, a white-capped soda vendor decants a bottle into a paper cup, beneath the headline POUR OUT [THE] POP BOTTLE PERIL!

To this day, of course, caps are removed from plastic soda and beer bottles at the point of sale, or the beer is decanted into a plastic cup, so that the fan who purchases a cold one is not simultaneously armed with alcohol and weaponry. Though we can't any longer produce it by unscrewing tops ourselves, that little wisp of water vapor that escapes the beer bottle when the cap is removed—like gun smoke curling from a Colt .45, or a ghost levitating from a cartoon corpse — is quietly mesmeric to many of us who grew up working in ballparks.

By the end of the decade, beer and baseball were happily remarried. In 1939, when the bachelor Ruppert died of phlebitis at age seventy-one, in his twelve-room apartment on Fifth Avenue, alone but for a staff of servants, his fortune was estimated at $100 million. In life, he was both Croesus and colossus, and now his casket was borne by honorary pallbearers from the twinned worlds of baseball (Ruth, Gehrig, Wagner, McCarthy) and beer (including Rudolph Schaefer, president of the Schaefer Brewing Company, a frequent sports sponsor whose most famous advertising slogan — "The One Beer To Have When You're Having More Than One" — was a jocular invitation to binge drinking).

In nationwide obituaries, the Colonel was remembered for his menagerie of monkeys — he kept a score of capuchins on his country estate — and stable of horses. He was also recalled as a lifelong bachelor and collector of antiquities. Lest anyone get the wrong idea, the *New York Times* obituary stressed his many manly pursuits, exemplified by baseball and beer and his unmistakable taste in interior decor. "He was distinctly of the masculine type, and this was reflected in his business office, which was paneled in dark wood," it read, before delivering the coup de grâce: *"There were no curtains."*

When those first reports of Ruppert's death began to circulate, police were dispatched to guard the block on which he lived. Twenty-five officers were required to control a public clamoring to pay its respects, for the Colonel had become an unlikely man of the people, a millionaire who gave the masses what they wanted: beer and baseball, direct descendants of bread and circuses.

From St. Patrick's Cathedral, Ruppert's body was driven twenty-eight miles north, to Kensico Cemetery in suburban Valhalla, where he was interred in the Ruppert family vault — a great, columned mausoleum. There he rides out eternity in the company of Lou and Eleanor Gehrig, not to mention Harry Frazee, the man who sold him Babe Ruth. Ruth himself is almost next door, in the adjacent Gate of Heaven Cemetery, where visitors still decorate his headstone with baseballs, beer cans, and bottle caps.

It wasn't until 1939, the year of Ruppert's death, that beer and baseball found connubial bliss on the radio. That season, the Yankees, Dodgers, and Giants first broadcast their ball games and that medium entered its golden age. And it was golden: Beer quickly became baseball's single biggest sponsor and was ubiquitous. Dizzy Dean was hired to call all home St. Louis Browns and Cardinals games for KWK in 1941, and to shill for Griesedieck beer on the air. When English teachers in Missouri publicly criticized his appalling grammar—base stealers "slud" into second—Dean was unmoved. "This beer outfit that hired me to learn the people baseball thinks I can talk all right," he said.

So powerfully patriotic was the combination of baseball and beer that the Columbia Brewing Company, St. Louis brewers of Alpen Brau, ran ads in the 1942 World Series program in which the redbird from the Cardinals uniform front—the one inspired by Allie May Schmidt—perched menacingly on Hitler's shoulder. It looked alarmingly like Poe's raven on the bust of Pallas.

"There's only one flag that you and your team mates are ever going to run up in the game you started," the Cardinals mascot tells the Führer. "It's the white flag of surrender."

Like Dean in St. Louis, doing both the Browns and Cards, Jim Britt in Boston called all Red Sox and Braves home games, urging Narragansett beer on his listeners. In the Bronx, Mel Allen bowed to his beer sponsor every time he called a Yankees home run a "Ballantine blast." When a Cincinnati Red homered onto the sundeck at Crosley Field, Waite Hoyt would say, "He hit it into Burgerville," a reference to Burger Beer, "The Beer That Brings You Baseball." These announcers became so synonymous with their sponsors that many had to be replaced when a team switched breweries.

Waite Hoyt would retire from the Reds when the team abandoned Burger as its beer sponsor. When Goebel gave way to Stroh's as the Tigers' beer patron, announcer Van Patrick stepped aside for Ernie Harwell. Harwell came from Baltimore, where he shilled on air for National Beer in his first three seasons. When the Orioles transferred sponsorship to Gunther Beer, National's unholy rival, Harwell naturally feared for his job. Gunther only retained him when fans petitioned the brewery on his behalf.

It could all be very confusing to a spectator trying to practice brand loyalty. In March 1953, when brewing titan August A. Busch Jr. bought the St. Louis Cardinals for $3.75 million from Fred Saigh — whose fifteen-month sentence for income tax evasion made owning the team problematic — Anheuser-Busch became proprietor of a team sponsored by rival Griesedieck. Worse, the Cards played in Sportsman's Park, which they rented from the Browns, whose games were sponsored by Falstaff.

More confusing still, Busch immediately bought Sportsman's Park for $800,000 from Browns owner Bill Veeck, and renamed it Budweiser Stadium. On April 10, six days before the Cardinals' first home game, commissioner Ford Frick strongly urged a name change, and the place became Busch Stadium instead, saving announcers from having to present Cardinals baseball, from Budweiser Stadium, brought to you by Griesedieck.

Busch's Anheuser-Busch brewery produced fewer than six million barrels a year, about the same as Joseph A. Schlitz, its rival for being the nation's biggest beer producer. The Busch name was so renowned for beer that the name change to Busch Stadium was inconsequential to the Woman's Christian Temperance Union. "You could toss up the three B's," said its president, Mrs. D. Leigh Colvin.

"Call it Beer Park, Budweiser Park or Busch Park and they all mean the same thing. No athletic park ought to be named for a brewer because everybody knows that beer and athletics don't mix."

Many others agreed. United States senator Edwin C. Johnson of Colorado introduced a bill that would subject clubs owned by breweries to federal antitrust laws. Johnson happened to be president of the Class A Western League, and didn't like that Anheuser-Busch was broadcasting Cardinals games (and Budweiser ads) over 120 stations, many of them in minor-league markets, "with total disregard for local ball clubs and breweries."

Baseball had been "prostituted," Johnson said, and become an "adjunct of the brewing business."

By then, many baseball broadcasts were two-hour beer ads. In St. Louis, the microphone flag bore not the station call letters but the words GRIESEDIECK BEER. The Ballantine sign above the scoreboard in right center field at Shibe Park was sixty feet across. Eighty-six different church and civic groups appeared before the liquor board in Baltimore in December 1953 to lobby against the Orioles, newly moved from St. Louis, getting a license to sell beer at Municipal Stadium. The Orioles' president, Clarence Miles, informed the board by telegram that denying the application to sell beer would put the team's very existence in jeopardy.

Baseball and beer were by then difficult to tell apart. In 1957, the new president of the Woman's Christian Temperance Union described baseball broadcasts as "beercasts." "Baseball has become beerball," Mrs. Glenn G. Hays of the WCTU said the year the Dodgers fled Ebbets Field and its overburdened urinals. "What was once the national pastime now appears to have become the star salesman of the beer barons, while club owners wonder why public interest and patronage have declined. Baseball is being taken from a wholesome spectator and sandlot sport into the realm of a national problem that includes alchoholism and drink-caused juvenile delinquency."

Beer was already the single biggest advertiser on televised base-ball in 1944. By 1961, only the Los Angeles Dodgers lacked a brew-ery sponsor. Even the expansion Mets had signed a five-year deal with Rheingold to sponsor their broadcasts, though they wouldn't play a game until the following season.

The vast majority of games were still played in the day, an invita-tion to indolence and hooky. "Beercasts of the game try to convince anyone who hears or sees them that it's the right thing to do to sit in front of the set and get drunk while viewing or listening," said Mrs. Hays of the Woman's Christian Temperance Union, but in fairness, fans were also encouraged to get drunk *at* the game, while sitting in the bleachers.

Connie Mack Stadium in Philadelphia didn't sell beer until 1961 — the Volstead Act still echoed there — but fans were allowed to bring their own. The Phillies, in 1956, sought a license to sell it in paper cups, a request made more urgent when Phillies fans rained beer bottles and cans onto the Giants during the second half of a doubleheader that April, causing the interruption of the game. Two nights later, with twenty police added inside the park, a thirty-six-year-old man was arrested for walking out of the left field bleachers to engage a player in conversation.

From the time the Braves arrived in Milwaukee in 1953, fans were also allowed to bring their own beer into County Stadium — "six packs, coolers, half barrels" — and they did, for eight libertine sea-sons. That era ended before the 1961 season, when the county passed an ordinance banning BYOB at the ballpark. The Braves still sold beer, twelve-ounce bottles decanted into paper cups, but the ban on bring-your-own appeared to pay quick dividends when a "small-scale riot" broke out during a game on June 24 of that season, Braves and Cubs fans pelting each other with beer cups. There were four arrests, but it could have been worse, had those cups been cans instead. (Or, God forbid, half barrels.)

But attendance at Braves games declined by nearly four hundred thousand fans during the 1961 season. A citizens' group formed—the "walking wets"—to "repeal" the Braves' "prohibition." After all, a six-pack of beer could be had for a buck outside the stadium, but it cost $0.30 a cup on the inside. The law was discriminating, said county board supervisor Cornelius Jankowski, against the "working man." With attendance declining by another four hundred thousand fans in 1962, the county board voted that June to repeal the ban, allowing fans once again to bring their own beer.

Whether beer was legal or illegal, sold or not sold, brought in or bought on-site, quaffed in bottles or poured into cups, fans were going to get drunk. Beer was a baseball constant. On Opening Day of 1964, the Braves' penultimate season in Milwaukee, "several fans ran onto the field, some to shake Willie Mays's hand and some to slide into second base." And that was a Wednesday afternoon in April.

The Washington Senators, meanwhile, had taken the Solomonic decision to ban beer sales in the grandstand, while offering it in the bleachers, where the umpires were suitably out of range. Its high price—$0.35—was deemed a suitable deterrent, as was the benign vessel it came in: a paper cup.

In Washington as in Milwaukee, baseball had found the perfect delivery system: the waxed-paper cup. Emptied, inverted, and stomped on just right, it made a sound like a gunshot, but could not otherwise be made to mimic a weapon. With its bottom removed, it became a megaphone.

The waxed-paper cup was bottomless in other, more important ways. It allowed for the cheap and prodigious dispensing of tap beer. When the Braves moved to Atlanta following the 1965 season, and Milwaukee got a new franchise five years later, the new club fully embraced beer culture, calling itself the Brewers and employing a lederhosened mascot—Bernie Brewer—to slide from a beer barrel into a frothing stein of beer after home team home runs. Lest the team mascot bathing in beer be seen as an invitation to inebriation, the club created a cartoon drunk called "the Two Fisted Slobber," whose appearance on the scoreboard—bubbles issuing from his nose—was meant to encourage responsible drinking. Instead, the Slobber quickly became a folk hero, his every appearance drawing applause.

Fortified with waxed-paper cups, the Brewers offered Ten Cent Beer Nights. They were so popular—unlimited beer at rock-bottom prices—they had to be abandoned, replaced by a coupon system, in which each fan could have only three beers, each of which came completely free of charge. "We threw out the ten-cent beer night for a lot of reasons," owner Bud Selig said in 1974. "The main reason was the obvious one—drunkenness."

That year, 1974, the century-old codependency of baseball and beer came, as it were, to a head. On May 22 in Milwaukee, Tigers slugger Willie Horton was twice showered with beer after hitting a two-run homer to beat the Brewers. This was what the waxed-paper cup had wrought: Players and umpires were no longer bottled, enduring instead the less dangerous but profoundly undignified beer shower. Where once fans retained the beer and then threw the receptacle, they now retained the receptacle and threw the beer.

A week later, in Arlington, the Texas Rangers and the Cleveland Indians engaged in an eighth-inning brawl that lasted ten full minutes. Upon returning to the dugout, Cleveland catcher Dave Duncan was given a beer shower by fans. Duncan tried to lead a delegation of Indians into the stands to confront those responsible, but was restrained by police.

It was with some anticipation, then, that the two teams next met six days later, June 4, in Cleveland, on what was widely advertised as Ten Cent Beer Night. Such was the lure of cheap Stroh's—which ordinarily sold for $0.60 a pop—that 25,134 people came to Municipal Stadium on that Tuesday night, roughly three times the Tribe's average attendance. Many arrived already inebriated, to judge by the firecrackers and smoke bombs that were detonated early on. In the top of the second, a woman bounded onto the field, bared her breasts in the on-deck circle, and then tried without success to kiss home plate umpire Nestor Chylak. At inning's end, forty more fans ran across the field, some of them turning somersaults.

In the fourth inning, as Rangers designated hitter Tom Grieve circled the bases after homering, a naked man sprinted onto the base paths and slid into second. Other streakers would follow, one wearing a single sock. Which isn't to suggest that beer was responsible for all of the night's mayhem. It was a bottle of Thunderbird, after all, that narrowly missed the head of Rangers first baseman Mike Hargrove. But one fact was inescapable: Sixty-five thousand cups of beer had been sold by the bottom of the ninth inning, when the Indians had the winning run on third base with two outs in a 5–5 game.

That's when several fans jumped the outfield fence and—high on Stroh's—endeavored to remove the cap, glove, and uniform shirt of Rangers right fielder Jeff Burroughs. Many other fans poured over the wall, like an invading army, bearing knives, chains, and pieces of their former seats. Tribe pitcher Tom Hilgendorf was hit on the head with a metal folding chair. Both teams, armed with bats, ran from the dugout onto the field to defend their teammates from the drunken mob. When umpire Chylak was also hit in the head by a folding chair, he abandoned the game, forfeiting it to the Rangers, after which all three bases were spirited away by spectators.

"We're lucky somebody didn't get stabbed," Rangers manager Billy Martin said afterward, while Indians skipper Ken Aspro-monte feared that the seventy-four-year-old franchise might yet be given the death penalty. "Cleveland may have lost a ballclub tonight," he said.

"We could have gotten killed out there very easily," Chylak said in the relative safety of his dressing room. By way of evidence, he displayed, in his bloody hand, a weapon he'd retrieved from the field: a beer bottle concealed inside several paper cups. Here was a visual history of ballpark violence in a single diabolical device: the beer bottle, and the cup that replaced it.

All of this is to say that the $8 beer, as a barrier-to-entry of ballpark inebriation, has proved beneficial to the modern fan, though few have thanked the owners for it. The comically high cost of stadium beer, of course, has had an even more salubrious effect on those owners, not least the Busch family, which was selling just under six million barrels of beer when it bought the Cardinals in 1953. On the twenty-fifth anniversary of that purchase, in 1978, Anheuser-Busch was selling thirty-five million barrels annually, and by 1987—when the Cardinals hosted the World Series, and Gussie Busch was pulled by Clydesdales through the outfield at the second incarnation of Busch Stadium—the brewery was doing seventy million barrels a year. Those Budweiser Clydesdales had become, by then, ubiquitous advertising icons.

When the Cardinals opened their third iteration of Busch Stadium in 2006—fifty-three years after Gussie Busch backed away from the name Budweiser Stadium—naming a ballpark for a beer had long since lost its taboo. The Colorado Rockies played in Coors Field, in the home state of the late Senator Edwin C. Johnson, who had opposed the sale of the Cardinals to a family of brewers.

When that sale was being mooted, an editorial in the *St. Louis Post-Dispatch* approved: "Mr. Busch gives every evidence that he thinks of the Cardinals as a baseball club and not as a device for selling beer."

It was both. By 2008, Anheuser-Busch was producing one hundred million barrels a year and the brewery was sold to InBev for $52 billion. Anheuser-Busch had become the nation's twenty-second-largest advertiser, and its endless TV and print and radio spots—its omnipresent stadium signage and sports sponsorships—were part of an annual marketing spend of $1.36 billion. By then, calling the ballpark Budweiser Stadium was scarcely necessary.

Beer bottles had become plastic, stand workers removed the caps at the point of purchase to inhibit their use as projectiles, and most teams offered alcohol-free "family sections," which Ryne Duren had long lobbied for. But beer and baseball were still inseparable. Over the years, a deep irony had developed. The only time many fans put their beer down at a ball game was at the playing of the national anthem, when once that tune was a cue to pick up one's beer and start drinking.

In 1766, a group of men began meeting fortnightly in London at the Crown & Anchor pub on the Strand, for drinking and singing and general conviviality. This new gentlemen's club took as its name the Anacreontic Society, after the Greek poet Anacreon, bard of wine and lust, and a man so prodigiously bibulous that he was widely reported to have died from a grape pip lodged in his windpipe. (He didn't.)

Ralph Tomlinson, president of the Anacreontic Society, wrote a theme song for the club. It was called "To Anacreon in Heaven." Tomlinson's lyrics suggested that women and drinking were, as one might imagine, the principal topics of conversation at the Crown & Anchor, "where my good fellows we'll learn to entwine / The myrtle of Venus and Bacchus' wine."

Tomlinson's words were set to music by another club member, John Stafford Smith, and "To Anacreon" quickly became a popular drinking song on both sides of the Atlantic, through the Revolutionary War and beyond, remaining familiar as late as the next hostilities between the two combatants, in the War of 1812.

During that war, on the night of September 13, 1814, an American attorney named Francis Scott Key was aboard the HMS

Tonnant, a British troopship in Chesapeake Bay, to negotiate the release of an American prisoner. For twenty-five hours, four miles from land, Key was forced to watch the British navy bombard Fort McHenry, in his native Baltimore, not knowing if it—and his hometown—had been captured in the night.

The next morning, by dawn's early light, Key saw the American flag yet waving over Fort McHenry, and on returning to Baltimore wrote a poem—"Defence of Fort McHenry"—to commemorate the battle. He gave the poem to Captain Benjamin Eades, of the 27th Baltimore Regiment, who printed more copies, one of which he took to a tavern next to the Holliday Street Theatre. There, in a bar, the poem was first read and then sung—as Key had specified it should be, in an instruction on the published copies—to that familiar melody: "To Anacreon in Heaven."

"Defence of Fort McHenry"—it was a music store that first published it under the title "The Star-Spangled Banner"—didn't officially become the national anthem of the United States until an Act of Congress made it so in 1931. But long before then it was played at baseball's most august occasions—at the opening of new ballparks and the raising of pennants, most of which coincided with Opening Day.

In 1897, before a Phillies–Giants opener in Philadelphia: "The players paraded across the field company front, and then raised the new flag, while the band played 'The Star Spangled Banner.'"

The following spring, before a rain-dampened crowd of 12,000 at the Polo Grounds eagerly awaiting a Giants–Braves game: "The opening ceremonies were not unlike previous years," as the *New York Times* reported. After the players paraded around the perimeter of the field: "The teams parted at the home plate, and then, doffing their caps, retired to the bench. The band, however, stopped at home plate, and when the enthusiasm had subsided, rendered 'The Star Spangled Banner.'"

Two weeks later, across town in Brooklyn, to celebrate the club's new Washington Park, Charles Ebbets's young daughter May raised a flag as the Twenty-Third Regiment Band played the national anthem before the game. "Thousands of persons forgot baseball at this stage and stood up with uncovered heads. The wildest enthusiasm prevailed."

And so it was that long before the turn of the century, spectators were rising and removing their caps before a ball game, if only on Opening Day and other special occasions. By 1902, the Seventh Regiment Band marched around the Polo Grounds prior to the Giants–Phillies opener playing "There'll Be a Hot Time in the Old Town Tonight," before stopping in front of the grandstand, falling silent, and striking up the anthem. "It was a noticeable fact that nearly all of the 18,000 rooters rose to their feet, and many of them uncovered when the national anthem was played," went the *New York Times* account. "It was 3:30 o'clock sharp when Umpire 'Hank' O'Day tossed a new ball into the field and the baseball season of 1902 was on."

The anthem was played again at the Polo Grounds on Opening Day of 1905 when the Giants raised a blue pennant whose gold letters proclaimed them CHAMPIONS BASEBALL CLUB OF NATIONAL LEAGUE 1904. "The Star-Spangled Banner" was played before games at the grand openings of Shibe Park in 1909 and Ebbets Field in 1913, among many other occasions. It was played, abortively, at the Baker Bowl in Philadelphia during the 1915 World Series, when fans *thought* they spotted President Wilson and his fiancée, Edith Galt, enter the ballpark. By the time the couple had arrived for real, play had begun and the bands had been banished from the field.

In 1916, Wilson ordered that the anthem be played at military functions. Two years later—with America engaged in World War I, ballplayers getting drafted, and the World Series moved back to early September by government decree—it was played before the Cubs came to bat in the bottom of the seventh inning of Game 1 at Comiskey Park, which the Cubs had rented out for its larger capacity.

Flag at Ebbets Field, Opening Day, April 14, 1914. *(Library of Congress)*

(This game is frequently—and mystifyingly—cited as the first time the anthem was ever played at a major-league baseball game, though it was nothing of the sort.) And though "The Star-Spangled Banner" was played throughout the Series, in Chicago and again in Boston, when the Series had shifted to Fenway Park, it wasn't until the next World War that it became a staple before all games.

Rud Rennie, an artilleryman in World War I, was by World War II a baseball writer for the *New York Herald-Tribune*. In 1942, Rennie was thrilled by the new practice of standing for the anthem at every game. "It reminds us that we're in a war," he said. "We need to be reminded at every opportunity. And remember that this goes on in every big league park every day that there's a ball game on foot."

Ever since, this tune composed as a cue for Londoners to lift their drinks has been exactly the opposite for American sports fans. It is the only reliable cue for them to put down their beers, and but for a moment.

Chapter 7

"THE REDHOTS WARMED WITH MUSTARD SAVED MANY A LIFE"

So the fan has removed his cap, and the cap has been removed from his beer—by the concessionaire, to prevent the bottle from being used as a missile—and that fan is now hungry.

Had that fan been in Brooklyn on August 22, 1867, when the Eckford Baseball Club hosted the Athletics of Philadelphia—two leading teams of the day—he would have been spoiled for choice. "Mr. Cammeyer again had the grounds in fine order, and Sam Lewis attended to the inner man in the manner for which he is well known," went the game story of the *Brooklyn Daily Eagle* correspondent, who evidently hadn't eaten on his way to the grounds. "Sam's chowder is becoming celebrated. There is another institution coming prominently before the ball-playing public, and that is the cocoanut-candy man—'fifteen cents a quarter of a pound, ten for five cents.'"

While Sam Lewis attended to the inner man, Charles Hercules Ebbets took care of his other appetites. In Brooklyn in 1883, when the Dodgers began life as the Atlantics, the twenty-three-year-old

Ebbets printed his own scorecards and sold them at Washington Park, "disposing of them to fans before the ink was dry."

At the same time, a twenty-seven-year-old milkman immigrated to the United States from Derby, England, and settled with his wife and sons in Niles, Ohio. There, Harry Mozley Stevens went to work in a steel mill, and later as a door-to-door salesman of books. When *Irish Orators and Oratory* proved difficult to move in Middle America, Stevens tried to find work more consonant with the interests of his new nation.

Attending a baseball game in Columbus, Stevens thought the scorecards on offer there were confusing. They were also devoid of advertising. He set about designing a better and more lucrative one, filled with paid ads. He bought the rights to be the exclusive scorecard provider at the Columbus ball grounds, and eventually expanded into the big leagues, moving to Pittsburgh and then to New York, where he got the Polo Grounds concession in 1892. "Harry Stevens always has some new idea on tap," *Sporting Life* noted two years later. "He is preparing the score card and it will be profusely illustrated.... His latest scheme is to attach a ballot to each card, so that the cranks can vote for their favorite players."

By then, Charles Ebbets was no longer printing his own scorecards. He had moved on, in rapid succession, to become a ticket taker for the Brooklyn club, and later club secretary, team president, briefly its manager, and most famously the owner of the Brooklyn Dodgers and namesake of baseball's most beloved ballpark.

Stevens, on the other hand, went all in with concessions. He couldn't help but notice—on arrival at the Polo Grounds as the "champion score-card seller of America"—that the ballpark's food was an afterthought. For the better part of a decade after he moved to New York, ham-and-cheese sandwiches were the sole option at the Polo Grounds as an accompaniment to beer, which cost $0.05 a serving in thick glasses with handles.

Harry M. Stevens, left, with Polo Grounds builder John Foster, center, and Giants owner John Brush, 1911. *(National Baseball Hall of Fame Library, Cooperstown, NY)*

Fans needed something to eat. Many fans brought their own food, for eating or otherwise. In 1895, a spectator "who thought perhaps that Fred Roat was hungry threw a chunk of bologna sausage at his head," according to the *Sporting Life* account of an Indianapolis Indians game that June.

In St. Louis, by some accounts, Browns owner Chris Von der Ahe served bunned sausages at his saloon, and introduced them to patrons at Sportsman's Park, in keeping with its other novelties: the Shoot-the-Chutes water slide behind the right field fence, the open-air beer garden, and the Wild West Show, the non-game-day horse races that lay waste to the playing field.

Owners elsewhere did what they could to encourage the thirst of their patrons. In baseball as at the circus, peanuts were a staple from the start, for spectators and participants alike. "His success this season in lining out the ball has filled Pete Browning with joy and increased his insatiable appetite for hot roasted peanuts," reported

Sporting Life in 1890. The Washington Senators hired one of their former players, Edwin Yewell, as their concessionaire in 1891 because he "had experience in the matter of printing score-cards and selling peanuts and soft drinks to base ball crowds sufficient to let him know what sort of service such folks want."

Peanuts were cheap and plentiful, if insufficiently delicious. Or so thought a German immigrant named Frederick Rueckheim, who created—with the help of his brother Louis—a confection of peanuts, popcorn, and molasses. "Cracker Jack" was an instant sensation when the brothers introduced it at the 1893 World's Fair in Chicago. Three years later, on the Phillies' scorecards in Philadelphia—among the ads for bicycles and cigarettes and unguents described as "toilet requisites"—was a small box that asked: "Have You Tasted Cracker Jack? The New Confection. So Good!! Try It!! The More You Eat The More You Want. 5c Per Package. Sold Everywhere. Exclusively On These Grounds."

Peanuts required no such hard sell. They weren't just popular but popul*ist*. When Richard Olney, secretary of state under Grover Cleveland, attended games in Washington in 1896, the *Boston Daily Globe* noted: "He declines to be a special guest of the management, but prefers to sit on the left field bleachers, where he can eat peanuts, kick at the umpire and root for the home team. To see the secretary of state at a ball game, he would never be taken for the great diplomat of this generation."

Owners kept sacks of peanuts stacked like sandbags in their ballparks, securing them against the ravenous appetites of their customers and employees alike. In Brooklyn, where Charles Ebbets had risen to the presidency of the Superbas in 1900, pitcher Iron Man McGinnity raided the team's concession stores after starts. "McGinnity's one weakness is peanuts," reported the *Brooklyn Daily Eagle*. "After every game in which he pitches he invades the office of Secretary Simpson and demands his reward in the shape of a bag of the

Virginia product. On the days when he is not called on to pitch he does not demand the toll."

When President Taft cheered on the Senators on April 19, 1909, he and Vice President James Sherman shared a nickel bag of peanuts in their box. Peanuts and Cracker Jack were inseparable—from each other, and from the national game. They were baseball in a nutshell, thanks to a man named Jack Norworth.

Norworth was a vaudevillian and Tin Pan Alley songwriter who had never before attended a major-league baseball game on that day in 1908 when he was riding the Ninth Avenue elevated train past the Polo Grounds, whose marquee announced the day's Giants game. In less than an hour on the train, on a scrap of paper pulled from a pocket, inspired by the sight of the advertised game, Norworth wrote a song that included the lines "Buy me some peanuts and Cracker Jack / I don't care if I never get back."

"How did I know about peanuts and Cracker Jack?" Norworth said years later. "I saw bush [league] games as a boy and got the 'feel' of the game." The lines were set to music by Norworth's writing partner, Albert Von Tilzer, who likewise had never seen a game live. "Take Me Out to the Ball Game" was a smash from the moment of its release. Thirty-two years later, on a day he was honored for writing baseball's unofficial anthem, Norworth went to Ebbets Field to see his first big-league game.

As baseball fare, not everything worked as well as peanuts and Cracker Jack. Ballpark tripe grills declined as the American appetite for stomach lining did the same. But by 1902, Harry Stevens had settled on at least one inviolable item. He sold hot dogs on cold days at Giants games, and their appeal was pretty instantly universal. "At the counters in the rear of the Polo Grounds," he later recalled, "you would find a prominent banker eating a frankfurter and drinking a glass of beer, and beside him would be a truck driver doing precisely the same thing."

"Take Me Out to the Ball Game" songwriter Jack Norworth, dressed to the nines, at a stage door. *(Library of Congress)*

Hot dogs, from very early on, became the game's staple food. The only proper way to watch the World Series, wrote *Chicago Tribune* baseball writer H. S. Fullerton in 1906, was by "eating a red hot in the first inning, a cheese sandwich in the second, a bag of popcorn in the third, drinking a white pope in the fourth, eating a ham on rye in the fifth, another red hot, another cheese sandwich, another ham on rye." Hot dogs weren't inducing coronaries, at least in the near term—they were doing something like the opposite: In the chill of that October, the paper's Charles Dryden wrote, "The redhots warmed with mustard saved many a life."

The following October, at Bennett Park in Detroit, as the Tigers hosted the Cubs in the World Series, "Ernie Whelan's 'red-hots' at 10 cents each were in great demand." Among their devotees was the owner of the Cubs. As he watched his team win the fifth and final game in Detroit, Charles Murphy took no chances at being left empty-handed, sitting "close to the hot dog counter."

Given the ravenous appetites he helped awaken, Stevens had become by 1908 so wealthy—a multimillionaire when the average annual income was less than $700—that he tried and failed to buy the Brooklyn club from Ebbets. By then it was hard to imagine that either man, never mind both, had begun their baseball careers as printers of scorecards. Stevens by then owned the concessions at both Boston ballparks, and Madison Square Garden and Saratoga Race Course.

A fixture at those parks in his bow tie and boater hat, Stevens was more recognizable than many of the men on the field. When the 1912 World Series opened at the Polo Grounds, a small contingent of Red Sox fans were brave enough to attend. "With heads erect the Hub horde marched to their places in the stands back of first base never flinching under the taunts that were heaped upon them in company with a fusillade of sandwiches," wrote one newspaper correspondent. "There is a suspicion that Harry Stevens, holder of the sandwich concession at the Polo Grounds, had something to do with the planning of that fusillade." That Stevens sold out of 100,000 sandwiches on a day that 35,730 came to the Polo Grounds remains a wonder, but then he was a salesman of abundant charms.

He was great company, despite having a propensity to quote long stretches of Shakespeare and the Bible from memory. In his office at the Polo Grounds, Stevens frequently hosted sportswriters postgame. While the day's take was being counted out, he poured them a drink from his liquor stash. It was, in the words of one scribe, "the only place I've seen where they keep the money out in the open and the liquor in the safe."

And yet his largesse toward writers and other unfortunates balanced a predatory instinct for making money. When umpire Bill Klem, not ordinarily camera-shy, turned his back on photographers on his way into Fenway Park before Game 3 of the 1914 World Series, a writer joked: "Harry Stevens giving away his peanuts wouldn't occasion more surprise."

"He charged high prices for his goods," wrote his friend John Kieran. "He would wrestle a man from here to San Francisco for a dime if he thought it was his."

Stevens couldn't rake those dimes in fast enough. He and others continued to experiment with stadium comestibles and their delivery. In 1914, at the new Weeghman Park in Chicago, vendors used a long-handled basket to pass hot dogs to patrons, and in turn to collect their money. The device, like a church collection basket, completed the metaphor of ballpark as cathedral, in a place soon to be renamed Wrigley Field.

The cocoanut-candy man of 1867 was long gone, but Boston Braves fans in 1915 were urged to buy Huyler's candies individually — Lemon Sour Drops for a nickel, Old-Fashioned Molasses for a dime — or better still in bulk. "Ask the Boys," the program urged, "for a pound of assorted chocolates and bonbons supplied directly to the ground fresh daily." A box of chocolates turned out not to be the ideal treat in the midday sun of an urban August, but again, ballpark cuisine was in its early adolescence.

When a sportswriter complained on a cold day at the Polo Grounds in 1916 that there was no hot beverage on offer, Stevens introduced coffee with great success. Popcorn, on the other hand, failed to catch on in New York — except as a spectacle, the popped kernels blown around a glass display case that resembled a snow globe. As a self-taught Shakespearean scholar, Stevens was acutely aware of the theater of the ballpark. His vendors, wearing crisp white coats and hats, had to pass inspection before every game.

During Prohibition, baseball fans in grudging acceptance of soda but still in search of a vice bought cigars for $0.15 or $0.20. But peanuts, and to an even greater extent hot dogs, remained far and away the most popular wares of the Harry M. Stevens company. Stevens leased land in Virginia to grow the peanuts he hawked at the Polo Grounds, Ebbets Field, Yankee Stadium, Madison Square Garden, and Churchill Downs, among many other places. Stevens was the most prominent publisher of baseball scorecards and game programs, though his predecessor in scorecards, Charles Ebbets, took back the food concessions from Stevens at Ebbets Field in 1923. Two years later, when the One Great Scorer came to mark against his name, Ebbets died a wealthy man in his room at the Waldorf-Astoria, testimony to the fact that few men went broke selling concessions to baseball fans.

Hot dogs grilling outside Ebbets Field before World Series Game 2, October 6, 1920. *(Library of Congress)*

Though certainly the most famous, given his proximity to the press in New York, Stevens was not alone in expanding the palate of the baseball fan. The St. Louis Cardinals and Browns hired Blake Harper, who transformed the concessions operation at Sportsman's

Park, which brought in $100,000 a year to that ballpark at the dawn of the Depression. A reporter in 1930 was dizzied by the menu: "Ice cream, éclairs and bricklets in three flavors; peanuts, near beer, draught and bottled and served at an old-time bar with a brass foot rail; hot fish sandwiches on Fridays; boiled egg sandwiches; cheese sandwiches; ham sandwiches; chicken salad sandwiches; tongue sandwiches; candy; chewing gum; cigars; cigarets; potato chips; pretzels; popcorn; soda, all flavors, and Coca-Cola; coffee; frozen all-day suckers for the knothole gang; shoe shines; artificial roses and autographed souvenir baseball bats." Vendors were provided with lockers and showers, and every one of the hawkers—50 to 125 were employed per game—had to "bathe, don a clean jacket and cap and pass inspection before going into the stands to sell."

These vendors were exclusively men. An 1862 law in New York City prohibited women from "waiting on, attending in any manner or furnishing refreshments to the audience or spectators at any place of public amusement." (New York legislators didn't move to repeal the law until 1977, by which time a few female vendors had already infiltrated Shea Stadium.)

No, the vendors were all men, and those men sold hot dogs. The actor Humphrey Bogart said, "A hot dog at the ballpark is better than a steak at the Ritz," though Harry M. Stevens didn't have to choose, having practically parlayed a ballpark hot dog *into* a steak at the Ritz. He lived in a succession of luxury hotels—never the Ritz, but the Savoy, the Waldorf, and the Belmont. He died at the Murray Hill Hotel in 1934, at age seventy-eight, having made an empire of food and scorecards. And though his letterhead listed him as "Caterer and Publisher," and his company continued to grow—it would be bought by the food-service giant Aramark in 1994—there was no mistaking his greatest legacy. "He realized the importance of the frankfurter," the *New York Times* announced in the fourth paragraph of his obituary. "Eminent sports writers joined in crowning him as the 'Hot-Dog King.'"

Yankee Stadium vendor selling soda in glass bottles. *(National Baseball Hall of Fame Library, Cooperstown, NY)*

If the Hot-Dog King had an heir, it was Thomas G. Arthur, patriarch of another family of concessionaires, Arthur Food Services of Los Angeles. When the Dodgers moved west from his and their native Brooklyn, Arthur held the food concession at the LA Coliseum, where they would play for four years. To celebrate the team's move into Dodger Stadium in 1962, Arthur introduced a foot-long hot dog of the kind he enjoyed in his Coney Island youth. When people impertinently suggested that the new dog was nothing close to a foot long, Arthur renamed it, for the sake of veracity, a "Dodger Dog." It became the most famous and for many seasons the best-selling sausage in all of baseball, if not the world.

People could not eat them fast enough. No less than Cary Grant told Arthur he needed to install a grill nearer to the high-priced

dugout seats at Dodger Stadium for quicker delivery and the constant aroma of grilled sausage. This desire for instant hot-dog gratifi-
cation would not be fully satisfied until the late 1990s, when some
teams began to fire bunned hot dogs directly into the crowd, from a
$7,000 air gun with a range of three hundred feet. The devices
weren't foolproof—dogs destined for the upper deck sometimes
broke apart over the grandstand, raining processed meat onto
spectators—but they satisfied an ever more voracious public.

By the 1980s, for $1.75, Orioles fans at Memorial Stadium were
offered two hot dogs in a single bun. To speed the passage of beer
down the gullets of those same fans, a Baltimore beer vendor named
Perry Hahn invented a handheld electrical device that cleanly decap-
itated aluminum beer cans, removing the lids whole and allowing
him to more quickly decant the contents into plastic cups. This flair
for innovation was born of necessity among hustling vendors. In the
same spirit, in 2000, a peanut hawker in Triple-A Columbus would
first toss his wares to a client and then throw him a slit tennis ball,
into which the customer would insert his money.

Many of these vendors became famous in their own right, none
more so than Elmer Dean, who lived with his father, Albert, in a
single room of a boardinghouse in Depression-era Houston, where
he threw bagged peanuts at Houston Buffaloes fans with a cry of
"Hey, lady, wanna buy a goober?" While Dean was pitching peanuts
in the Texas League, his younger brothers, Dizzy and Daffy, were
pitching baseballs for the St. Louis Cardinals. "He was as good as
us," Dizzy said, "except he threw his arm out pitching them damn
peanuts." Called to the big leagues to sell peanuts at Sportsman's
Park in 1936, Elmer returned to the Texas League after only a few
days, concluding: "People in St. Louis don't like their peanuts mixed
with baseball."

Like Dean, Roger Owens began his baseball career as a pitcher—
at Manual Arts High School in Los Angeles—before peanut vend-

ing brought him fame, if not quite fortune. In his autobiography, the aptly named *Working for Peanuts,* Owens recounted his rise from hawking sodas in the Dodgers' first year in Los Angeles to becoming—over the next forty years—as familiar and renowned as many of the celebrity "season-peanut-holders" to whom he threw his prepaid goobers.

As Jackie Price once had with baseballs, Owens could—with one hand—throw three bags of peanuts to three separate customers. He traveled the country with his peanuts and was picked out by the cameras on *Monday Night Football* selling nuts at a Dallas Cowboys game. He pitched his wares in Washington, D.C., at the presidential inauguration of peanut farmer Jimmy Carter. "One grows 'em, one throws 'em," noted a press release from the National Peanut Board, on which Owens sat, though not literally, for baseball's best vendors never seemed to sit at all. Owens once sold 2,400 bags of peanuts in a single game, though as a peanut-vending iron man he had competition in Dodger Stadium. Hal Schiff began selling at Shibe Park in Philadelphia for Connie Mack in 1937 and was still vending peanuts in Chavez Ravine four decades later, having changed teams, like so many ballplayers before him.

Another old-timer, "Peanut Jim" Shelton, iconic in Cincinnati in his top hat and tails, worked every Reds home game for forty-three years, a streak that ended only after he was mugged and hospitalized in 1976. He was eighty-six years old.

Peanut Jim was not to be confused with another top-hatted vendor, Ray (the Birdman) Jones, who wore a top hat with a working water spigot while flogging pennants at Texas Rangers games.

Their bronze busts will never be displayed in Cooperstown, but these men were part of the game's fabric, their distant cries heard in the background between pitches on baseball broadcasts from the beginning of radio into the age of color television.

And for some, vending was the first rung on a very tall ladder.

Charlie Grimm was a peanut vendor at Sportsman's Park in St. Louis before becoming a player, manager, and broadcaster. Another St. Louis vendor, Bill Walsingham, became vice president of the Cardinals. When Fred Saigh was forced to sell the team in 1953, Walsingham was his first-choice buyer. "He is a St. Louis native and worked his way up from a peanut vendor at the ballpark," said Saigh, defying Elmer Dean's verdict that St. Louisans did not care to mix baseball and goobers.

For many others, vending was their only aspiration in baseball. It offered life in a nutshell. Three generations of the Jacobs family sold peanuts outside Gate A at Fenway Park from its opening in 1912 through the remainder of the twentieth century—the peanut cart held down for forty-four of those years by George (the Peanut Man) Jacobs. When he died, in 1988, the Red Sox held a moment of silence.

At Wrigley Field, Dan Ferrone sold beer—and in later years, a lighter load of peanuts—for more than fifty years, beginning in 1938. Manny Gluck, program vendor at Gate 4 of Yankee Stadium, worked fifty consecutive home openers, from age fourteen until his death in 2005, by which time he had obtained—had *attained*—vendor badge number 1. (If it wasn't quite as famous as the employee number 1 badge that Steve Wozniak was awarded over Steve Jobs at Apple, the badge was every bit as coveted at Yankee Stadium.)

When I went to work stabbing dogs for the vendors at Met Stadium in 1979, with no desire to do anything else in life, Walter McNeil had already been selling beer there for eight years of what would be a long run. He moved to the Metrodome when the Twins left the Met in 1981, and on to Target Field in 2010, when the Metrodome was abandoned. By then, McNeil was long celebrated in the Upper Midwest as "Wally the Beer Man," a sobriquet that appeared beneath his likeness on baseball cards and bobbleheads, and in TV commercials. During a Twins game in 2010, his fortieth season in the big leagues, McNeil unwittingly sold beer to an under-cover nineteen-year-old decoy in a police sting operation. Twins fans wore "Free Wally" T-shirts, and a jury eventually did just that, finding McNeil not guilty. But the seventy-six-year-old retired anyway, a reminder—if one were needed—that the Italian word for *bottle* is *fiasco*.

Purveyors of peanuts, beer, hot dogs, and soda would have work forever. Through various vogues—for fried chicken and cake slices and ham sandwiches—those staples have endured for more than a century as baseball's four food groups. The fifth Beatle of ballpark food didn't make the scene until 1978, when its abrupt appearance was met with confusion. While preparing its readers for the 1978 All-Star Game at Jack Murphy Stadium, the *San Diego Evening Tribune* had to explain the Padres' newest delicacy: "Nachos [are] corn chips with cheese and peppers on them."

Among the manifold curiosities on display at the Superdome in New Orleans on September 15, 1978—Frank Sinatra, Liza Minnelli, and Sylvester Stallone, to say nothing of Muhammad Ali and Leon Spinks, who were contesting the heavyweight championship of the world that night—nachos drew their share of rubberneckers. There, too, "spectators could buy Nachos Grande," wrote the *St. Petersburg Times* columnist Hubert Mizell, "a Mexican dish that amounted to little more than Fritos covered with warm cheese sauce, for $1.60."

By Christmas, the nacho agnostics had largely been converted. At college football's Fiesta Bowl, at Sun Devil Stadium in Tempe, Arizona, hot dogs were displaced by a swinging, salsa-dancing, leisure-suited interloper from the Southwest. "The traditional ball-park culinary staple was second fiddle at the Fiesta Bowl," wrote the correspondent for the *Kingman (Arizona) Daily Miner*. "Its replacement? Why nachos.... That's right, nachos. The crispy tortilla chips were served with hot cheese sauce."

In American stadiums and arenas, nachos were the thin edge of the cheddar-wedge, opening the door to fish tacos, Rocky Mountain oysters, garlic fries, sushi, toasted ravioli, and all other manner of regional and ethnic exotica. Its "cheese" sauce—the yellow of a school bus, with the viscosity of forty-weight motor oil—was frequently ersatz "cheez." But then nowhere was baseball's propensity for willful misspelling more fully and joyously realized than at the concession stand.

To the game's litany of Twi-Nite doubleheaders and Edge-U-Cated Heels, concessionaires brought Hi-Brow beverages, Marv-O orangeade, Redi-Orange soda, Chik-N-Baskets, Bar-B-Cue Pork, Bar-B-Q Beef, Lik-Em Peanuts, Choco-Pies, Melo-Crown cigars, By-a-Choc hot cocoa, Hygrade Red Hots, Krun-Chee Potato Chips, Sno-Cones, and Snax Peanuts.

Incarcerated in the walk-in freezer of the main commissary at Met Stadium, a thirteen-year-old boy newly employed by the Minnesota Twins had plenty of time to contemplate the cases of Northland Dairy's Big Dip Ice Milk Frosty Malts that came with those wooden spoons that looked little oars, and were every bit as transporting. At the Met, the only ice cream alternative to a Frosty Malt was orange sherbet, also from Northland Dairy. (Orange was a groovy accent to baseball's color scheme in the 1970s, through Charlie Finley's orange baseball and the Sunkist soda that was offered as the only alternative to Coca-Cola at Met Stadium as late as 1981.)

By then the Frosty Malt was in retrograde. As a cultural phenomenon, it received a fitting send-off from Steve Goodman, who had written "City of New Orleans" for Arlo Guthrie, "You Never Even Call Me by My Name" for David Allan Coe, and "Banana Republics" for Jimmy Buffett, but is best remembered in his native Chicago for "A Dying Cub Fan's Last Request," which he first played in 1983, a year before leukemia took his life at thirty-six. "Give everybody two bags of peanuts and a Frosty Malt," Goodman sang, "and I'll be ready to die."

As a cold confection, the Frosty Malt—like the much-loved Cool-A-Coo ice cream sandwich at Dodger Stadium—lost its place of supremacy to the ice cream sundae served in a miniature, inverted, souvenir batting helmet, which ingeniously combined two of man's favorite diversions: sports memorabilia and whipped cream dispensed from an aerosol can. From the moment of its mandated adoption by major-league players, the batting helmet almost instantly crossed into pop culture, and not just as a vessel for soft-serve sundaes. It had passed from protective device—the armored cap of Dr. Dandy, the Beanproof Cap of Foulproof Taylor—to piggy bank, lampstand, and Helmet Day giveaway.

In short, the helmet had become a baseball "novelty," a word that once evoked joy buzzers, whoopee cushions, and plastic vomit, but came to embrace—on Peg-Board stands of American ballparks— an endless array of branded ephemera: pearl-handled knives, cigarette lighters, lowball glasses—items often more appropriate to grizzled men with mortgages and marital problems than wide-eyed boys.

The godfather of the modern baseball novelty trade began his career as so many titans had, vending hot dogs. Danny Goodman, son of a milkman, also sold birch beer at Double-A Brewers games at Athletic Park in Milwaukee in 1926, working for Charlie and Louis Jacobs, who ran the concessions at ballparks and burlesque theaters. (Their business would eventually become the catering giant Sportservice, Inc.)

Goodman worked the burlesque circuit, too, standing in the aisles to hawk "Marsh chocolates, manufactured by the Marsh Candy Company and known throughout the world." Many of those chocolate boxes, he promised, contained a Wescott Watch, from the Wescott Watch Company of Wescott, Connecticut. There was no Marsh Candy Company, or Wescott Watch Company, or Wescott,

Connecticut, for that matter, and the few boxes of ordinary candy that *did* contain a cheap wristwatch were marked by a rubber band and always "sold" to a shill in the audience, who invariably returned it to Goodman.

As for baseball, the crowd in Milwaukee during Prohibition was 95 percent male—some days there wasn't a single woman in the stands—and those men had their choice of four items: hot dogs, peanuts, soda, and near beer.

At eighteen, Goodman moved up the Jacob brothers' chain to Baltimore, where he worked for a man named George Weiss. Together they learned many ballpark truths, among them: Never vend Popsicles from a tub filled with dry ice, a lesson learned when Goodman's inventory on a hot day was quickly reduced to sticks and syrup.

By 1932, Goodman and Weiss had traveled together to the top of Double-A baseball. Goodman had become the concessionaire for the Newark Bears, where he tried with limited success to persuade Weiss, the new Yankees farm director, that there was an appetite, even during the Depression, for something other than food and drink. Namely, team trinkets and apparel.

"I used to disagree with George because I've always been a guy who felt he could instinctively read the public and its tastes pretty well," Goodman said of Weiss. "People like to identify with sports heroes and winning teams and they will buy things like T-shirts and pennants if you give them style and value for their money."

"Stick to hot dogs," Weiss replied. "We make two cents clear profit on every one."

Until then, "novelties" were largely restricted to programs, scorecards, and seat cushions. Goodman used to soak the grandstand before games in the minors. "A guy had a choice of a 12-cent cushion," he said, "or ruining a two-dollar pair of pants."

Goodman would not be ignored. "Someday," he told Weiss, "novelties will be bigger than hot dogs, or even peanuts."

Weiss did allow Goodman to sell pennants, badges, and the oxy-moronic one-size-fits-all cap. Goodman was the first man to flog caps at the ballpark, he often claimed, adding: "So far nobody has ever challenged that statement." He bought them at wholesale for a quarter and sold them for a dollar. When Prohibition was repealed, Goodman opened a bar under the stands at Ruppert Field, named for Jacob Ruppert, whose Ruppert Beer sold for $0.20 a glass. Newark also offered hard liquor by the drink, the first baseball club — claimed the *Sporting News* in 1980 — ever to do so.

In 1937, Goodman persuaded the Curtiss Candy Company to donate a case of Baby Ruth bars to any player who hit their sign, which players did frequently. Among those players was my great-uncle Buzz, who was traded from Brooklyn to the Yankees before the 1936 season and assigned to Newark. (Perhaps the Bellevue-bound teenager who stole his uniform pants from the Ebbets Field clubhouse that February had had a premonition that Buzz would never again need those Dodgers knickers.) He and the rest of the Bears had no pressing desire to receive 240 Baby Ruth bars every time they hit a double. So Goodman bought the candy bars back from the players and sold them at a profit in the park.

So innovative was Goodman that, in 1938, the concessionaire was recruited away from Weiss. Bob Cobb, the owner of the Brown Derby restaurant, summoned Goodman to a more receptive market for the selling of his dreams. And so Goodman went to work for the Hollywood Stars, Cobb's team in the Pacific Coast League.

Cobb was a forthright businessman. "Bob Cobb," Goodman told Jim Murray, recalling his days as a burlesque vendor, "was the kind of a guy who *would* put a watch in every box."

Novelties were not entirely new as Goodman worked to explode the market. At Briggs Stadium in Detroit, Tigers fans in 1939 could purchase "Souvenir Miniature Louisville Sluggers With Autographs of Famous Players." Felt pennants were also growing in popularity.

But Goodman, in Hollywood, recognized that team hats and T-shirts conferred a kind of secondhand celebrity on those who bought them, an effect heightened by the countless real celebrities in attendance at Gilmore Field. Cobb himself was a famous figure, and famously innovative. He invented the Cobb salad and provided tableside telephone service at the Brown Derby, the only restaurant on earth where such a practice existed, except in the movies, where diners were frequently interrupted mid-meal with an urgent piece of telephonic exposition.

The men who made and starred in those movies, whose caricatures hung on the walls of Cobb's restaurant — Spencer Tracy, Gary Cooper, Bing Crosby, Walt Disney, Cecil B. DeMille, Jack Benny, and George Burns — were among the minority shareholders in the Hollywood Stars, and frequent visitors to the park. Shareholder Bill Frawley worked two miles from Gilmore Field, at Desilu Studios on Cahuenga Boulevard, where he played Fred Mertz on *I Love Lucy*. Fred, Ethel, and Lucy famously ate at the Brown Derby, in a booth next to William Holden, in an episode called "L.A. at Last!"

If the Stars drew ten thousand fans to the brand-new Gilmore Field, Goodman would sell thirteen thousand kosher hot dogs and four thousand hamburgers bought fresh from the Farmers Market behind the ballpark at Third and Fairfax. Recognizing the appeal of decent food served quickly, Goodman would pitch oil companies on the idea of serving hot dogs and sandwiches at their service stations. He was flatly turned down. That staple of the gas-station convenience store — shriveled franks rotating on a little heat-lamped Ferris wheel — would have to wait another two decades to take hold.

At Gilmore Field, Cobb insisted that the ballpark food be on a par with what he served in his restaurants. And it was. Fans who purchased Goodman's hot dog were offered a choice of whole wheat, white, or rye roll. He put prizes in the peanut bags, to emulate Cracker Jack. The coffee was brewed for hours, to meet the standard of the Brown Derby, whose clientele was sometimes indistinguishable from the crowd at the ball games.

Indeed, when CBS broke ground on its lavish Television City studio complex in 1951, and Lucille Ball ceremonially lit the construction site, she did so directly across from Gilmore Field. Hollywood stars now only had to cross the street to watch the Hollywood Stars. And they did.

Jayne Mansfield became a kind of mascot. George Burns put his arm around the concessionaire for a picture in the game program, whose caption claimed the comedian "gulps Goodman's hot dogs by the gross."

Bob Hope and Milton Berle were among the comedians in a pregame celebrity baseball exhibition to benefit Damon Runyon's cancer charity. The game was organized by Danny Goodman, who chaired the entertainment committee at the Friars Club in Beverly Hills and knew, from that role, that publicity almost always trumped dignity. And so on April 1, 1950, the Stars wore shorts—and rayon shirts—to play the Portland Beavers. As with every other deviation from conformity in baseball history, it was met with ridicule. When Hollywood manager Fred Haney walked to the plate to exchange lineup cards, Portland skipper Bill Sweeney met him there dressed in drag and carrying a mop.

A year earlier, in 1949, the Stars had even petitioned the Pacific Coast League, asking for a ten-minute intermission after the fifth inning of every game, ostensibly so fans could stretch but in fact so they could spend money at Goodman's glorious concession stands. To provide cover for this ruse, the Stars' groundskeepers applied gratuitous maintenance to the diamond. And so began the baseball tradition of "dragging the infield" while spectators queued at the food and novelty stands.

By then, Goodman's old boss in Newark, George Weiss, had risen to the general manager's chair for the world champion New York Yankees, who were entering a golden decade with an announcement. "In answer to popular demand of the fans," read a notice in 1950 game programs, "the Yankees have created this season a new department: Yankee Souvenirs."

The team had embraced Goodman's long-ago advice to flog programs, caps, signed balls, and photos and—for the first time in 1950—something called a Yankees "sketchbook," or yearbook. All of these were made available either by mail order (write to "Yankee Stadium, Bronx, N.Y.") or at "one of the many gay souvenir stands" in the Yankee Stadium lobbies.

A multitude of new suburban homes going up in postwar America were in need of decor, and the Bombers were happy to oblige. "All of these souvenirs are ideal gifts for baseball minded youngsters or treasures for club rooms and dens," the team promised. In addition, fraternal clubs and church groups could arrange to pick up and return highlight films of the 1949 World Series simply by turning up at Yankee Stadium, as if it were a branch of the New York Public Library.

Under Weiss, the Yankees won the World Series nine times between 1949 and 1962. Every pennant won sold countless more felt pennants at Yankees souvenir stands, where the team, by 1963, led both leagues in the sale of baseball's signature novelty: the bobble-head doll.

By the time Danny Goodman introduced them to baseball fans, bobbleheads were already an ancient novelty, often known as "shakers" or "nodders."

"Someone came to me from Japan in 1958 with a bobble-head doll," Goodman recalled thirteen years after the fact. "I was the first one that had it."

The first one in baseball, he meant. To underscore their timeless appeal, doll collectors like to point out the bobblehead's cameo appearance in "The Overcoat," Nikolai Gogol's short story published in 1842. "The collar was low," Gogol wrote of his protagonist, "so that his neck, in spite of the fact that it was not long, seemed inordinately so as it emerged from it, like the necks of the plaster cats which wag their heads and are carried about on the heads of scores of image sellers."

Danny Goodman surrounded by Dodgers novelties, including bobbleheads, at Dodger Stadium in 1971. *(Larry Sharkey, copyright © 1971, Los Angeles Times, reprinted with permission)*

When Goodman issued the first bobbleheads to baseball fans at Gilmore Field, they were rotund and cherub-cheeked, with a permanent smile on each face. The early generic baseball bobbleheads bore a slight resemblance to Goodman himself, who looked like the kind of caricature that hung on the walls of the Brown Derby. He was short and dapper, with a long nose, swept-back hair, and a jutting lower lip that called to mind a benign version of the Penguin from *Batman*.

In the winter of 1957, when the Dodgers were moving to Los

Angeles, Goodman made the unsolicited suggestion that the team play its inaugural season in Wrigley Field, with little more than twenty thousand seats. "Turn 'em away, if necessary, every time," Goodman said of the fans. "Then they'd really whip up even greater interest, which would pay future dividends."

And though Walter O'Malley didn't take Goodman's advice—the Dodgers would cross the county and play in the cavernous Coliseum—he did hire the visionary upon arriving in Los Angeles. The club already had its food concessionaire—Thomas Arthur, busy dreaming up the Dodger Dog—so O'Malley appointed Goodman the Dodgers' director of advertising and promotion, a role he settled into at the Coliseum, where he set about selling everything imaginable for an owner eager to do just that. "Business reasons," O'Malley said of the hire. "If just half his friends show up, we'll sell out every game." When the Friars Club finally got around to feting Danny Goodman, Ronald Reagan emceed the event, which saw Jack Benny and Chico Marx roast their friend.

After thirty years in the business, Goodman was finally stepping on a stage suitable to his outsized ambition. At the Coliseum, Goodman sold not just Dodgers caps and shirts, but also Dodgers bugles—he ordered twenty thousand of them, at a buck apiece, on which Dodgers fans would play "Charge!" When kids began to beat one another over the heads with them, Goodman was forced to withdraw the bugles, but he still had countless other novelties to flog.

There were forty-five different items at fifteen separate novelty booths. "We'll have 12 different hat styles," he told the *Los Angeles Times* before the Dodgers played their second season at the Coliseum, "ranging from a snazzy black-and-white Dodgers Tyrolean number, to Mexican Panamas and peek-a-boo bonnets."

A manufacturer of plastic products began stamping out plastic hats with the Dodgers logo on them. Goodman offered them for sale at the Coliseum—they were immediately a hit—and soon other teams did the same. They proved so popular that the plastics manufacturer abandoned its other lines and devoted double shifts exclusively to plastic baseball hats.

"There'll also be Dodger piggy banks," Goodman promised, "Dodger bath towels, Dodger pillow cases, Dodger bolo ties, Dodger cigarette lighters, bandannas, scarfs, ties, pencil sets, jackets, bracelets, binoculars, money clips, Indian belts..."

There were dolls, eight-inch homages to Duke Snider and Don Drysdale, costing three bucks apiece. They were so lifelike, Goodman swore, "you'll think you've bought a new boarder." As promised, there were piggy banks and pillowcases, film and flashbulbs, bath towels and buttons.

At the Coliseum, Goodman and the Dodgers offered more merchandise than any other team in the nation, and every one of those keepsakes offered fans a sense of belonging as well as a whiff of glamour. "Dodger fans don't buy hats or jackets to protect themselves, but simply to be seen wearing them," he told interviewer Jeane Hoffman in 1959. Indeed, the team sold more shade hats at night games than at day games.

During the 1959 World Series, in the shadeless Coliseum, he sold one hundred thousand straw hats in three games. He always insisted that he could have sold a hundred thousand more. That Series, played in Los Angeles and Chicago, was the tipping point for sports novelties, Goodman insisted. In the Coliseum, in front of countless marketers and advertisers from every industry, Goodman's manifold branded products flew. "Not long after that," he would say near the end of his life, "the breweries had their own mugs and caps, the airlines had model planes and luggage, the racetracks had jockeys' caps instead of baseball caps and everybody had our T-shirts with their names on them."

In homage to his old team, Goodman staged the first annual "Hollywood Stars Night" before a Dodgers home game in 1958, featuring luminaries like the three-foot-nine actor Billy Barty. "I'll give you stars you've never heard of," Goodman had promised Dodgers PR director Red Patterson, and he certainly delivered.

Those "stars," if O'Malley got his way, would soon play in baseball's grandest theater. In 1959, the Dodgers owner submitted a request to the Los Angeles City Council to have 192 acres of Chavez Ravine rezoned for commercial use. Twenty of those would be occupied by the ballpark, and another eighty-four acres were required for parking. That left nearly ninety acres on which the Dodgers hoped to build "concentric rows of novelty and souvenir stands, several restaurants, including a Hawaiian luau layout, and a complete auto service center."

The service center survived. The orange Union 76 ball—rising like a second sun beyond the outfield wall at Dodger Stadium—would become familiar to generations of Dodgers fans. But the rest of the plan was rejected, councilmen fearing that O'Malley was planning a "downtown Disneyland" for his captive audience.

It didn't matter. Deprived of their concentric circles of souvenir stands, the Dodgers and Danny Goodman sold, in the confines of Dodger Stadium, glossy photos, bathrobes, baby rattles, blankets, bracelets, playing cards, record albums of radio calls, vinyl Windbreakers, parasols, and underpants. In 1961, O'Malley bought the Dodgers their own airplane, a four-engine Lockheed Electra II turboprop called the *Kay O*—after his wife, Kay O'Malley—and had it repainted with a baseball on the cockpit and the Dodgers script resplendent on the tail. The plane cost O'Malley $2.8 million, but Goodman managed to sell the *Kay O* back to Dodgers fans every day, as a model airplane kit. (A sunburst on the box read, "Your Revell model plane kit is made especially for Danny Goodman Concessions and can only be obtained from them," which was to say: *him*.)

The team's mail-order catalog was promoted on air during games, satin jackets offered in the satin tones of Vin Scully, whose voice had a mesmeric effect on children listening in the evening, in darkened bedrooms, their transistor radios issuing the siren call of "another Danny Goodman Special." These specials — usually a package of three surplus trinkets, offered at a price of $2 — netted the Dodgers about $0.14 apiece, Goodman told his friend Phil Elderkin of the *Christian Science Monitor*. But every special that was shipped out contained a color catalog of two hundred Dodgers items, and 90 percent of those catalogs were used on a future purchase, for more expensive merchandise.

That inaugural season at Dodger Stadium, 1962, Goodman and team publicist Red Patterson persuaded O'Malley for one game to give away Dodgers caps free of charge. The game sold out and the souvenir baseball caps did missionary work for the club. "The kids get the cap free, take 'em home and other kids see the caps and they want 'em," Goodman said of the loss leader. "It sort of stimulates interest." That same year, the Los Angeles Angels moved into Chavez Ravine for four seasons as the Dodgers' tenant, and Goodman became their concessionaire as well, selling ladies' aprons emblazoned with TO HECK WITH HOUSEWORK, I'M GOING TO SEE THE ANGELS PLAY and wipe-clean reusable dry-erase scorecards. No idea was too crazy, except for those that were.

"I turn away more people than you could imagine," he said. "Every guy who comes in here thinks he has the greatest idea. One guy last week wanted to sell me a Dodger kite. 'If you can't sell 'em,' he told me, 'then buy 50,000 of 'em for a give-away night.' Can you imagine what would happen if we handed out 50,000 kites? Kids would be flying kites all over the park. Another guy wanted to sell me Dodger boomerangs. I don't even want to think what might happen with something like that."

By then, bobblehead dolls had followed Goodman from the Hollywood Stars into the big leagues. In his office at Dodger Stadium, Goodman kept a full set on his desk. George Weiss might have said no to him in Newark, but the bobbleheads, in Los Angeles, would always nod their assent.

At Dodger Stadium, Goodman was creating the future, and not just of baseball. "Why would anyone think it unusual to pick up a hat or a sweater when he's at the ball game?" he asked Sid Ziff of the *Los Angeles Times* in 1962. "They go to drugstores for everything from automobile tires to hardware as well as their medical supplies. Years ago, who would have expected luxury cafes and complete restaurants in the ballparks? I think eventually we'll have full-scale shopping centers inside the parks. After all, we're dealing with a captive audience for three or four hours. Eventually, we'll be taking advantage of it."

Some of his ideas worked too well. In the 1970s, when beach balls began to blight the field of play at Dodger Stadium, it killed Goodman to remove those items from sale at his stands, except that those stands were still heaving with every conceivable kind of product.

When batting helmets became mandatory in 1971, for instance, Goodman had long ago recognized the potential of plastic hats to serve as ambassadors that spread the gospel of the Los Angeles Dodgers.

And so he did likewise with plastic batting helmets. In their first season of mandatory use, Goodman staged Helmet *Weekend*, May 28 through 30, buying and warehousing 150,000 souvenir Dodgers helmets at a cost of $110,000, secure in the knowledge that Dodgers fans from Oxnard to Long Beach would be buying more of those and all manner of other Dodgers swag on their next visit to Chavez Ravine.

For fans unable to visit, Danny Goodman Concessions shipped satin Dodgers warm-up jackets all over the world, each one bearing Danny Goodman's signature on the wash tag, in the same leaning script as the Dodgers uniform. Sammy Davis Jr.'s had SAMMY on the back, stitched in white. Every star who walked into Dodger Stadium walked out bedecked in Dodgerana, among them Frank Sinatra, Don Rickles, Walter Matthau, and Jack Lemmon. One memorable evening, a limousine pulled up to second base and disgorged Dean Martin, who wore a glove on one hand and held a cocktail in the other.

By 1976, when Tommy Lasorda took over as Dodgers manager, freeing Walter Alston to ride his motorcycle in Ohio, it was sometimes difficult to tell who was benefiting more when celebrities donned Dodgers gear: the gear, or the celebrities? Asked in 1979 who would win the National League West, comedian Jonathan Winters—renowned as a Cincinnati Reds fan—knew the right answer: "The Dodgers will win their division," Winters said, "because Danny Goodman gives me a free pass."

By then, Goodman's ancient prophecy had come to pass: Novelties were bigger than peanuts. Having begun his career vending hot dogs to a Milwaukee crowd as male as a monastery, Goodman lived to see women—and men—shopping for clothes at the ballpark. "Today women represent about 40 percent of the crowd," he said in 1980, "and they buy about half of everything we sell."

That year, in addition to hosting the All-Star Game, the Dodgers held more promotions than any team in baseball ever had. Fans were invited to T-Shirt Night, Baseball Card Night, Fireworks Night, Wristband Night, Helmet Weekend, Poster Day, Jacket Weekend, Batting Glove Day, Ball Day, Photo Album Night, Camera Day, Old-Timers Day, the Dodger Family Game, Country Music Day, two Businessmen's Specials, three Teen Nights, Fan Appreciation Day, and—as ever—Hollywood Stars Night.

The following summer, the dwarf actor Billy Barty was playing in his twenty-fourth consecutive Hollywood Stars game, and seven-foot-two Kareem Abdul-Jabbar joined him on the celestial roster, whose members had to bat against that summer's biggest Los Angeles celebrity, who just happened to be a Dodgers pitcher. Danny

Goodman had already fed the flames of Fernandomania by stocking the stadium with thirty-five thousand Fernando Valenzuela bumper stickers, fifteen thousand Fernando Valenzuela pennants, and ten thousand Fernando Valenzuela dolls. They found their way all over the Southland, and those that didn't were dressed up as "Danny Goodman Specials" and mailed out into the world by Danny Goodman Concessions.

Goodman worked in his Dodger Stadium office, festooned with pennants and piggy banks and his own army of yes-men—that multitude of bobbleheads—from 6:00 a.m. until 10:00 p.m., if there was a night game. Afternoons, he'd play cards and nap at the Friars Club. A bachelor, Goodman took his dinners at Chasen's or the Brown Derby, whose founder departed this world in 1970 for his eternal rest at Forest Lawn Memorial Park in Glendale, where the restaurateur still hobnobs for eternity with the Hollywood elite, among them Walt Disney, Clark Gable, Humphrey Bogart, Spencer Tracy, and Jimmy Stewart.

In 1983, at the age of seventy-four, Danny Goodman joined his Hollywood colleagues in the great beyond. Souvenir pennants flew at half-staff in every boy's bedroom in America.

Goodman was interred at Hillside Memorial Park, where he still rubs elbows with actors and athletes. In Hillside's own Map of the Stars—a directory called *Distinguished Residents of Hillside Memorial Park and Mortuary*—Goodman appears alphabetically between Sid Gillman and Hank Greenberg. "He is credited with virtually inventing the sports souvenir marketing industry," goes his entry. "Among his promotions were bobblehead 'shaker doll' Dodgers given away at games."

His legacy endured, too, in Dodger Stadium's annual Hollywood Stars game, which survived—as low-wattage bulbs are known to do—well into the twenty-first century, long after Gilmore Field had been razed and Television City had expanded onto its former lot. There, in the 1980s, CBS erected two new soundstages, Studios 36 and 46. In the latter, on the ground where the Hollywood Stars once played, Hollywood "stars" now performed as contestants on the reality show *Dancing with the Stars,* whose luminaries were often obscure at best. Danny Goodman—"I'll give you stars you've never heard of"—would have been pleased.

What he might have made of twenty-first-century baseball is another question entirely. Goodman lived to see "novelties" eclipse peanuts and hot dogs, as he'd predicted, and even to see Dodgers caps colonize those parts of the world that remained blissfully ignorant of the Dodgers themselves. But he departed this world before concessions became a Frankenstein's monster—a frank-and-stein monster—that no torches or pitchforks can ever subdue.

In the new millennium, immediately after pennant and World Series victories, players pulled on souvenir caps and T-shirts designed to commemorate the very championship that was being celebrated by the pulling on of those commemorative caps and T-shirts. Those caps and T-shirts were then offered for sale to home viewers in the very next commercial break. The celebratory caps and T-shirts designed for the losing team, meanwhile, were often shipped to foreign-aid organizations, destined for citizens of developing countries, in what amounted to the ultimate Danny Goodman Special.

He didn't make the interlocking *LA* on the Dodgers cap quite as famous as the conjoined *NY* of the Yankees, but then Goodman had helped make the Yankees' ubiquitous merchandising machine by whispering in George Weiss's ear all those years ago. Yankees yearbooks—introduced with the rest of the Souvenir Department in 1950—had already reached their peak of popularity by 1981, when George Steinbrenner had to withdraw fifty thousand copies from stadium stands (in his photo in that year's edition, the Yankees owner—owing to an excess of red in the printing process—appeared to be wearing lipstick).

It was just as well that those yearbooks disappeared, as the acquisitive fan was by then already overburdened. Program in hand, cap on head (after the playing of the anthem), possessed of hot dog and beer and possibly a sundae—the soft-serve at sea in a capsized plastic batting helmet—there was nothing left to do but to take one's seat, a fraught proposition in any age of baseball.

Chapter 8

ROW C, SECTION 42, SEATS 3 AND 4 AT THE POLO GROUNDS

On the Fourth of July, 1950, Barney Doyle made his way down Row C of Section 42 in the left field grandstand at the Polo Grounds, the cigars in his shirt pocket fortifying him for the baseball doubleheader ahead. The fifty-four-year-old freight sorter from Fairview, New Jersey, brought a guest, thirteen-year-old Otto Flaig, a neighbor's son. By the end of that season, 17 million people would attend major-league baseball games in 16 ballparks (compared to 73.4 million in 30 parks in 2011) and most would make the same instant calculation that Doyle did when confronted with two identical seats: Which one of us will sit in *this* one, and which one of us will sit in *that* one? Doyle eased his bulk into Seat 3. The boy sat in Seat 4.

At half past noon, as the Brooklyn Dodgers emerged for batting practice on a brilliant green field, Doyle turned—scorecard in hand—to speak to Flaig. Then he abruptly pitched forward, blood pouring from his left temple.

"What's the matter?" Flaig said.

Doyle didn't answer. When policemen were hailed, a fan in Row B reported having heard, moments before, a sound like a paper bag

251

popping. Someone sat Doyle up, but he splayed sideways, across the next seat back. Which is how a brazen newspaper photographer found him: face to the sky. If not for the blood running down his neck and into his shirt, Doyle might have fallen asleep warming himself in the sun.

An ambulance was dispatched from Harlem Hospital and a doctor declared Doyle dead. Then officers removed his body and took Flaig into protective custody. In that instant, standing-room patrons in the overflow crowd of 49,316—anticipating a glorious day of baseball between the Dodgers and the Giants—rushed to fill the vacant seats.

Those seats at the Polo Grounds were made by the American Seating Company of Grand Rapids, Michigan—"Furniture City"—the epicenter of mass-produced furniture in the United States. When three civic leaders there sat down for a local school board meeting one evening in 1886, they did so in the children's desks, which they found poorly designed and ill suited to a long school day. The board members resolved to improve their students' posture and sight lines by building a more comfortable chair, attached to the desk as a single unit. The result was the first product of the American Seating Company, which quickly built seats for other schools, and for opera houses in McPherson, Kansas, and Leadville, Colorado. By 1909, in addition to schools and theaters, it was supplying the seats for the new Forbes Field in Pittsburgh, the first ballpark to eschew wood in favor of fire-retardant concrete and steel.

From then on, whenever baseball owners talked of putting fannies in the seats, those seats were likely from the American Seating Company, which supplied Comiskey Park in Chicago in 1910, Fenway Park in Boston in 1912, and Chicago's Weeghman Park, later renamed Wrigley Field, in 1914.

When the company delivered seats to the glorious new Yankee

Stadium in 1923, those seats ranged from seventeen to nineteen inches wide. It was this style of seat that Barney Doyle squeezed himself into at the Polo Grounds in 1950. His seat had two widely spaced horizontal slats as a backrest. Some aisle seats in the grand-stand at the Polo Grounds had the Giants' interlocking *NY* elegantly rendered in iron, but Doyle's seat had only two snub-nosed elbow rests, further pinching him in.

The seat bottoms were wooden slats, made of elm. By 1950, Dutch elm disease was reducing the supply of such seats — the Elm City of New Haven, Connecticut, had already lost a great many of its stately shade trees — and growing rear ends were rendering them too small and insufficiently sturdy.

Within eight years, when both teams on the field that Fourth of July had departed New York for the West, the American Seating Company would make baseball's first plastic seats, for the Los Ange-les Coliseum, inaugural home of the Los Angeles Dodgers, a name unthinkable to the spectators at the Polo Grounds in the summer of 1950.

But then so much was about to change in America in that first decade after the war. On the evening of December 1, 1955, when Rosa Parks refused to give up her seat on a city bus in Montgomery, Alabama, that seat was made by the American Seating Company, which also made the desks that American students were being instructed to hide under, at the height of the Cold War, in the event of nuclear attack.

When the nation's capital opened its own new ballpark in 1961 — called District of Columbia Stadium, but later renamed for the late Robert F. Kennedy — research by the American Seating Company suggested that the average American rear end had grown three inches wider since Yankee Stadium went up thirty-eight years earlier.

All of which is to say that Doyle, in the ghastly photograph of him taken at the Polo Grounds on July 4, 1950, scarcely fit into his obsolescent seat.

Doyle hadn't always been a spectator. He had once been, in a phrase of Teddy Roosevelt's, "the man in the arena," boxing professionally in his youth, then managing a young heavyweight fighter named James Braddock in the 1920s in New York City, back when Foulproof Taylor was haunting gyms asking fighters to "Kick me here."

By the time Braddock achieved global fame as the "Cinderella Man"—defeating Max Baer in 1935 for the world title he would eventually lose to Joe Louis—Braddock had long since ditched Doyle for another manager, Joe Gould.

By 1950, Doyle had settled into a comfortable senescence as a spectator, a fan of the New York Giants, whose games he attended as often as he could at their ballpark in Harlem, from which he was taken—on that Fourth of July, before a single pitch had been thrown—to the Office of the Chief Medical Examiner downtown.

There, a dapper seventy-two-year-old man named Thomas A. Gonzales studied Doyle's body. Gonzales had worked in the OCME since its creation in 1918, the first office of its kind in the United States. He and his predecessor as chief medical examiner, Charles G. Norris, were pioneers in American forensic medicine. In his thirty-two years on the job, Gonzales had seen, or successfully diagnosed, nearly every conceivable manner of earthly exit.

A 1939 profile of Gonzales in *Life* magazine listed, a little too enthusiastically, some of the more exotic of the city's seventy-five thousand annual deaths. In the year preceding the profile, a man was crushed in a revolving door. Another was killed by the kick of a child. "More than 70 women died during or after criminal abortions," *Life* reported, "and for reasons which no one in the C.M.E.'s office pretends to understand, an abnormally high percentage of the victims were named Dolores."

And yet what Gonzales saw on July 4, 1950—a bullet that dropped from the clear blue sky before a baseball game—was a first. If the circumstances were unusual, though, the forensic details were prosaic, at least for New York: A .45-caliber slug had entered Doyle's left temple on a downward trajectory and lodged in his brain, killing him instantly.

As detectives fanned out on Coogan's Bluff, the high promontory that overlooked the Polo Grounds from a quarter of a mile behind home plate—affording a clear view of the outfield seats—the Dodgers and Giants resumed their famous rivalry. Between games, players asked sportswriters for details of the shooting, some expressing fear that they might have been targets. Dodgers second baseman Jackie Robinson, having broken baseball's color line three years earlier, had more reason than most to fear. Of his teammates, he said: "They were talking more about the shooting than the game."

Police questioned dozens of children who were playing on the bluff. That evening, as officers searched the empty ballpark for any bullets that might have missed their targets, detectives questioned a slight fourteen-year-old boy. He wore tortoiseshell glasses and lived with his great-great-aunt at 515 Edgecombe Avenue, a six-story walk-up 1,120 feet above the Polo Grounds on Coogan's Bluff.

In that apartment, police found three .22-caliber weapons, but not one that might have fired a .45-caliber slug. After three days of denying any involvement, the junior-high student, Robert Mario Peebles, confessed that he'd found a .45-caliber handgun in Central Park the previous winter, a single bullet in its chamber.

He saved that slug for six months, firing it into the air from the rooftop of his building in celebration of Independence Day. In doing so, he was exercising what Charles Howard Hinton, inventor of the baseball gun, once called "the deeply implanted love of shooting which exists in every boy."

The Polo Grounds viewed from Coogan's Bluff. *(National Baseball Hall of Fame Library, Cooperstown, NY)*

There was a high parapet that fronted the rooftop, making it impossible for Peebles to have aimed the gun. He fired it at a forty-five-degree angle from behind a shelter enclosing the rooftop stairwell. Newspapers across America that week ran a photo of a New York detective standing atop that roof, reenacting the shot, a perforated white line tracing a terrible parabola from the rooftop of 515 Edgecombe to Section 42 of the Polo Grounds, where it fell on Barney Doyle in Seat 4.

A similar photograph ran in American newspapers the following season, only the dashed white line traced the arc of a baseball being struck by Giants third baseman Bobby Thomson. This line, too, ended in the left field grandstand at the Polo Grounds, where Thomson's home run beat the same Dodgers for the National League pennant on October 3, 1951.

The story in the October 4, 1951, editions of the *Daily News* pronounced Thomson's home run—without evident discomfort by anyone who composed or read the headline—THE SHOT HEARD 'ROUND THE BASEBALL WORLD. It instantly entered into lore, slightly shortened, as the Shot Heard 'Round the World.

That phrase was borrowed from "Concord Hymn," the Ralph Waldo Emerson poem commissioned to commemorate the Battles of Lexington and Concord, the first battles of the American Revolution, which led to the fireworks that marked the Independence Day that Robert Peebles celebrated by firing his pistol into the air.

Those two shots at the Polo Grounds—one heard "'round the world," one heard only by a few fans in left field—have had a very different afterlife. The metaphorical shot, fired by Thomson, became perhaps the most famous moment in baseball history, a touchstone for everyone from Sonny Corleone (gunned down at a toll plaza in *The Godfather* while the game played on the radio) to Don DeLillo (who made it the opening set piece of his novel *Underworld*).

The real shot, which killed Barney Doyle, was quickly forgotten.

In the 1950s, the Washington Senators sold, at novelty stands at Griffith Stadium, "gun pencils," in the form of bolt-action, single-shot rifles, that dispensed lead into the scorecard the way real guns did into Apaches in the Westerns that played on TV.

When the National League expanded from ten to twelve teams in 1962, and the fledgling New York Mets moved into the Polo Grounds—filling a void left by the Giants and Dodgers, both departed to California and its pristine toilets—they hosted the other expansion team on June 22. The Houston team that visited the Polo Grounds that day was called the Colt .45s, named for the same caliber of weapon that had killed Doyle twelve years earlier in the same park. Sewn to the front of the visitors' jerseys was a .45-caliber pistol that had just fired a .45-caliber slug. The smoke curling from its barrel formed the *C* in COLTS.

By then, Doyle was a distant memory. About the only spectator who seemed not to have forgotten that Fourth of July in 1950 was Flaig, the thirteen-year-old guest of Doyle, whose brief time in the protective custody of police proved galvanic.

Flaig died, of a liver ailment, on July 31, 1992, aged fifty-five, on what was to have been his first full day of retirement from his job as police chief of Teterboro, New Jersey.

And that is where the story of Barney Doyle would have ended, except that on July 4, 1985 — thirty-five years to the day after he was killed — thirty-four-year-old Joanne Barrett, nearly five months pregnant, attended a game at Yankee Stadium. She was with her husband, Kevin, and their two sons, in the upper deck of the stadium, a quarter mile from the site of the old Polo Grounds.

Those seats, thanks to the renovation of Yankee Stadium in 1974 and '75, were more capacious — 22 inches wide, with 29½ inches of "row spacing," the industry phrase for legroom — but of little comfort to Barrett in light of what happened in the sixth inning that night.

In that inning, with the Yankees leading the Twins 3–2, something shattered Barrett's right hand. To judge by the popping sound heard in the park — to say nothing of the hole in her hand — it was a bullet. Police thought it was fired from inside the stadium. They combed the park for a bullet but never found one. Barrett was taken to a nearby hospital, where Yankees owner George Steinbrenner — born on the Fourth of July — called to offer his condolences. These were apparently insufficient, as Barrett announced her intention to sue the Yankees.

Police never found a suspect, or the mystery bullet that passed through Barrett's hand. She pronounced herself too traumatized to ever again attend a baseball game, then promptly withdrew from her unwelcome stay in the spotlight.

Three days after the game, rifling through her handbag while checking out of the hospital, Barrett found, among the usual detritus — Kleenex, car keys, compact — the copper-colored bullet. It had come to rest in her purse.

Even on purely baseball terms, none of these was the shot heard 'round the world, nor even the shot heard 'round New York City. That shot rang out a century and a half ago, when an officer named John McDowell of the 29th Precinct of the New York Police Department was walking a beat in Manhattan.

Tom Shieber, senior curator of the National Baseball Hall of Fame, pieced together what happened that terrible night from contemporary newspaper accounts:

At 3 o'clock in the morning on January 8, 1877, Officer John McDowell was walking down Seventh Avenue when he noticed something amiss at Courtney's Liquor Store. A light was on and the door had been forced open, so the officer entered. There he found three burglars with their loot: $120 worth of cigars. One of the burglars, a 19-year-old named James Farrell (sometimes referred to as George Flint), attempted to escape. As he rushed past McDowell, the policeman struck him with his club. The burglar drew a revolver and fired, the bullet hitting McDowell behind his left ear and passing out his right temple. While the other burglars escaped, the seriously wounded officer managed to wrestle Farrell to the ground, at which point a number of other officers came upon the scene and arrested the burglar. The heroic police officer eventually recovered from his wounds and was given $1,000 for his bravery by the Trustees of the Riot Relief Fund. Additionally, McDowell was awarded the New York City Police Department Medal of Valor.

That medal, and the bar marked VALOR from which it was suspended, were linked by a small charm, custom designed by Tiffany & Co.

In the language of typography, this charm formed a ligature: essentially, two or more letters joined together to form a new character. In this case, an *N* was imposed over a *Y* to form the startling new character now recognized the world over on the caps and home uniforms of the New York Yankees.

Nobody is certain how—or even if—the Yankees came to embrace the police medal charm, though the Yankees' publicity department pointed out that a man named Bill Devery joined the NYPD in 1878 (and became its chief twenty years later). From 1903 to 1915, Devery was a co-owner of the New York Highlanders baseball team, which occasionally went by the name Yankees.

What is certain is that the club adopted a linked *NY* as its logo in 1909. And that a century later, the *New York Times,* having reviewed hundreds of New York City police reports, concluded that the Yankees logo was the one piece of apparel common to the greatest number of New York street criminals. "Dozens of men and women who have robbed, beaten, stabbed and shot at their fellow New Yorkers," the *Times* reported on its front page, "have done so while wearing Yankees caps or clothing."

The paper never noted the violent nineteenth-century root of the linked *NY* logo, nor of the irony inherent in its becoming, in the twenty-first century, an icon of street crime in the city.

The Yankees' interlocking *NY* graces the exterior of aisle seats in the self-styled "Legends" section at Yankee Stadium, the luxurious moat of 1,800 upholstered seats that stretches from third base to first base. Those seats are twenty-four inches wide, with thirty-nine inches of legroom and teak armrests. When the stadium opened in 2009, the best of those seats were priced at $2,500 per game. They were built to accommodate—in more ways than one—the fattest of fat cats.

About the only thing those seats have in common with the seat Barney Doyle died in is their city of origin, for they were designed and manufactured by the Irwin Seating Company, headquartered in Grand Rapids, Michigan, since 1908. Like its intracity rivals, American Seating (which equipped Radio City Music Hall), Irwin has also built seats for great American theaters, among them Carnegie Hall. And those theater seats provide a two-century snapshot of the average American's expanding stature.

Theater seats in the 1890s were eighteen inches wide with twenty-four inches of legroom. That was the industry standard, according to a 2010 study by Theatre Projects Consultants, a firm that designs performing arts venues. Twenty-first century theaters require seats that are twenty-three inches wide, with thirty-five inches of legroom. Between 1910 and 2010, the average American's height grew by five inches, according to the Centers for Disease Control. In just the forty years from 1960 to 2000, the average adult's weight increased twenty-four pounds, or 15 percent. In theaters, seats are bigger and thus fewer, with a higher ticket price.

"The floor area that held 20 seats in 1900, and 13 seats in 1990, today holds 10 seats," stated the study by Theatre Projects Consultants. The primary reason, the report concluded, is obesity.

Stadium seats are no different. They've grown bigger and fewer and more expensive. But despite their wider dimensions, seat makers and spectators alike want them to resemble the seats of a century earlier. On the hundredth anniversary of Fenway Park, Red Sox fans sat in seats still made by the American Seating Company. And though those seats were plastic, they were slatted at the back, to resemble the originals.

The seats at Citi Field, home of the Mets, were made by the Irwin Seating Company, and slatted at the back, too. As the National

League team in New York, the Mets are heirs to the Dodgers and Giants, the two teams playing at the Polo Grounds that fateful day in 1950. To reflect their heritage, the Mets had Irwin make the slatted seats at Citi Field a deep green, in homage to the Polo Grounds, where Barney Doyle died in his deep-green seat on that hot Fourth of July, so many years ago.

Chapter 9

RECESSIONAL

Fans exiting the Polo Grounds that tragic Fourth of July in 1950 did so to the usual urban soundscape of car horn, bus wheeze, and the overhead thunder of an elevated train, the IRT's Ninth Avenue El—the "Polo Grounds Shuttle"—rumbling onto its second-story platform at 155th Street and Eighth Avenue.

That music was the only music, the Giants having abstained from a growing trend of the past decade—a live pipe organ to play their patrons home.

Philip K. Wrigley had introduced baseball's first organ to his eponymous ballpark in Chicago on April 26, 1941, with organist Roy Nelson playing classical music before and after the Cubs' 6–2 loss to the Cardinals. In doing so, Wrigley was emulating the indoor arenas of the day, most conspicuously the one across town, Chicago Stadium, whose monstrous Barton organ—played by a bald and blade-thin Dane named Al Melgard—leaked through radios nationwide during the 1932 Democratic National Convention, when Melgard's rendition of "Happy Days Are Here Again" became the party's theme song.

The organ maker Dan Barton of Oshkosh, Wisconsin, had principally built instruments for the great movie palaces of the silent-film era, when the organ scored every star from Garbo to Chaplin. It was a movie-palace organ that Barton constructed for Chicago Stadium in 1927, the year Al Jolson and *The Jazz Singer* introduced the talkie and began the demise of the silent-screen starlet—to say nothing of the silent-film organist. Among the latter was Gladys Goodding, who played for the Loew's chain in New York City, whose many jewels included the pharaonic wonder of the Loew's Pitkin Theater on Pitkin Avenue in Brooklyn.

Born and orphaned in Macon, Missouri, Goodding moved to Manhattan in 1922, when she was twenty-nine, with aspirations to be on the stage—in musical comedy or light opera—rather than beneath it. But she was newly divorced, and had two young children, and by the time she had taken up residence at the Belvedere Hotel on West 48th Street, across from Madison Square Garden, Goodding was content to pay the rent by playing for other actors.

When Madison Square Garden owner Tex Rickard died in 1929, the arena temporarily trucked in a pipe organ for his memorial service. Rickard was a fight promoter who had built the third iteration of the Garden in 1925 and acquired for it, a year later, a National Hockey League franchise to compete with the Garden's first hockey team tenant, the New York Americans. Everyone called Rickard's new team "Tex's Rangers," and the name stuck. At his memorial service, Rickard lay in state on the arena floor, in a silvered-bronze casket, the organ providing a funereal air for the ten thousand visitors who lined Eighth Avenue between 49th and 50th Streets, a fitting turnout for a man who was then, and may yet remain, sport's most successful purveyor of hype.

Under his stewardship, the Garden fancied itself the world's most famous arena. (When Rickard built an arena in Boston in 1928, he called it "Boston's Madison Square Garden," a name mercifully pruned to "Boston Garden.") To be worthy of its own epithet,

MSG needed an organ to compete with such modern wonders as the Cleveland Public Auditorium, which had a $100,000 organ with 10,010 pipes and 150 stops. It was the largest ever built by Ernest M. Skinner & Company, and everything about it was exceptionally loud. It drowned out the speakers at the 1924 Republican Convention, but there was no danger of the same happening at that year's Democratic Convention, as the *Times* noted, for that would take place at the soon-to-be-replaced Madison Square Garden, which was bereft of an organ. Even the name of the Cleveland organ—the Magnum Opus 328—sounded ominous, quite possibly dangerous, like a handgun.

As they did in the silent movie houses, these organs complemented the theater of sports. At Chicago Stadium, Al Melgard used the massive Barton both to stir and calm the city's fans. When a riot broke out after a boxing match, Melgard stunned the crowd into peace by playing an earthshaking rendition of the national anthem. In his hands, "The Star-Spangled Banner" sounded more like Bach's *Toccata and Fugue in D Minor*—the music we associate with Dracula's castle and silent horror films—as Melgard's vibrato-rich rendition shattered lightbulbs and a row of windows in the stadium.

This was perhaps more power than was strictly necessary in a musical instrument whose primary purpose was to divert crowds during hockey fights. And so a Chicago polymath named Laurens Hammond set about inventing a pipeless organ. He already had a variety of creations to his name, including a silent, spring-driven "tick-less" clock; anaglyph glasses, with one red lens and one green, for the viewing of 3-D movies; and the Hammond Automatic Bridge Table, which magically shuffled and dealt four bridge hands in the way that Roger Owens would, in a single motion, throw three bags of peanuts to as many customers at Dodger Stadium.

On April 15, 1935, at the Industrial Arts Exposition in New

York's Radio City Music Hall, Hammond tore the tarp off the revolutionary Hammond organ. It immediately wowed the music world, including Pietro Yon, organist at St. Patrick's Cathedral, and George Gershwin, who ordered one on the spot. Madison Square Garden finally succumbed, too, installing a Hammond and then installing, behind it, Gladys Goodding, who had only to cross the street from the Belvedere to go to work.

At hockey and basketball games, Goodding used the organ as a wry commentary on players—as a form of musical heckling—in the way that Melgard did in Chicago. When thirty-eight-year-old Eddie Shore and the rest of the New York Americans took to the ice to face the Blackhawks in 1940, Melgard serenaded Shore with "Darling, I Am Growing Old."

When the Blackhawks were delayed getting into New York for a game against the Rangers, Goodding returned the favor, filling a two-hour delay with songs like "Waitin' for the Train to Come In" and "Give Me Five Minutes More." Baseball—a silent movie without a soundtrack—was missing out on a great deal of fun.

And so Wrigley installed an organ at Wrigley Field in 1941, to popular acclaim. Then the following spring, Dodgers general manager Larry MacPhail put a state-of-the-art Hammond organ in at Ebbets Field, where he hired Goodding. A stout woman approaching her fiftieth birthday, Goodding also sang the national anthem on most days, accompanied by herself on organ.

In Brooklyn, the organ was not quite an immediate success. At the start of that first season in 1942, a seventy-year-old former music teacher named J. Reid Spencer, who lived three blocks south of Ebbets on Lefferts Avenue, sued the Dodgers for violating the borough's noise ordinance, claiming that Goodding's organ recessionals after Dodgers games roused him from his afternoon naps.

For some Flatbush killjoys, the organ was the last straw. "We've taken everything in stride—double-headers, night games, parking, everything," said an Ebbets neighbor named Lillian Strongin. "But this atrocious music atrociously played is the limit."

"We like the music," countered Mrs. John Lawlor. "My 90-year-old mother who lives opposite the ballpark thinks it's grand."

Spencer, the plaintiff, begged the court not to think of him as "a crabbed man. I like to think I am not." But the infernal calliope, he said, also made it impossible for the cop in the apartment below him to sleep when preparing for his night beat, and for the infants of the building to take afternoon naps.

Gooding received the lawsuit in her customary good humor, and even was inspired to biting musical satire by the litigation. She turned up sheet music for a 1914 composition called "Canzonetta in E-flat Major," written by the plaintiff, retired music teacher J. Reid Spencer himself, and promised: "I'll play this next Tuesday when the Dodgers return home."

And so she did. The judge, meanwhile, threw out the case when he noticed that Reid had to cup a hand to his ear even to hear the courtroom proceedings. Gooding was thus given license—literally and metaphorically—to pull out all the stops.

Her songs sent out coded messages, inside jokes, and poison darts. She knew April 23, 1951, was Warren Spahn's thirtieth birthday. When the Braves ace pitched fifteen and two-thirds innings at Ebbets Field that afternoon and still took a 2–1 loss, Gooding waited until the left-hander walked slump-shouldered from the mound before playing "Happy Birthday to You."

Her rendition of "Three Blind Mice," played as the umpires convened before a game at home plate, upset crew chief Bill Stewart, to whom she apologized afterward.

During rain delays, "Let a Smile Be Your Umbrella" rang out. When the Dodgers lost Game 7 of the 1952 World Series to the Yankees, she played "Yankee Doodle" and—by way of apology—"(What Can I Say) After I Say I'm Sorry?" Whenever Dodgers reliever Fireman Hugh Casey saved a game, fans exited—whether they knew it or not—to "Casey would waltz with the strawberry blonde," the refrain from "And the Band Played On." The song took on a terrible poignancy in 1951, when a Brooklyn woman named Casey in a paternity suit. From his hotel room in Atlanta, where he'd been demoted to the minors, the pitcher phoned his wife. As she pleaded with him on the phone, Casey took his own life with a gunshot to the throat.

By tailoring her music to each player, Goodding pioneered what came to be known as "walk-up" music. When Los Angeles native Duke Snider came to bat, Goodding pounded out, "California, Here I Come"—a selection that would take on a terrible poignancy of its own on September 24, 1957.

That Tuesday night, the Dodgers played their final game in Brooklyn. Only 6,702 spectators bothered to show, but Goodding gave them—and any open-windowed apartment dwellers within three blocks—an elegy in minor keys. Her playlist grew inning by inning into a lover's lament: "Am I Blue?" gave way to "After You're Gone" and "Please Don't Ask Me Why I'm Leaving." "Que Sera Sera" bled into "Thanks for the Memories." "How Can You Say We're Through?" yielded to "When I Grow Too Old to Dream." After the Dodgers had beaten the Pirates 2–0, she played "May the Good Lord Bless and Keep You" as the Ebbets grounds crew reflexively groomed the infield, in the manner of a chicken that doesn't yet know it's headless.

And then "Auld Lang Syne" played as the closing credits rolled on baseball in Brooklyn, if not quite on Gladys Goodding, who continued to play at Madison Square Garden until 1963, when she died of a heart attack on a Monday, having played the Knicks' win over Cincinnati the previous Saturday night.

Her bench at the Garden was filled by organist Eddie Layton, who added Yankee Stadium to his duties in 1967, when the hide-bound Bombers finally installed their own Hammond. His was a very 1970s kind of rock stardom, right down to the signature captain's hat—Layton owned a twenty-six-foot tugboat—he wore nightly while playing to fifty thousand people and amplified by fifty thousand watts. Like other baseball organists, Layton even had his own original hits. It was Layton who composed that four-note progression—B-flat, F, G, A—that repeats over and over, and faster and faster, until reaching its climax of "Duh-duh-duh-*DEEP*-dee-*dum—CHARGE!*" Decades later, it remains instantly recognizable (and inexplicably unacclaimed).

The Dodgers, meanwhile, struggled to fill Goodding's girdle in Los Angeles, briefly alighting on a film scorer from 20th Century studios named Chauncey Haines Jr., who had once been an organist in that city's grand silent-movie houses.

This was baseball's baroque period, the middle 1960s and '70s, the ballpark organ's golden age. Its Bach may well have been John Kiley, whom the Red Sox hired in 1953. Like Goodding, Kiley had once been a silent-film organist, at the Criterion Theatre in Roxbury, Massachusetts. By 1975 he was a Boston institution—"the only man to play for the Celtics, Bruins, and Red Sox"—equally nimble of finger and mind. When Carlton Fisk homered for the Sox in the twelfth inning of Game 6 of the '75 World Series—waving the ball fair with the broad gestures of a silent-film star—Kiley played him home to Handel's "Hallelujah Chorus."

Kiley doubled as a choirmaster, but that wasn't unusual; the men and women who provided the soundtrack for '70s baseball were a diverse collection of lounge lizards and church organists. The Pirates plucked Vince Lascheid from the Colony Restaurant in suburban Mt. Lebanon, and his own playlist embodied this high-low dichotomy: "Superstar" from *Jesus Christ Superstar* for Roberto Clemente, "Talk to the Animals" for Bob Moose.

Shay Torrent commuted from Santa Barbara to Anaheim to play every Angels home game, a round-trip of 350 miles, in that icon of SoCal '70s cool: a VW bus. When a power failure knocked the lights out at Anaheim Stadium in 1979—but failed to silence the Big A organ—Torrent played "You Light Up My Life."

And they did. Organists lit the lives of those whose ears were sufficiently sophisticated (or sufficiently unsophisticated, in many cases) to connect the tune they were hearing to the spectacle they were witnessing. When a streaker ran across the field at Veterans Stadium in 1972, Phillies organist Paul Richardson performed a musical emasculation: "Is That All There Is?"

At Jarry Park in Montreal, the great Fernand Lapierre composed and played "La polka des Expos," a Gallic-Polish mash-up that was one part francophone, two parts sousaphone. During conferences on the mound, Lapierre entertained the Expos faithful with "Parlez-moi d'amour" ("Talk to Me of Love"). It's the song Sam is playing when Ilsa first walks into Rick's in *Casablanca*.

All these organists upheld Gladys Goodding's grand tradition of gentle mockery. Nancy Faust of the White Sox was particularly adept at Gooddingesque puns, playing Olivia Newton-John's "Physical," for instance, when introducing shortstop Omar Vizquel. She was also heiress to Al Melgard's seat at Chicago Stadium behind the mammoth six-deck Barton organ, a devilish instrument that finally found, after half a century, its own Faust.

By tailoring music to individual athletes, these organists were playing their own elegy—though they had no way of knowing that at the time. In St. Louis, Ernie Hays, profane maestro of the Busch Stadium organ, played Franz Liszt's "Hungarian Rhapsody No. 2" when Cardinals reliever Al (the Mad Hungarian) Hrabosky entered games. The organ—this staple of early horror films—was creating its own monster: a growing expectation that every on-field act would be preceded by music, or accompanied by music, or followed by a musical punch line.

Those of us filing into the Met for Minnesota Twins games in the 1970s had our own walk-up music, the pregame standard of "Satin Doll," by Duke Ellington, played with a Vegas vibe and bounce by Ronnie Newman. In fact, Newman had worked in Vegas and Tahoe with Ella Fitzgerald and Mel Tormé, not to mention Lenny Bruce, which was appropriate, as the organist was opening in Bloomington for another comedy act, the Minnesota Twins.

Newman got the gig, for fifty bucks a game, in 1977, the year of *Saturday Night Fever*, when players and fans both wore double-knits during the games, and occasionally white shoes and belts. The Twins right fielder was called Disco Danny Ford. It was the last possible time in America that "Satin Doll" could be considered a stadium anthem, played on organ to pump up an audience for a sporting event.

The song was already a quarter-century old that summer, composed in 1953, when baseball was still preeminent in American life. A photo from the middle '50s shows Ellington batting against his bandmates in the parking lot of a Florida motel whose marquee — ASTOR MOTEL — COLORED — makes a useful right field foul pole. Behind him, parked sideways, his tour bus doubles as a backstop.

By the time my parents and brothers and sister and I were attending Twins games at the Met — sitting down the third-base line, the seven of us descending in height like organ pipes — Ellington was dead. But his ghost was resurrected in the summer of 1977, first by Ronnie Newman, and then by Stevie Wonder, whose Ellington tribute song — "Sir Duke" — went to number one that glorious June.

On the broiling Sunday of June 26, the Met was sold out for its first Jersey Day, a Danny Goodman–pioneered promotion in which the Twins, in the unfamiliar position of first place, handed out cotton replica home jerseys bearing the number 29 of Rod Carew, the team's only star. But what a star he was.

Carew treated the batter's box as a crime scene, as if determined not to leave prints. Toward that end, he wore *two* red batting gloves, like ruby slippers for the hands. What had drawn ridicule for Ken Harrelson had become, in a decade, an emblem of cool. But even in the gloves, Carew barely gripped his Louisville Slugger C243, squeezing it ever so lightly around the thin handle, as if it were an icing funnel he was using to decorate a cake. A wad of tobacco bulged the right cheek of the left-handed hitter, pulling the skin taut beneath his right eye, the one nearest the pitcher, the better to see what was coming. As kids in Bloomington, we did the same thing, wadding lunch meat in our cheeks instead of tobacco. Buddig brand pressed pastrami worked best, sliced thin as onionskin.

In his familiar style—one hesitates to call it "inimitable," since every child in the Twin Cities could and did imitate it—Carew went 4-for-5 that Sunday afternoon for the Twins, and raised his average for the season to .403. From my seat in the left field bleachers, I could lower a brown thermos jug to the center field commissary, where my brother Jim was working inside as a sixteen-year-old manager. He would fill it with Sunkist orange soda at half-hourly intervals and lob it back to me, a baseball grenade of a different kind.

Two weeks later, Carew was simultaneously on the covers of *Time* and *Sports Illustrated,* posing on the latter with Ted Williams, the last man to hit .400, thirty-six years earlier. That summer was a brief moment in the national spotlight for the Twins, and my hometown, and the ghost of Duke Ellington. And then it passed. By July, "Sir Duke" had yielded its number one spot in the Top 40, stepping aside for the disco juggernaut of "I'm Your Boogie Man"—and, though we didn't yet know it, making way for the modern age.

Carew was the league's Most Valuable Player but fell twelve points short of .400. The Twins reverted to form, finishing in fourth place in the American League West, 17½ games behind the Kansas City Royals. All through that season, and the next—when the Twins won only seventy-three times—the unsinkable Ronnie Newman played "Satin Doll" in a jazzy, jumpy style, a joyous carnival calliope for 787,000 paying customers.

At the end of that season—on September 28, 1978, with his team in Kansas City, nineteen games behind their opponents— owner and general manager Calvin Griffith spoke to the Lions Club in Waseca, Minnesota. In his remarks, as reported by *Minneapolis Tribune* writer Nick Coleman, who was in attendance, he called Carew a "damn fool" for accepting "only $170,000" to play for the Twins.

He disparaged newlywed catcher Butch Wynegar—who spent too much time, in Calvin's estimation, chasing his bride around the bedroom—and several other players by name. But then every player in baseball was lesser than Carew, who had sewn up his seventh American League batting title that weekend. And then, fatefully, Calvin Griffith was asked at the Lions Club if he would ever again move the franchise that his father had owned in Washington.

Six years after Clark Griffith died in 1955 and bequeathed the Senators to him, Calvin had moved the team to Minnesota. "I'll tell you why we came to Minnesota," Calvin told the Lions Club audience that evening in Waseca. "It was when I found out you only had 15,000 blacks here. Black people don't go to ball games, but they'll fill up a rassling ring and put up such a chant it'll scare you to death. It's unbelievable. We came here because you've got good, hardworking, white people here."

The Twins were still in Kansas City for the season's final series when the remarks were reported to the players. Carew declined to comment. But he spoke the following day, the final day of the season, and also as it happened his thirty-third birthday. "I will not come back and play for a bigot," Carew said. "I'm not going to be another nigger on his plantation."

And he didn't return, departing for the Angels before the 1979 season, which is the season I joined the Twins, at age thirteen, with "Satin Doll" leaking through the sealed door of the walk-in freezer of the main commissary behind home plate, my front left tooth halved by a thrown baseball, so that I resembled the hockey players that my brothers had scissored out of *Goal* magazine and taped to a wood-paneled wall in our basement.

In the days after Griffith's Lions Club speech, Wynegar called the sixty-six-year-old owner a "damn fool." Dan Ford demanded a trade and joined Carew in Anaheim, where Disco Danny had the best year of his career, driving in 101 runs in 1979. I was largely oblivious to the social upheaval at the Met—high as I was on grill gas, Red Man, and the commissary's FM radio pumping out Supertramp and REO Speedwagon.

But a cultural shift was taking place. Players were asserting their independence, and brooking no bullshit on matters of race. Latin players—or American players with Latin surnames—did not want to hear "The Mexican Hat Dance" played on an organ every time they came to bat, no matter how jaunty the rendition.

Once literally in a lofty position—the organ loft at Chicago Stadium loomed over the audience like a weather system—the organ was falling from its place of prominence. In the first years after the Twins moved indoors to the Metrodome in 1982, Ronnie Newman played from a pit beneath the playing surface and watched the games through a periscope, "Satin Doll" emerging from the subterranean lair like a Bond villain.

The notes would drift up to my own lair, in a concession stand at the Metrodome, where I worked for a single season, my father rolling the odometer forward by one year on my birth certificate so that I appeared to be eighteen, old enough to sell beer.

From my window in that stand, I could gaze longingly at the press box door. It was only thirty feet away, just across the concourse, a fast-flowing river of people that seemed uncrossable to a seventeen-year-old aspiring writer. I had no earthly idea how to get from this stand to that one, from roller grill to keyboard.

When the Twins were on the road, I watched them play on our basement TV and wrote game stories on my mom's Royal typewriter. You had to strike the keys hard, as if trying to ring a bell on a carnival midway. Which is exactly what I was doing, the bell of the carriage return ringing at the end of every line.

Three years after I graduated from college, as a young baseball writer for *Sports Illustrated*, the Twins made the 1991 World Series and I covered it. I was living in New York, but when the Series was in Minneapolis, I stayed in Bloomington, in the house I grew up in. When the Twins won Game 7 against the Braves, late on a Sunday night at the Metrodome, I returned to that house and wrote the story for *SI*, in the same basement where I used to compose Twins stories on my mother's Royal typewriter. And all through that sleepless night, ears still ringing from the crowd noise, they rang with something else, too: "Satin Doll," and the unforgettable carriage return of my mother's Royal.

Ronnie Newman was still playing for the Twins that year. In 1977, "Satin Doll" was a nostalgic nod to the 1950s. By the 1990s, it had become a nostalgic nod to the 1970s.

By the late '70s, when Ernie Hays was playing "Hungarian Rhapsody No. 2" for the Mad Hungarian in St. Louis, entrance music had become a novelty. By the late 1980s, when Indians reliever Ricky Vaughn was bursting out of the bullpen to "Wild Thing" in the movie *Major League,* walk-up music had become common in the Show. By the time the Twins and Braves were contesting that 1991 World Series, the majority of ballpark music was recorded: contemporary hits—pop, heavy metal, and hip-hop—booming over the PA system.

Newman played "Satin Doll" until 1998, when he was finally driven out by the tyranny of the compact disc. He was making $98 a game at retirement, a $48 raise on his starting salary in 1977. In two decades, he played "Satin Doll" 1,775 times, in as many consecutive games, without a sick day, but that summer of '98 ballpark organs were playing their own funeral recessional. Trevor Hoffman, the San Diego Padres' indomitable closer, began entering games to AC/DC's "Hell's Bells," whose opening gongs whipped the crowd into a diabolical state of excitement. The entrance quickly became known as "Trevor Time." Everyone wanted his own signature song.

In Boston, John Kiley had already retired, in 1989, after four decades at Fenway. Jane Jarvis was retired after fifteen years with the Mets, having previously played for the Milwaukee Braves. Nancy Faust played forty-one years with the White Sox before retiring in 2010, Ronnie Newman twenty-one years with the Twins before he left the stage. They were all—in the words of the home run call—going, going, gone.

The Dodgers eventually found their West Coast Gladys Goodding, in the form of two women: Helen Dell in the '70s and '80s, Nancy Bea Hefley in the '90s and noughties, forty years between them at Chavez Ravine, the way Walter Alston and Tommy Lasorda managed for forty-four years between them. But then the Dodgers had a special reverence for organs and the women who played them.

To everyone else, the organ had become quaint. Even parks that retained them reduced their time to pre- and postgame interludes, players and spectators preferring the new tradition of walk-up music.

In 1999, following the success of "Hell's Bells" in San Diego, Yankees closer Mariano Rivera began emerging from the bullpen at Yankee Stadium to Metallica's "Enter Sandman," signaling—in the final year of the last millennium—lights out to hitters, but also to ballpark organists.

At the same time—in the last decade of the twentieth century and the first decade of the twenty-first—new ballparks were being built to resemble old ones, or what we think the old ones must have felt like, but never did. In 2009 the Mets opened Citi Field, with an enormous rotunda meant to invoke the tiny one at Ebbets Field, done in that ballpark's red brick and limestone. The rotunda gave way to those deep-green seats that evoked the Polo Grounds.

But even nostalgia has its limits. So the club abandoned the Ebbets aesthetic at the bathroom doors, installing 725 toilets, 374 of them for women and 351 for men. Two hundred and forty of these were eco-friendly waterless urinals. The Mets would never have to move for want of adequate plumbing. O'Malley lived to see the irony of the National League team in New York making its home in a place called Flushing.

The word *nostalgia* comes from the Greek *nostos* (homecoming) and *algos* (pain). Like other "-algias"—*neuralgia* comes to mind—it was coined as a medical affliction, homesickness so acute as to cause physical anguish. I felt something resembling that in 2010, when my hometown Twins moved into Target Field, their new ballpark, and played outdoors in Minnesota for the first time since their last game (and mine) at the Met in 1981.

When I traveled to Target Field in its inaugural season, and approached the $522 million ballpark on foot, I was met first by a bronze statue of Rodney Cline Carew. It had none of Carew's lightness of touch—it was heavy, leaden, not the wisp that was Rodney Cline at the plate—and omitted the bulge from his front cheek, the

Red Man wrapped in bubble gum. This was no doubt intentional, Carew having quit chewing after finding a growth in his mouth in 1992, and enduring a reported $100,000 in dental work. A baseball tradition brought by farm boys to the big leagues a century earlier was emphatically uncool in the twenty-first century.

Not far from Carew's statue was another one, of Calvin Griffith in a business suit, holding a baseball in his upturned right hand. The baseball was both emblem of his life's work and object of his greatest trauma, when fans celebrating the '24 World Series win in Washington overwhelmed the young batboy and made off with his horde of horsehide.

Still farther outside the stadium, 520 feet from home plate, stood an enormous sculpture of an old fielder's glove, rising up in greeting, the way my grandfather's catcher's mitt seemed to reach for me from its grave of packing peanuts. The 1,500-pound glove at Target Field was every bit as ancient, from the benighted age before the Wilson A2K, when every glove resembled the Hamburger Helper mascot. Its index finger was connected to the thumb by a narrow bit of webbing, as if waving heavenward to Bill Doak. As I passed, a family of four nestled comfortably into its pocket for a picture.

Passing into Target Field through Gate 29—another homage to Carew—fans filed past concession stands selling water for $4 a bottle and beer for $7.25. Calvin Griffith would have found this scarcely believable, and his father even less so.

On June 29, 1941, after Griffith Stadium had run out of soda during a doubleheader against the Yankees—the temperature nearly one hundred degrees, before a full house of thirty thousand, with DiMaggio hitting safely in his forty-first and forty-second consecutive games to break George Sisler's American League record—fans complained that rogue vendors were selling ice water to Senators fans. Owner Clark Griffith denied the very possibility that his vendors would take advantage of fan thirst in this way, shaking down customers for water at $0.10 a glass on a hot summer day. (It wouldn't have been the first robbery of the day. That same afternoon, between games of the twin bill, is when DiMaggio's beloved Betsy Ann bat was stolen from the Yankees dugout.)

But a brief investigation by Griffith revealed that his vendors had indeed exploited the day's heat: Ice had been sold for a quarter, ice water for a dime, lukewarm water for a nickel. The owner fired the vendors, apologized in the press, and the scandalous practice of charging for water ceased immediately. If it also planted a seed in the owner's head—sports fans will pay for just about anything, and one day owners will charge $4 for bottled water—he never said so publicly.

At Target Field, Jacob Ruppert would have stared in slack-jawed wonder at the various brands of beer on offer, thirty-four different varieties, dispensed in concession stands and luxury boxes, at seats, and in two stadium pubs. Men drinking there would be deprived of the communal experience of that ballpark staple, the trough-style urinal, which doesn't comply with local building code. But no matter. In one of those stadium pubs was a ballpark organ, with Sue Nelson at the wheel. She apprenticed with Ronnie Newman at the Metrodome, and took over his scaled-back duties in 1998. A dozen years later, the organ was making a small comeback, in a minor key, recalling that distant time when the only woman in the park was the organist.

On this night, though, half the crowd was composed of women, and more than half the restrooms. Of the 667 toilets, 401 of them were in ladies' rooms. There were, separately, dedicated spaces for nursing mothers, though the Twins allowed fans to BYOB when it came to baby bottles.

The team's Clubhouse Store was a Danny Goodman dream

sprung to life, 4,800 square feet of retail space open daily, whether the Twins were home or not. Goodman's prophecy of fifty years earlier — "I think eventually we'll have full-scale shopping centers inside the parks" — had come to pass.

And yet, that captive audience had so much more to captivate it. The video scoreboard covered 5,757 square feet, capable of conveying 4.4 trillion shades of color. There was free Wi-Fi in the stadium, bringing instant replays and real-time box scores to my phone. Eventually, fans could post their own Twitter messages to one of the scoreboards from their seats. Some of those seats had wooden backs, made from ash by the Irwin Seating Company. And that ash was not the only Proustian callback to a vanishing past: After decades of infidelity at the Metrodome, the Twins had returned to the Schweigert hot dogs of Met Stadium, the pork-and-beef hot dogs of my youth, and theirs.

Of course, there were also Cuban sandwiches, empanadas, pork chops on a stick, walleye fingers, wild rice soup, and all manner of other culinary exotica. But the staples continued to thrive, and for five bucks, and three innings of nonstop nagging, a boy or girl could still get an ice cream sundae in an inverted batting helmet.

The opponent on this night was the Brewers, and they wore a sprig of barley on their caps, and the Budweiser roof deck in left field literally loomed over the proceedings, its red letters against the black sky like a sign from the heavens to drink. And yet nobody was throwing beer bottles. Indeed, there were no bottles to throw. The only aspersion aimed at the umpires was the sign on their dressing room door, labeled not only in English but in braille.

Those umpires were under greater scrutiny than ever before in their history. In addition to the usual TV and smartphone cameras, three dedicated cameras were permanently mounted in the stadium — indeed, in every stadium — and trained on their strike zone. Those cameras tracked the ball from the nanosecond it left the pitcher's hand until it crossed the front edge of home plate. This information — including speed, trajectory, and location of the pitch, accurate to within one inch and one mile per hour — were instantly transmitted to a computer, and then onto thousands of other computers and television screens, for real-time second-guessing of umpires by both fans and the umpiring overlords at Major League Baseball.

This system, called PITCHf/x, was developed by the same company that gave televised football its great Edisonian innovation: the yellow line that indicates first downs.

So baseball's retro craze had been tempered by the codependent revolutions of technology and statistical analysis. But as I found my seat, beer in hand, then rose for the national anthem — turning toward the flagpole salvaged from the Met — none of that was on my mind. For there, suddenly, was the field, gorgeous in contrasting shades of green.

Two and one-half acres of turfgrass had been cut from a farm in Fort Morgan, Colorado, and shipped overnight to Minneapolis, on nineteen refrigerated trucks, driven with the urgency of medical couriers transporting live organs for transplant.

"The history of every nation is eventually written in the way it cares for its soil," Franklin Roosevelt said in 1936, and so it is with the nation of baseball. The first shovel in the ground at Target Field was a silver spade bolted to a Louisville Slugger.

The soil, more than 90 percent sand, was lovingly tended by Larry DiVito, though the Twins' spring training home at Hammond Stadium in Fort Myers, Florida, was still tilled by eighty-year-old George Toma, who became a head groundskeeper as a seventeen-year-old high school senior in 1947, for the Indians farm club in Wilkes-Barre, Pennsylvania. There, he studied under Cleveland's head groundskeeper, Emil Bossard, who had begun his own career right here, in the Twin Cities, in 1913, as groundskeeper for the St. Paul Saints. In the century that followed—from 1913 in St. Paul to 2012 in Fort Myers—there was an unbroken line from Bossard to Toma, the Evers-to-Chance of Twins ballpark grass.

Bossard was the son of a Swiss plumber who immigrated to Minnesota in 1892 and opened a hardware store in St. Paul, where Emil was put to work. While delivering lumber to Lexington Park, the boy was recruited to fill in for an inebriated groundskeeper and remained for twenty-three years. In 1936, Bill Veeck brought him to Cleveland, where Bossard and his crew wore straw hats thrown onto the field by Indians fans celebrating home runs. They should have been wearing Indians uniforms, for Bossard's crew accounted—by Veeck's own reckoning—for a dozen victories a year.

When sinkerballer Bob Lemon pitched, Bossard softened the infield, saturating the dirt in front of home plate so that any ball driven into it would quickly die. When the speedy White Sox were in town, he loosened the dirt around first base, depriving runners of a fast start. Teams that played small ball found it difficult to bunt: The ball kept rolling foul, Bossard having peaked the base paths.

Outside Target Field was a statue of another Twin, Hall of Famer Harmon Killebrew. When Killebrew was a boy in Payette, Idaho, playing ball with his two brothers in their front yard, his mother would complain they were wrecking the lawn. Killebrew's father, also named Harmon, replied, "We're raising boys, not grass."

But Emil Bossard defied that bit of wisdom, raising grass and boys at Municipal Stadium, and doing a masterful job of both. In 1940, White Sox owner Grace Comiskey asked Bossard to send one of his sons to Chicago, hoping genes would have an effect. Gene took the job there, at age twenty-three, but his brothers Harold and Marshall remained in Cleveland. They would sit in the scoreboard with Bob Feller's 20-millimeter gun scope, which the pitcher had used as an antiaircraft gunner on the USS *Alabama,* and steal the signs of opposing catchers.

The Bossards moved the fences in and out in Cleveland, depending on the opponent. The pitcher's mound rose and fell like the stock market. The visitors' bullpen mound was raised, so that opposing pitchers then throwing from the actual mound felt like they were pitching from a trench.

Emil retired from the Indians in 1956 and was succeeded by his son Harold, who was succeeded by *his* son Brian, who went on to conjure grass for the Padres and the Yankees. In Chicago, Gene Bossard worked for forty years in the manner Emil taught him. Ken Harrelson of the Red Sox once laid down a bunt at Comiskey Park that stuck in the swamp in front of home plate, only half visible, like a golf ball that had fried-egged itself in a sand trap. When the home plate umpire asked Bossard to explain the pond in front of the plate, the groundskeeper removed his cigar, shrugged, and said, "The hose broke."

Gene Bossard was succeeded in Chicago by his son Roger. Emil's grandson became renowned in his own right in the world of sports—indeed, in the world at large—as "The Sodfather." Among his many side projects, he conjured soccer fields in the sand for the Saudi royal family, to whom he seemed a desert sorcerer.

George Toma, meanwhile, grew grass on plywood for the 1994 World Cup, and it was from this kind of unpromising soil—a hardware store in St. Paul—that Emil Bossard grew a family tree whose branches reached into every major-league ballpark across a century. Acolyte Toma got his first big-league job in Kansas City in 1957, working for Charles Finley and the A's, repeating all the tricks he learned from Emil. Toma branched out into football, working every Super Bowl played through 2012, and published an autobiography in which he wrote: "Is there another Emil Bossard on the horizon? Not that I have seen."

In fairness, how could there be? Bossard has been credited with inventing the tenpenny-nail drag for grooming the infield, creating protective screens for batting practice pitchers, and even putting bases on stakes, the better to anchor them into the ground.

Previously, as Ty Cobb recalled in his autobiography, "bases were left out until they were spiked apart. They weren't anchored and strapped down firmly, giving you a solid cushion for sliding. Those sawdust bags would shift a foot or more when you tore into them."

Those shifting bases were canvas sacks, offered "stuffed" or "unstuffed" by the A. J. Reach Company, whose official guide in 1910 noted unstuffed bags "can be filled with sand or hay, and after the game emptied." When Babe Ruth circled the bases for the '27 Yankees, those bases were stuffed canvas. It was a minor-league club executive named Jack Corbett who patented a better base—rain-resistant, and tapered at the bottom so as not to turn up at the edges. The Jack Corbett Hollywood Base debuted in the big leagues in 1939, and its fifteen square inches of quilted white rubber remains the only base used in Major League Baseball.

Those bases are anchored by six-inch stanchions, brainchild of Emil Bossard, who was also by some accounts the first to stripe the grass, using a heavy roller dragged behind the mower to bend the blades toward and away from the sun, creating contrasting light and dark shades, as on a vacuumed carpet.

This technique lay dormant until the 1990s, when Milwaukee groundskeeper David Mellor mowed a pattern into the outfield at County Stadium to disguise damage from a concert there. By the time Mellor was director of grounds in Boston, striping jack-o'-lanterns and socks and American flags into the grass at Fenway Park, mowing patterns were customary throughout baseball. Even artificial turf fields were striped. Red Sox fans could submit their own mowing patterns, via the club's website, and Mellor would choose one to cut into the field at Fenway.

Target Field on this night was checkered like a tablecloth, laid for a vast banquet.

Minnie and Paul pulsing with neon at Target Field in Minneapolis. *(Ffooter/Shutterstock.com)*

And so the familiar ritual began, with a pitch. The pitch was tracked and measured by three cameras, from pitcher's hand to catcher's mitt. This space-age technology didn't obscure the fact that the two principals in this drama were still called a battery, vestige of a previous technological revolution.

The word *battery,* in baseball, derived from Foulproof Taylor's old vocation, telegraphy, which consisted of a transmitter and a receiver, a pitcher and a catcher.

The pitcher and catcher looked, on this night, not all that different from their forebears. True, their uniforms were no longer instruments of torture. Their pants were tailored to reach their shoe tops, obscuring their socks entirely, though some players flashed high socks, in homage to the game's origins. Stirrups had all but vanished from every level of the game. Batters came to the plate in armor, their shins and forearms shielded without any stigma whatsoever. Ryne Duren's rose-tinted sunglasses had given way to red-tinted contact lenses that made the wearer's eyes glow like feral animals. Maple bats whipped through strike zones framed by electronic monitors that instantly conveyed information to flat screens and laptops.

But the umps still made the calls, the ball still looked as it did a century earlier, and the Arizona Diamondbacks still had a cow femur mounted on a railing in their dugout, for the bone rubbing of bats.

The gloves were still made of leather, though not always, and not entirely. On June 16, 2011, Yankees pitcher Brian Gordon took the mound in New York wearing the first all-synthetic glove in major-league history, without a stitch of leather. It was the brainchild of an artist named Scott Carpenter, who handcrafted gloves from a man-made microfiber called Clarino. The gloves were stuffed with wool, but Carpenter also offered a synthetic stuffing, for vegan shortstops. Each of his gloves was five to ten ounces lighter than its rawhide equivalent, and tailored to the player's hand, and still only one player in history had worn one by 2012, owing not just to existing contracts with leather-glove manufacturers but to 140 years of tradition. Synthetic gloves are scent-free. Even the big leaguers who wore synthetic back panels on their gloves preferred a leather pocket, allowing them to do what I did when my grandfather's catcher's mitt arrived in the mail: place it over my nose and mouth and inhale.

And so the game played on, literally hidebound but somehow ever changing. Carpenter lived and worked in Cooperstown, of all places, where the glove he made for Gordon was enshrined nearby, behind glass in the Hall of Fame.

The last forty-eight miles of the drive to Cooperstown, from my home in Connecticut, is a stretch of rural roads that runs past stands of trees, past grazing cows, past horses and sheep and — just on the outskirts of town, overlooking Otsego Lake—the estate of August Anheuser Busch. The land was purchased by the brewery magnate at the turn of the previous century, when Otsego County was the nation's finest region for growing hops. In good times, before he fell ill and took his own life with a shotgun in 1934, Busch entertained the neighbors with trained elephants performing on the lawn.

On my drives to Cooperstown, every ingredient necessary for a baseball game, then, was just beyond the car window: cow, horse, sheep, tree, and hops. Which is to say ball, bat, glove, grass, and beer.

As forty thousand of us sat in Wi-Fi'd wonder watching the game in Minneapolis, on infinite flat screens and smartphones and even— when strictly necessary—with the naked eye, I couldn't help but marvel at how we got here. A ball hand-sewn in Costa Rica was whipped round the horn, recalling another epic journey, to say nothing of baseball's own, embracing culture, commerce, technology, race, romance, murder, travel, war, and screwballs of every variety.

Baseball was the world on a plate—home plate. And it was all set down before me on the checkered tablecloth of Target Field.

For all its novelty, Target Field still had bleachers that bleached and shadows that crept and a tarp that rolled out when the skies opened up. The first time that happened, after twenty-eight seasons indoors, Twins fans looked up in disbelief and loudly applauded the heavens.

Under the stars, I silently did the same, and felt a sharp pang of memory. Not a day had passed since I was ten that I hadn't thought of baseball, or at the very least baseballs. And I still couldn't eat a snow cone at Target Field—or drink any other hot or cold beverage— without a sharp pain in my left front tooth, thirty-four years after it was snapped in half by a thrown baseball, an ever-present reminder of my failure to catch a ball at first base for the Bloomington Athletic Association Braves in the summer of 1976.

Baseball had literally made an impression on me, even before that employee ID card arrived on my thirteenth birthday, bearing the Twins' mesmeric logo of Minnie and Paul shaking hands.

That logo was the centerpiece of the new Target Field. On a magnificent sign above the center field bleachers, the cartoon ball-players wore belted flannels and tall socks. Like Babe Ruth and Cy Young before him, Paul leaned on his bat for support. Framed by the silhouette of my home state, the pair shook hands. They were forty-six feet tall and pulsing with neon.

Somewhere down the third-base line, so was I.

ACKNOWLEDGMENTS

Early in the research of this book, I made a late-autumn drive from my home in Connecticut to the National Baseball Hall of Fame in Cooperstown, New York, with my then seventy-seven-year-old father riding shotgun. After four hours in the car, we arrived to find a paper note taped to the Hall's front door: CLOSED TODAY.

Unlike other shrines, the Baseball Hall of Fame closes only three days a year—Thanksgiving, Christmas, and New Year's—but snowmelt from a November storm threatened the region with flooding. So Dad and I passed a windswept moment on the front steps, jiggling the locked front door, feeling like Clark and Rusty Griswold in National Lampoon's *Vacation,* denied entry into Walley World by the animatronic moose.

Mercifully, the Hall reopened the next day, and I set foot for the first time in its wonderful library, where visitors are obliged—as in other solemn rituals—to don white gloves. These gloves, proffered at the front desk, turn everyone who wears them into Mickey Mouse. In that and subsequent visits, I spent several white-gloved days poring over file folders so endlessly absorbing they risked swallowing me whole.

In one such folder of flaking, yellowed news clippings devoted to baseball concessions, I found a silver foil hot-dog wrapper. When Tom Shieber, the Hall of Fame's senior curator, happened by and snatched it out of my hand to archive elsewhere, I suddenly envied this man whose job necessitated a file drawer devoted to ballpark hot-dog wrappers. (He writes engagingly about many of his discoveries on his *Baseball Researcher* blog at baseballresearcher.blogspot.com.)

Shieber's colleague Bill Francis is a Hall of Fame researcher in every sense of that phrase. I'm indebted to Bill for answering every one of my queries with great skill and good cheer. No subject—from the urinals at Ebbets Field to the bring-your-own-beer policies in major-league ballparks—was too inane for Bill to field. Or if it was, he never told me. Because he knows something about every-thing, from baseball to the British guerrilla artist Banksy, stumping him became a personal challenge.

When thirst for knowledge gave way to thirst for beer, Bill took me to the Doubleday Café on Main Street. On our own, my dad and I discovered Cooley's Stone House Tavern on Pioneer Street, where we were fortified with Guinness and grilled cheese.

Freddy Berowski made time for me in the National Baseball Hall of Fame Library—officially the A. Bartlett Giamatti Research Center—and ensured that a mountain of folders (and a pair of white gloves) were waiting on arrival.

I'm also grateful to the Hall of Fame's director of research, Tim Wiles, who coauthored *Baseball's Greatest Hit,* an evocative book about "Take Me Out to the Ball Game." Wiles graciously offered to house my (now extensive) research on Jimmy Boyle at the Hall. He and all the staff in Cooperstown saved me from many errors in this book. Any that remain are mine.

Pat Kelly, the Hall of Fame's photo archivist, helped to bring the manuscript alive with pictures of many of the principals. The Library of Congress is another invaluable photo resource as well as a national treasure.

Speaking of bringing things to life: John Parsley at Little, Brown shares an enthusiasm for things lost and things found, and a Dr. Frankenstein–like belief that we can reanimate the dead. John was the first person to suggest there was a book in the objects of baseball—the first to realize that my grandfather's mitt could tell a broader story. His deft editing and enthusiasm for the subject were invaluable.

I'm likewise indebted to Michael Pietsch for his interest in the project, and to Malin von Euler-Hogan for her endless assistance.

Carolyn Haley is a thoughtful copyeditor who improved the manuscript. Karen Landry improved everyone's improvements.

I'm grateful as ever to Esther Newberg, for her twin love of books and baseball (though in which order those belong, I cannot say).

Baseball Reference (baseball-reference.com) is a bottomless resource for anyone writing about the game, as is all the good work done by the Society for American Baseball Research (SABR.org).

It's not possible to write about baseball uniforms without feeling Paul Lukas—author of the Uni Watch column for ESPN.com—looking over your sleeve-patched shoulder. Marc Okkonen's epic book on baseball uniforms (*Baseball Uniforms of the 20th Century*) was a good point of entry on that subject. Noah Liberman's book on gloves (*Glove Affairs*), and two books on the Louisville Slugger (*Crack of the Bat* by Bob Hill and *Sweet Spot* by David Magee and Philip Shirley), are likewise engaging on those subjects. Peter Morris's two-volume epic, *A Game of Inches,* is a fascinating account of baseball's origins and evolution.

Joe DeMartino is a former Linotype operator for the *Brooklyn Daily Eagle,* whose offhand memories about the long waits at urinals at the Ebbets Field men's room of his youth inspired chapter 6.

Thanks to the staff of the Brooklyn Public Library, who helped both in person and online, with its archive of the *Daily Eagle.*

The online archives of *Sporting Life* and *Baseball Magazine* maintained by the LA84 Foundation were also indispensable.

My friend Jim Badorek tipped me off to the story of his relative Ted Pisk.

My editors at *Sports Illustrated* excused my occasional absence.

Diane Taylor is a lovely writer who has blessedly maintained the memory of Foulproof Taylor, her great-uncle, in every sense of that adjective. Diane was kind enough to share stories and photographs of Foulproof with me.

Jimmy Boyle and his wife, Clare, raised three children on the west side of Cincinnati. One of them is Pat Boyle, my uncle, who has kept his father's mitt and scrapbook and stories alive, and passed all of them along to me. My aunt Ann (Boyle) Burns shared letters, photographs, and above all memories of her father. Ann and Pat's big sister is my late mother, Jane (Boyle) Rushin, who loved baseball and Cincinnati and the point at which they intersected in the Cincinnati Reds. It was my mother who encouraged me to read and to write, and to get a job at Metropolitan Stadium. This book is the product of all those urgings.

Pete Rose was another product of Cincinnati's west side. When he beat the Mets with a home run in the twelfth inning of Game 4 of the 1973 National League Championship Series, my mother danced around the shag carpet of our family room in Bloomington, Minnesota.

In my mind's eye, she never stopped.

NOTES

Introduction

6   **guard the team's supply of baseballs:** R. J. Lesch, "Eddie Brannick," SABR bio, http://sabr.org/bioproj/person/f0d59a5f.

8   **stolen a bouquet of bats and my Uncle Buzz's uniform pants:** "Boys in 'Bats' Theft Raid Ebbets Field," *New York Times*, February 11, 1936.

9   **Clark Griffith invented the screwball:** Leavengood, *Clark Griffith*, 23.

13   **Bob Casey informed fans:** Associated Press, "17,697 at Minnesota Ball Park Evacuated over Bomb Threat," *New York Times*, August 26, 1970.

Chapter 1

20   **sixty-one baseball-shaped gefilte fish:** "Hank Greenberg Didn't Have a Last Shot in the Dark at Ruth's Record," *Sports Illustrated*, June 14, 1982.

20   **Laura Bush commissioned a cake:** Bush, *Spoken from the Heart*, 191.

21   **"What Christy Mathewson could do to the Germans":** United Press International, "Ingenuity of Germans," *Northern Indianian*, April 1, 1915.

21   **invented a hand grenade:** *Yellowstone News*, September 30, 1916.

22   **"If America ever goes to war":** "London Correspondent of the *Washington Star*: Bomb Throwing by Hand," *St Joseph's News-Press*, August 9, 1916.

22   **"Our boys already excel":** "Captain Fish Writes from France," *New York Times*, May 5, 1918.

22   **"He threw in a peculiar fashion":** Evers, "Teaching the Poilus How to Play Baseball."

23   **"This hand grenade throwing is great exercise":** Nort, "A Message from the War Front."

24   **one went off in his right hand:** Associated Press, "Marine Hero to See Game," *New York Times*, October 7, 1944; "Marine Hero in Cards' Dugout," *Youngstown Vindicator*, October 8, 1944.

25   pitcher Dave Ferriss was photographed: "Baseball-Shaped Tear-Gas Grenade Strikes 'Em Out," *Popular Science*, October 1945, 121.

25   "The Chinese, lacking America's baseball tradition": Associated Press, "Chinese Reds Have Resurrected the Grenadier," *The Day* (New London, CT), January 22, 1951.

25   Dr. Cecil C. Fawcett patented a lethal baseball grenade: "Hand Grenade, Baseball Style, Designed for Easier Throwing," *New York Times*, September 15, 1956.

25   "Pedro Ramos will trade a baseball for a hand grenade": United Press International, "Baseball Sí, Politics No, Ramos Says," *Pittsburgh Press*, April 11, 1961.

26   "The man who hit the Pearl Harbor home run": Associated Press, "Admiral Who Directed Attack on Pearl Harbor Killed on Saipan Island," *St. Petersburg Evening Independent*, July 14, 1944.

26   "teargas grenade...that skitters around": "Army Studying Radar Set That Can See Through Wall," *Washington Star*, February 15, 1971.

27   "Among college boys": Hinton, "A Mechanical Pitcher."

27   "whenever men wished to impel a ball": Ibid.

28   "The baseball is placed in the barrel of the cannon": "The New Baseball-Pitching Gun," *New York Times*, March 12, 1897.

28   "There was a muffled report": "Too Long to Load," *Boston Daily Globe*, January 11, 1897.

29   "Batters having accustomed themselves": "Played Ball with a Gun," *Daily True American*, June 11, 1897.

29   shot baseballs out of the Chester County Courthouse: Carson-Gentry and Rodebough, *Images of America*, 6.

30   "As regularly as the ball teams visited Washington": "Schriver's Feat," *Sporting Life*, September 1, 1894.

31   "[A] ball was thrown from one of the small windows": "Only One Hundred Singers," *Washington Post*, January 10, 1885.

31   "I'd never try a stunt like that again": "Akron Man Captained Washington's First Pennant Winning Nine," *Akron Beacon Journal*, May 22, 1932.

31   "He talked of arrests": "Schriver's Feat."

32   the ball was discovered by Gibson's son: "Baseball Caught by Gabby Street in Monument Drop Rediscovered," *Washington Post*, January 12, 1964.

32   "might as well try to stop a bullet": *The Reach Official American League Base Ball Guide 1910*, 258–59.

33   "other things besides Torso murders": *Brooklyn Daily Eagle,* from an undated clip on file at the National Baseball Hall of Fame Library.

34   "They looked like aspirin tablets": "Drop Zone," *Cleveland Plain Dealer,* August 20, 2003.

35   "jumped into my arms": Anderson, "When Baseballs Fell from the Sky."

35   "It looked like an aspirin": "Joe Sprinz, Hit by Ball Dropped from Blimp," *San Jose Mercury News,* January 25, 1994.

36   "This is the end of that kind of a stunt": August 10, 1939, in an otherwise unidentified newspaper clipping in the National Baseball Hall of Fame Library.

36   "monstrous flies": Kahn, *October Men,* 53.

37   "I get mad at the ball players": Red Smith, *New York Herald-Tribune* column carried in *Stars and Stripes,* March 19, 1963.

37   "He liked his snakes": Veeck and Linn, *Veeck as in Wreck,* 108.

38   Max Bengersen retrieved a ball: "Boy Wounded Fatally by Annoyed Man," *New York Times,* July 27, 1902.

38   Gillis and two other Whales: "The Last Whale," *Sports Illustrated,* February 3, 1964 (Gillis died in Phoenix in 1964 at age eighty-eight).

38   Christian Koehler clambered over that fence: "Boy Killed by Hammer Throw at Practice," *New York Times,* October 1, 1904.

39   Harris fumbled for a baseball: From a description in the Heritage Auctions press release, March 22, 2006.

39   "Whooooa. It's *the ball*": "McFarlane Paid $3 Million for McGwire's 70th Home Run Ball," *Washington Post,* February 9, 1999.

41   "It is rather disconcerting": "New Rule Idea," *Sporting Life,* January 18, 1913.

41   Charlie Weeghman wearied of fighting: "Editorials," *Baseball Magazine,* October 1916.

41   "I don't know whether you or Shettsline": "Boy Who Got Ball in Stands Found Not Guilty of Larceny," *New York Times,* July 20, 1923; "Losing Proposition," *Philadelphia Weekly,* June 27, 2007.

42   "a one-round knockout of a gent": "Every Day Is Flag Day at the Ball Parks," *New York Times,* May 16, 1942.

42   the hides of thirty-five thousand horses: "Inside Story of Baseballs," *Popular Science,* April 1950, 161.

43   switched first to Bolivian horsehide: Mead, *Baseball Goes to War,* 78.

43   the powerhouse Cardinals lost 1–0: Associated Press, "Substitute Baseball Will Be Discussed," *Palm Beach Post,* March 5, 1943. The dead balata

baseballs of 1943—and the anemic scores they produced—were reported by the Associated Press, "Cincinnati Wins from Cards," *Tuscaloosa News,* April 23, 1943; Associated Press, "Change Made in Major League Ball," *Lawrence Journal-World,* April 24, 1943; Associated Press, "Test Shows 1942 Ball Liveliest," *Pittsburgh Press,* April 21, 1943; and Hynd, "The Inside Story."

44   **"One day in school":** "Stoughton Man Invented First Cover of Baseball," *Stoughton Sentinel,* April 3, 1909, Stoughtonhistory.com.

46   **"The famous baseball genius":** *St. Paul Pioneer Press,* quoted in Lamster, *Spalding's World Tour,* 3.

48   **"Talk about special Providence!":** Spalding, *America's National Game,* 511.

Chapter 2

53   **named after biblical figures:** James, *The New Bill James,* 45.

53   **"a howling drunk":** "Louisville Wins Easily," *New York Times,* July 13, 1887.

53   **an exceedingly rare unassisted pickoff:** Nemec, *The Beer & Whiskey League,* 240.

53   **"he played about fifteen feet off second base":** From an otherwise unidentified news clipping dated October 12, 1887, in Browning's player file in the National Baseball Hall of Fame Library.

53   **"The Gladiator drank more than was necessary":** From an otherwise unidentified news clipping dated October 18, 1890, in Browning's player file in the National Baseball Hall of Fame Library.

55   **a nickname bestowed by newspapers:** *Louisville Post,* June 17, 1891, cited in Von Borries, *American Gladiator,* 45.

56   **"all oiled and rubbed":** *Louisville Courier-Journal,* May 19, 1895, cited in Von Borries, *American Gladiator,* 119.

56   **Frank Bradsby so impressed J. Frederich:** Hill, *Crack of the Bat,* 50.

57   **slipped on an icy street:** "Bat Manufacturer Dies," *New York Times,* January 18, 1924.

57   **fractured another man's skull:** "Blow Causes Boy's Death," *Washington Post,* April 29, 1907, cited in Gorman and Weeks, *Death at the Ballpark.*

58   **"took up a batter's stance":** Hendley, *Al Capone,* 144.

64   **"hardly break stride saying hello":** Magee and Shirley, *Sweet Spot,* 71.

67   **Easton was hunting one day:** Gant, *International Directory of Company Histories.*

67 **Shroyer received United States patent...for his bat of steel:** *The United States Patents Quarterly*, 4.

68 **Testifying in a 1975 patent suit:** United Press International, "Aluminum Rapped as Bat Material," September 11, 1975.

Chapter 3

74 **"delicate garments":** "Glove Remains a Giant Target," *San Jose Mercury News*, July 9, 2007.

75 **"Cezanne painted apples":** Wulf, "Glove Story."

75 **"It's something I don't deny":** Oldenburg, *Oldenburg*, 11.

76 **"diamond palace":** "Unveiling Diamond Palace in Land of Sun," *Sporting News*, April 12, 1962.

76 **"one of the wonders of the West":** "Giants' Camp Is Oasis in Arizona Desert," *New York Times*, March 7, 1965.

76 **"Welcome to Franceesco Granday":** "Sauer's Gastronomical Feat Opens Giants' Farm Base," *Sporting News*, March 22, 1961.

79 **"the circular stitching peculiar to baseballs":** "Thousands Visit New Ball Park," *New York Times*, March 17, 1913.

82 **"national game of base-ball for men and boys":** "The Ball Up," *New York Times*, December 18, 1870.

83 **"a pair of buckskin mittens":** *Cincinnati Daily Commercial*, June 28, 1870.

83 **He was one of thirty-two thousand casualties:** *Washington Post*, January 12, 1908.

83 **"Allison was a gunner":** *Boston Daily Globe*, March 24, 1876.

85 **"gloves were unknown":** "Douglas Allison, One of Baseball's Pioneers, Tells How the Great Game Was Played Forty Years Ago," *Washington Post*, January 12, 1908.

85 **"if we fearlessly grasp a nettle":** Brookes, *Manliness*, 30.

86 **"The glove worn by [Waitt]":** Spalding, *America's National Game*, 475–76.

87 **Cornelius McGillicuddy's baseball journey:** Mack, *My 66 Years in the Big Leagues*, 17.

88 **"You had to catch the ball two-handed":** *Baseball Digest*, November 1972, reprinted from a story by Phil Elderkin in the *Christian Science Monitor*.

89 **"almost a copy of Bushong":** "Notes and Comments," *Sporting Life*, August 10, 1887.

89 **"an inshoot jellied the fingers":** "As It Used to Be," *Cincinnati Post*, May 28, 1926.

90 "a spring mattress on his left hand": Shafer, *When the Dodgers Were Bridegrooms*, 64.

90 "The Doctor was proud of this affair": "Ups and Downs of Catcher's Gloves," *New York Times*, January 24, 1915.

91 "When I shave my upper lip": Brian McKenna, "Doc Bushong," SABR bio, http://sabr.org/bioproj/person/5d4b5fe8.

91 he sent a version to the brand-new Baseball Hall of Fame: Vlasich, *A Legend for the Legendary*, 59.

92 "Boyle is fond of a joke": *Toronto Daily Mail*, December 19, 1891.

93 the blade had snapped off when it hit bone: "Blade in Ball Player's Shoulder," *Reading Eagle* (Pennsylvania), May 6, 1899.

96 "I have just received a sad letter": A copy of the letter is on file at the National Baseball Hall of Fame Library.

97 "A more honest and harder-working professional player": *New York Clipper*, December 16, 1882.

98 "a mattress for a Singer midget": Bud Shaver, *Detroit Times*, March 13, 1935.

98 "three lengths of barbed wire": Seidel, *Ted Williams*, 57, quoting Ring Lardner.

98 "There's a whale of a difference": "Major League Ball Teams Ready to Open Training Camp," *Palm Beach Post*, February 18, 1940.

99 "the smallest glove of any first baseman I know": John Kieran, *New York Times*, March 16, 1941.

99 seventeen fractures in Gehrig's hands: "Iron Bird Pursues Iron Horse in Baseball's Durability Race," *New York Times*, July 13, 1993.

99 "He took his glove and threw it": "Dahlgren Still Carrying Lou Gehrig's Glove," *Sporting News*, June 16, 1979.

100 "an extension of his own skin": Eig, *Luckiest Man*, 279.

100 "Almost every youngster here": "Memories Are Recalled by Bill (Spittin') Doak," *Sarasota Herald-Tribune*, February 8, 1953.

101 "leave tombstones out there": *Hartford Courant*, April 17, 1954.

101 "It would be foolish": "Leaving Glove on Field Old Habit, but Some Day—," *Baseball Digest*, January 1952, reprinted from the *Boston Globe*.

101 the unattended glove of teammate Topsy Hartsel: Nemec, *The Official Rules of Baseball Illustrated*, 46.

102 Nellie Fox hit a bloop: "Strange and Unusual Plays," http://www.retrosheet.org/strange.htm.

102 "gloves on the field look sloppy": "Baseball Reinstates Sacrifice Fly," *New York Times*, November 4, 1953.

104   "the A2000 gave you so much confidence": Liberman, *Glove Affairs*, 28.

104   "single greatest piece of sporting equipment": "Esquire Endorses," *Esquire*, November 2008.

104   "a masterpiece of man's creative urge": Dave Kindred, "Riding the Wave," in Smith, *Celebrating 70*, 181.

105   "the wreck of the Hesperus": Lane, "Ball-players Hands."

105   a promise to his mother never to swear: "From Classrooms to Boardrooms, Swearing Is Becoming More Commonplace," *Fort Worth Star-Telegram*, January 26, 1998.

105   landmark case *Hundley v. Commissioner of Internal Revenue:* The ruling is online at http://www.leagle.com/xmlResult.aspx?page=1&xmldoc= 196738748aitc339_1353.xml&docbase=CSLWAR1–1950–1985& SizeDisp=7.

106   Hundley's ascension in Chicago: Johnny Bench's conversion to one-handed catching is described in Furlong, "Johnny Bench: Supercatcher for the Big Red Machine."

107   "come through the Catcher's Mitt": Hall and Hall, *I Served*, 135.

108   "an immediate transformation in his outlook": "Lost and Found," *New Britain Herald*, October 23, 2009.

108   afflicted with hemorrhoids: Kurkjian, "Old-Fashioned Glove Story."

Chapter 4

109   "Tunnel workers crawled from the depths": Alan Feuer, "You Think This Is Hot?," *New York Times*, August 16, 2010, http://cityroom.blogs.nytimes .com/2010/08/16/way-back-machine-you-think-this-is-hot.

109   "terrible weapon of death": "Barney Morris Dead; Was Said to Be 109," *Brooklyn Daily Eagle*, July 3, 1901.

110   Edison Electric Illuminating Company: The ad for electric fans ran in the *Brooklyn Daily Eagle*, July 3, 1901.

110   wore their bathing suits on the streets: "Object to Bathing Suits for Wear in the Street," *Brooklyn Daily Eagle*, July 7, 1901.

110   the temperature dropped twelve degrees: "Elements Combine to Beat Champions," *Brooklyn Daily Eagle*, July 3, 1901.

110   BROILING SUN, WIND, RAIN AND HAIL: Ibid.

111   A horse had expired: *Brooklyn Daily Eagle*, July 3, 1901.

111   "When I played for Toledo": *Baseball Digest*, October 1957, 78, reprinted from the *Chicago Tribune*.

112   "I asked Hughes to come up": "Brooklyns Lose Two on Infield Errors," *Brooklyn Daily Eagle*, July 5, 1901.

112   **leeches were applied:** Ibid.

112   **he was pummeled:** "Cowardly Attack on Umpire O'Day," *Brooklyn Daily Eagle,* July 9, 1901.

113   **"Owing to the heavy weight flannels":** Advertisement in *Sporting Life,* March 7, 1896.

113   **"Charles Benson committed suicide while insane":** "Heat Drives Many to Their Death," *Atlanta Constitution,* July 10, 1897.

113   **Mike Grady and Brooklyn catcher Aleck Smith:** "Relentless Heat," *Spokesman-Review,* July 12, 1897.

114   **"might prove fatal":** "Frank Chance Has a Collapse," *Meriden Morning Record,* July 3, 1911.

115   **sold at auction for $62,213:** Chance's Cubs home jersey was Lot #590 in a Legendary Auctions offering, for which bidding closed November 19, 2009.

116   **"One of Hornsby's great features":** "Diamond Stars Decided Tailor Needed Asset," *Miami News,* April 28, 1929.

116   **"you wouldn't recognize old Casey":** "Casey Stengel Acquires Dignity Now That He Manages Boston," *Milwaukee Journal,* March 16, 1938.

116   **"The scratch is on the inside":** "Champs Begin to Hit Up the Pace," *Boston Globe,* July 4, 1905.

118   **Frank Bonner...died of blood poisoning:** "Death List of a Day, Frank Bonner," *New York Times,* January 2, 1906.

118   **nearly lost a finger:** *Pittsburgh Press,* December 27, 1907.

118   **Forrest Crawford died of it:** "Baseball Player Crawford Dead," *New York Times,* March 31, 1908.

118   **death of Yankees manager Miller Huggins:** *New York Times,* September 26, 1929.

118   **Waddell bruised one of his thighs:** *Meriden Morning Record,* May 8, 1913.

119   **"suffered such little things":** Associated Press, "Buck Newsom Claims Tough Luck Honors," *Calgary Herald,* July 13, 1938.

119   **join the boy in the great beyond:** "Grief of Coolidge at the Deathbed of Son in '24 Depicted by Doctor," *New York Times,* July 11, 1955.

119   **"the power and the glory of the presidency":** "Glory of Office Stolen by Death of Coolidge Boy," *Palm Beach Post,* March 8, 1929.

120   **Calvin Jr. had worn black socks:** Morgan and Tucker, *More Rumor!,* 89.

120   **calling Snodgrass "Spiker!" and "Dirty!":** "Postpone the Fourth Contest," *Pittsburgh Press,* October 18, 1911.

120   **Rabbit Maranville once entered:** "Maranville: Boston's Durable Shortstop." *New York Times,* June 1, 1931.

121 **"Partisan feeling here is very strong"**: "Snodgrass Hooted Out of Philadelphia," *New York Times,* October 20, 1911.

122 FRED SNODGRASS, 86, DEAD: *New York Times,* April 6, 1974.

122 **"ankle-chokers"**: Ballard, "Fabric of the Game."

123 **"First a layer of heavy underwear"**: Henry McLemore, "Sports Parade," *Painesville Telegraph,* August 3, 1939.

124 **"The uniforms were so uncomfortable"**: "Global Games," *Chicago Tribune,* July 13, 1995.

125 **Singleton's hives only intensified**: Associated Press, "Expos' Singleton Itching to Turn In His Uniform," *Oxnard Press-Courier* (California), July 5, 1972.

127 **Charles Ebbets suggested the league**: "Decision on Benton Is Left to Landis," *New York Times,* February 14, 1923. (The Baseball Hall of Fame database on uniforms, "Dressed to the Nines," is a magnificent resource, available online at http://exhibits.baseballhalloffame.org/dressed_to_the_nines/database.htm.)

128 **It was White Sox owner Bill Veeck**: "White Sox Add Name to Number on Road Uniforms This Season," *New York Times,* April 10, 1960.

128 **"We look like semi-pros"**: *Portsmouth Times,* March 23, 1960.

128 **home phone numbers on the uniforms**: Keene, *1960,* 41.

129 **Ted Kluszewski strode to the plate**: "Kluszewxi (Who?) Stirs Fans," *New York Times,* May 9, 1960.

129 **Another was Orlon**: A brief history of Orlon is available online at the DuPont Heritage Timeline, http://www2.dupont.com/Phoenix_Heritage/en_US/1941_detail.html.

131 **New Era Cap Company**: Watershed dates in New Era history are available online at http://pressroom.neweracap.com/category/13/Photos/page/172/History.aspx.

131 **Johnson asked the home plate umpire**: "Pirates Win World's Series," *Reading Eagle,* October 15, 1925.

132 **"wore his cap inside out at the Polo Grounds"**: "Big League Chatter," *New York Times,* August 16, 1932.

132 **stole his hat**: "Four Home Runs by Phillies Help Simmons Vanquish Giants, 6 to 2," *New York Times,* September 24, 1956.

133 **Khrushchev snatched the cap**: "Newsman Wins Nikita Over to Baseball Cap," *Lakeland Ledger,* February 25, 1960.

133 **"lovable piece of headwear"**: Charles McDowell, *Deseret News,* November 25, 1966.

134 **John Board was an usher:** "Ushers Have Spent Decades Helping Out Reds' Fans," *Cincinnati Enquirer,* October 4, 2010.

Chapter 5

139 **Fred Clarke, the player-manager:** "Hat Chatter: Fred Clarke Designs New Baseball Cap for Use in the Sun," *Men's Wear* 29 (May 11, 1910): 93.

139 **"We never heard of flip-down sunglasses":** Cobb and Stump, *Ty Cobb,* 57.

140 **"has taken to wearing smoked glasses":** *Sporting Life* 11, no. 3 (1888): 2.

140 **"No outfielder should balk at wearing sunglasses":** Cobb and Stump, *Ty Cobb,* 233.

141 **Dixie Walker borrowed teammate:** Broeg, *Memories of a Hall of Fame Sportswriter,* 17.

141 **"But it's the sun field":** "Where'll I Play Ruth, Wails Mr. McKechnie," *Milwaukee Journal,* February 28, 1935.

141 **because right was in the sun:** "Yankee Trio Has Edge in Field, at Bat," *San Jose News,* September 22, 1932.

141 **"they'd switch him with Bob Meusel":** "Casey Stengel 'Explains' Who Will Play Left Field," *Sarasota Herald-Tribune,* October 8, 1960; "Echoes from the Dugouts," *New York Times,* April 15, 1931.

141 **"no other sun field is quite so bad":** *Sporting Life,* January 23, 1897.

142 **"Sold Honus for $190":** DeValeria and DeValeria, *Honus Wagner,* 242. (In his biography of Fred Clarke—*Fred Clarke: A Biography of the Baseball Hall of Fame Player-Manager*—author Ronald T. Waldo puts the sale price of Honus the Mule at $100.)

142 **"Casey didn't tell me that":** "Return of the Sober Superstar," *New York Times,* July 10, 1994.

142 **Clarke sipped a bourbon highball:** Associated Press, "Wagner Greatest, Says Fred Clarke," *Miami News,* May 22, 1960.

143 **"Smoked glasses of late years":** "Keeler: The King of Right Fielders," *New York Times,* March 5, 1911.

143 **"Speaker, scorning the aid":** "2 Home Runs Help Yanks Beat Indians," *New York Times,* May 23, 1924.

144 **"But it didn't seem like he saw good":** Bryan Hoch, "Former Yankees Pitcher Duren Passes Away," MLB.com, January 7, 2011, http://newyork.yankees.mlb.com/news/article.jsp?ymd=20110107&content_id=16407444&vkey=news_nyy&c_id=nyy.

145 **eighty-pound bronze bust:** "For Rose and His Reds, It's Cobb or Bust," *Sports Illustrated,* May 6, 1985.

145   **a Southern Californian named Jim Jannard:** "Oakley's Founder Looks Like a Million—And Then Some," *Los Angeles Times*, August 10, 1995; "Luxottica, Oakley Shares Rise on $2 Billion Purchase," *Bloomberg*, June 21, 2007.

146   **"Pat Dougherty rubs mud":** Morris, *A Game of Inches*, 341.

146   **"Dougherty declares his reason for retiring":** "Pat Dougherty Quits Baseball," *New York Times*, February 17, 1912.

146   **State Bank of Bolivar:** *Sporting News*, May 9, 1940, 3.

146   **"Sandow Mertes tried that new sun field":** Morris, *A Game of Inches*, 341.

147   **Mertes had a beloved dog:** "Parting Remarks of Mr. Brannick," *New York Times*, February 12, 1940.

147   **two researchers at the Yale School of Medicine:** Brian M. DeBroff and Patricia J. Pahk, "The Ability of Periorbitally Applied Antiglare Products to Improve Contrast Sensitivity in Conditions of Sunlight Exposure," *Archives of Opthalmology*, July 2003.

148   **"I sweat too much":** Matt Fortuna, "Cedeno Fits In with Self-Made Mustache," MLB.com, July 7, 2010, http://mlb.mlb.com/news/article.jsp?ymd=20100607&content_id=10909448&notebook_id=10909702&vkey=notebook_pit&fext=.jsp&c_id=pit.

149   **"use of firemen and policemen":** "Pneumatic Head Protector," *Toledo Blade*, April 10, 1902.

149   **Reds pitcher Andy Coakley hit Giants catcher:** "Bresnahan Injured, Hit by Pitch," *Meriden Daily Journal*, June 19, 1907.

150   **Chapman stood in close to the plate:** "Beaned by a Pitch, Ray Chapman Dies," *New York Times*, August 17, 1920.

150   **"Headgear for ballplayers":** "Headgear for Players," *New York Times*, August 19, 1920.

151   **"I went from second tenor to baritone [sic]":** Robert L. Burnes, "Call Me Foulproof," *St. Louis Globe-Democrat*, 1961.

153   **"wore nothing but a white jockey strap":** "The Slugging Match," *Lawrence Daily Gazette*, August 8, 1893.

153   **"a tri-color belt of ribbons":** "Corbett Wins," *Philadelphia Record*, January 26, 1894.

153   **"an upward kick on Driscoll's groin":** "Queer Fight in Paris," *New York Times*, October 29, 1899.

153   **"Berger, the Poly catcher":** "Scholastic Base Ball," *Brooklyn Daily Eagle*, May 22, 1901.

154   **"The testicle being an exquisitely sensitive organ":** Lydston, *The Surgical Diseases*, 924.

154   **"Mr. D., single, aged twenty-eight years"**: *Medical Review* 27, 330. (Mr. D. had an operation to remove the testicle on December 3, 1892.)

154   **felled him like a tree**: "Hardy His Bad Inning," *Baltimore Sun,* June 26, 1907.

154   **"suffering from severe pains in the groin"**: "Rain Upsets Giants' Plans in the South," *New York Times,* March 31, 1908.

155   **"In moments of stress"**: "Claude Berry Was 'Ketcher' for Kid Teams," *Deseret News,* February 14, 1916.

156   **"There was a fresh cry"**: "World's Title Rests on Result of Today's Game," *Border Cities Star,* October 10, 1924.

156   **"the greatest thrill of her life"**: "Mrs. Coolidge Takes President to Game," *New York Times,* October 10, 1924.

156   **"The Prohibition gangsters sat at ringside"**: Burnes, "Call Me Foulproof."

157   **"HYPUS IGOE THROUGH THIS WALL"**: "Before Fight Camp Became a Suite Science," *New York Times,* March 1, 1987; "Stunt Either Painless or Brainless," *New York Daily News,* July 21, 1996.

157   **"Chairman Farley could save himself"**: Ed Sullivan, *New York Evening Graphic,* quoted in Taylor, *Prizefight Government.*

158   **Referee Jimmy Crowley began counting Schmeling out**: "Schmeling, Beaten, Wins Crown on Foul," *Baltimore Post,* June 13, 1930.

159   **Their waistbands, glove cuffs, and jockstraps**: "Jacob Golomb, 58, a Manufacturer," *New York Times,* August 25, 1951.

159   **"the trouble at first"**: Associated Press, "A Glove in Every Face," *St. Petersburg Evening Independent,* March 26, 1949.

159   **"I told Carnera to place his huge paws"**: Taylor, *Prizefight Government.*

160   **Pepper Martin never wore a cup**: "The Hot Corner: It's No Place for the Timid," *Baseball Digest,* August 1989.

160   **"He was just a lucky man"**: Feldman, *Dizzy and the Gas House Gang,* 50.

161   **"I saved you"**: Schoendienst and Rains, *Red,* 30.

161   **"a black and blue spot"**: "Board Bars Appeal of Tunney Ruling," *New York Times,* September 25, 1927.

162   **Foulproof and a film crew from Pathé**: Taylor, *Prizefight Government.*

163   **rushed to the side of the supine Cochrane**: United Press International, May 26, 1937.

164   **"I think some lighter guard"**: "'Bean Ball' Helmet Tested; Found Okay," *Pittsburgh Press,* June 1, 1937.

164   **"taking a look at the lop-sided caps"**: "Hill Learning to Field from Mack," *Washington Post,* August 1, 1937.

165   **"Throgmorton Slovinsky MacPhail"**: Taylor, *Prizefight Government,* 63.

165   "They wouldn't wear a thing": "Plastic Protectors Inside Caps Will Be Worn by Dodger Batters," *New York Times*, March 9, 1941.

166   "The objection I heard": Ibid.

167   "The man who invents a helmet that insures": "Connie Mack Prefers Slam-Bang Baseball, Favors Helmet Use," *Ellensburg Daily Record*, March 28, 1941.

168   HE DEVISED MANY METHODS: "Dr. W. E. Dandy Dies; Brain Surgeon, 60," *New York Times*, April 20, 1946.

168   "protective liners made of fibroid": "Lane Backs Crash Helmets," *St. Joseph's Gazette*, September 6, 1954.

168   "This sound without echo": Kahn, "Baseball's Secret Weapon."

169   "It was more difficult than people think": Associated Press, "Charlie Muse; Created Baseball Batting Helmet," May 17, 2005.

169   "Only sissies wore helmets then": "Cuomo Makes His Late-Night Debut," *Albany Times Union*, November 6, 1993.

171   Rickey's helmet concern: "Rickey Enjoys Last Laugh on Cap Idea," *Washington Observer*, September 12, 1957. (As the piece noted, "Some writers and players made a great joke of it.")

174   "Writers were running out of euphemisms": "A Hex of a Situation for Fisk," *Boston Globe*, June 12, 1974.

174   "I didn't think I was going to make it": "So Far, the A's and Their Elephant Have Yet to Lose," *Philadelphia Inquirer*, June 27, 1989.

175   baseball is tied with lacrosse: Romaine and Rothfeld, *The Encyclopedia of Men's Health*, 38.

176   not entirely safe: Associated Press, "Baseball Deaths Mount to Five," *St. Petersburg Times*, July 13, 1963.

176   eighteen-year-old Tom Douglas: "College Player Killed by Pitch," *Milwaukee Journal*, April 20, 1964.

177   saved by a $10.50 helmet: "Los Angeles: Helmet Saves Batter," *Eugene Register-Guard*, May 15, 1965.

177   "You trying to tell me something?": "Drysdale Dealing in Hard Hats," *Calgary Herald*, June 29, 1965.

178   NEAR DEATH and FATALLY HURT: "Benton Near Death; Cincinnati Pitcher Probably Fatally Hurt," *Milwaukee Journal*, July 30, 1913.

178   Herrmann...declined to pay: "Benton Will Not Be Paid While Injured," *Cleveland Morning Leader*, July 30, 1913.

178   "I'm afraid of motorcycles": "The Dangerous World of Mickey Lolich," *Sarasota Herald-Tribune*, April 6, 1969.

179   delivered—for a one-time fee: Davis, "The Man Behind the MLB Logo."

180 **ritually shattered it:** "The Poor White Sox Could Drown in the Sahara," *Sarasota Herald-Tribune*, May 11, 1971.

180 **Brian Barsamian, who had written:** United Press International, "Just Colorful Charlie," *Windsor Star*, March 17, 1970.

180 **"Under the lights it will be beautiful":** "Charlie O Adds 'Color,'" *Washington Observer-Reporter* (Iowa), March 17, 1970.

180 **Finley's fellow owners denied him:** "Colored Bases Agenda Item at Baseball Meeting Here," *Montreal Gazette*, July 28, 1970.

181 **"I have lost my sight":** "Conigliaro Suddenly Retires," *Eugene Register-Guard*, July 11, 1971.

181 **"This is certainly no sport for sissies":** "No Game for Sissies," *Family Week*, February 21, 1971.

181 **"It's too hot":** "Goldsworthy Enjoys Streak but Not His Headgear," *Calgary Herald*, February 16, 1971.

182 **died of a stroke:** *Argus-Press* obituary, November 12, 1975.

182 **"What the heck is *that?*":** Associated Press, "Twins' Inventive Doc Lentz Plans to Cash In This Time," *Baltimore Sun*, February 9, 1971.

182 **"If Evans had been wearing":** "Evans Still Hospitalized; But Vision Remains Clear," *Lewiston Evening Journal*, August 30, 1978.

184 **"People can say what they want":** "Mets' Wright Won't Get Big Head over Helmet," *Newsday*, September 2, 2009.

184 **"Sweetheart" and "Mrs. Harrelson":** "Some Hitters Feel Their Bare Hands Are Enough," *New York Times*, April 1, 2007.

185 **"an ordinary street glove":** *Sporting News*, May 12, 1932, cited in Morris, *A Game of Inches*, 448.

185 **"wears a golfer's glove":** "Brewers Get Gleeson, Grate for Pyle, Sinton," *Milwaukee Sentinel*, May 18, 1948.

185 **after rupturing a thumb muscle:** "Yankees to Use McDonald Tonight," *New York Times*, June 16, 1953.

186 **Hank Foiles wore one on his left hand:** "Bad Throw to First Base His Downfall," *Pittsburgh Press*, July 27, 1957.

186 **"feeling of compactness":** "Barber Got Tired in Sixth," *Baltimore Sun*, July 29, 1960.

186 **"Brandt has been wearing":** "Indians Get Newcombe," *Baltimore Sun*, July 30, 1960.

186 **wore a golf glove in batting practice:** Associated Press, "Kansas City High on New Shortstop," *Tuscaloosa News*, March 15, 1961. (From an Associated Press Wirephoto caption on March 2, 1962: "Jim Piersall [left], Washington outfielder who signed a $45,000 contract this week, largest in the history

of the Senators, slides his hand into a golf glove at the start of batting practice. Bob Johnson [right], infielder, also wears one of the gloves to prevent blisters." From an Associated Press story in spring training of 1963: "Center fielder Jim Piersall spent almost an hour hitting against the pitching machine, wearing a golf glove to prevent blisters." ["Marv Breeding Checks Into Senators Camp," *Sarasota Herald-Tribune,* February 26, 1963.])

186   Jim Gentile... removed his golf glove: Associated Press, "Gentile Ties AL Record Hits Fourth Grand Slam," *Eugene Register-Guard,* July 8, 1961.
186   "This happens about once a week": "Maris Hits No. 35," *New York Times,* July 16, 1961.
186   "It just feels good... six months and two days": "Terry Becomes a Giant Killer While Practicing on Chickens," *New York Times,* October 11, 1962.
187   wore a "golfer's glove" to great notice: "Wills of Dodgers Swipes 93d Base," *Milwaukee Journal,* September 19, 1962.
187   green golf glove: Red Smith, "Fools Rushed Out, Angels Rushed In," *St. Petersburg Times,* September 4, 1962.
187   "Though the idea will sound strange": "Headgear for Players."

Chapter 6

188   "with unfeigned horror": Fetter, *Taking On the Yankees,* 196.
189   "like a horse going to a horse trough": McKelvey, *The MacPhails,* 22.
189   "matter of public health": D'Antonio, *Forever Blue.*
189   "Public telephone booths will be distributed": "Ebbets Field Will Have Every Comfort for Brooklyn Patrons," *Sporting Life,* April 20, 1912.
189   "when completed Ebbets Field": Ibid.
190   E. J. McKeever & Bro.: "Stephen M'Keever Dies in Brooklyn," *New York Times,* March 7, 1938.
190   "the public urinals were fetid troughs": Kahn, *The Era,* 299.
190   "stench of perennially backed-up toilets": Eliot, *Song of Brooklyn,* 87.
191   "Brooklyn's slums have spread": "Walter in Wonderland," *Time,* April 28, 1958.
191   "treat baseball fans like cattle": Ibid.
192   "I want the folks to see me": "Candidates' Words Speak for Themselves," *Chicago Tribune,* November 29, 1999.
192   "The beer garden was considered in play": Hetrick, *Chris Von der Ahe.*
193   "The empty beer bottle made its appearance": "Baseball Plays a Golden Anniversary," *New York Times,* February 8, 1925.

193   "Interjected at suitable places": "Sullivan Fighting Drunk," *New York Times,* May 23, 1886.

194   "one of the best catchers in the game": *Sporting Life,* January 18, 1913.

195   "have not touched a drop to-day": "National Game Playing," *Brooklyn Daily Eagle,* May 18, 1884.

195   composed a poem on the spot: "Brooklyn Coppers Win at Base Ball," *Brooklyn Daily Eagle,* August 16, 1892.

195   shagging flies in a pasture: Callahan, *Carl Sandburg,* 11.

196   "who the bird was": "Baseball Players Aided by Football," *New York Times,* October 30, 1919.

196   Evans remained at his post: "Man of High Courage," *Montreal Gazette,* July 1, 1911.

196   "baseball as played uptown": "Spring Calendar of Fashionable Sports," *New York Times,* May 5, 1907.

197   accumulated by the hundreds beneath the grandstands: "Side-lights on the Game," *Baseball Magazine,* October 1916.

197   thirteen empty beer kegs: "Garry's Party All Messed Up," *Toledo News-Bee,* April 25, 1925.

198   "It didn't taste like that to me": "Labeled 'Sauerkraut'; Hadn't Taste of Beer," *St. Petersburg Evening Independent,* April 25, 1925.

198   Hack Wilson was busted in a midnight raid: "Hack Wilson Found in 'Beer Parlor' Is Taken to Lock Up," *Telegraph Herald,* May 24, 1926.

198   "they choose ginger ale": "Ball Fans Must Fast," *New York Times,* April 13, 1924.

199   beer kegs were delivered to Ruth's suite: Weintraub, *The House That Ruth Built,* 266.

199   turned Third Base...into its Roxbury Crossing branch: "Noted Baseball Saloon Turned Into a Library," *San Jose Evening News,* May 18, 1923.

199   "Maybe he will forget his disappointment": "Red Sox Sell Ruth for $100,000 Cash," *Boston Globe,* January 6, 1920.

199   "a Prussian formality to Ruppert": "The First Boy Wonder," *New York Times,* August 23, 1965.

200   "burdened with bottles": "Carnage of Innings Described by Cobb," *New York Times,* October 8, 1921.

200   "No more are empty beer bottles": "Says Cray L. Remington," *Rochester Evening Journal,* January 10, 1924.

200   "The patrons of the ball yards": "Paper Cup," *Washington Post,* April 3, 1933.

201   "A slightly inebriated gentleman": "Caught at the Plate," *New York Times,* September 14, 1924.

201 **"A man who throws a bottle":** "To End Ballpark Disorder," *New York Times,* September 3, 1920.

201 **Dodgers promised to raise grandstand ticket prices:** "To Stop Bottle Throwing," *New York Times,* July 9, 1922.

202 **knocked the bottom from the bottle:** "Yanks Beat Browns Before 30,000," *New York Times,* September 17, 1922.

202 **thirty thousand potential witnesses:** "Pop Bottle Mystery Solver Is Lucky Fan," *New York Times,* October 2, 1922.

202 **"Boys, let's go and refresh":** "Bambino Smiles, Shakes Hands," *St. Petersburg Evening Independent,* March 3, 1927.

203 **formed a cordon around Pfirman:** "Giants Down Cubs as Pop Bottles Fly," *New York Times,* September 13, 1927.

203 **"a long bar that dispensed hard liquor":** "Johnson Has Many Friends," *Providence News,* October 22, 1927.

203 **Indians manager Roger Peckinpaugh argued a call:** "Umpire Struck in Cleveland Badly Hurt," *Miami News,* May 13, 1929.

203 **much-concussed former umpire:** "Umpire Assaulted as Athletics Win," *New York Times,* May 12, 1929.

203 **"Give Colonel Jake Ruppert the right to make beer":** Associated Press, December 23, 1932.

203 **"my own brewery will be ready":** "Col. Ruppert Is Kept Busy," *Youngstown Vindicator,* November 15, 1932.

205 **His office would give a $5,000 reward:** "Play at First Provokes Riot," *Milwaukee Journal,* July 27, 1936.

205 **POUR OUT [THE] POP BOTTLE PERIL!:** *Sporting News,* September 26, 1935.

206 **twinned worlds of baseball...and beer:** "15,000 Pay Tribute at Ruppert's Rites," *New York Times,* January 17, 1939.

206 **"distinctly of the masculine type":** "Ruppert, Owner of Yankees and Leading Brewer, Dies," *New York Times,* January 14, 1939.

207 **"This beer outfit that hired me":** "Diz Dean Tells Off Critics," *Tuscaloosa News,* July 25, 1946.

209 **"Call it Beer Park":** United Press International, "Frick Cries over Beer," *New York Times,* April 11, 1953.

209 **"with total disregard for local ball clubs":** "Frick Opposes Broadcast Ban," *Middlesboro Daily News,* February 25, 1954.

209 **"adjunct of the brewing business":** Associated Press, "Ready to Sell Cardinals Claims Busch," *Ottawa Citizen,* May 26, 1954.

209 **denying the application to sell beer:** "Battle Opens For and Against Beer in Baltimore Stadium," *Washington Post,* December 29, 1953.

209   "Baseball has become beerball": "Baseball or Beerball," *Chicago Tribune,* July 3, 1957.

210   single biggest advertiser on televised baseball: "Sponsors Pay Record High for Baseball," *Eugene Register-Guard,* March 8, 1961.

210   The Phillies...sought a license to sell: Associated Press, "Giles Gets Rough with Phils Fans," *Spencer Daily Reporter* (Iowa), April 24, 1956.

210   a thirty-six-year-old man was arrested: Associated Press, "Says Umps Can Forfeit Games If Fans Riot," *Ludington Daily News,* April 19, 1956.

211   law was discriminating...against the "working man": "Walking Wets Win Right to Bring Beer," *Washington Post,* June 6, 1962.

211   "several fans ran onto the field": "Blame It on the Booze," *Oswego Argus-Press,* July 6, 1964.

211   Washington Senators...had taken the Solomonic decision: United Features Syndicate, "Suds Ban in All but Bleachers Fault of Solons Themselves," *Eugene Register-Guard,* June 20, 1957.

212   "the ten-cent beer night": "If Brewers Cancel Beer, 'Tis Something," *Pittsburgh Post Gazette,* June 6, 1974.

212   Dave Duncan was given a beer shower: United Press International, May 30, 1974.

213   "We're lucky somebody didn't get stabbed": "Spectators Cause Tribe to Forfeit," *Toledo Blade,* June 5, 1974.

214   "We could have gotten killed out there": Associated Press, "Umpire Hurt; Cheap Beer Costly to Tribe," *Reading Eagle,* June 5, 1974.

214   Busch family...was selling thirty-five million barrels annually: Johnson, "Sports and Suds."

214   "Mr. Busch gives every evidence": *St. Louis Post-Dispatch,* February 21, 1953.

216   There, in a bar, the poem was first read: "Francis Scott Key," *New York Times,* March 14, 1897.

216   "the players paraded across the field": "Baseball Season Opened," *New York Times,* April 23, 1897.

216   "The teams parted at the home plate": "On the Baseball Field," *New York Times,* April 16, 1898.

217   "Thousands of persons forgot baseball": "On the Baseball Field," *New York Times,* May 1, 1898.

217   "when the national anthem was played": "Big Day for Baseball," *New York Times,* April 18, 1902.

217   fans *thought* they spotted: "President's Fiancée Is Main Attraction," *Wilmington Star,* October 10, 1915.

218   "It reminds us that we're in a war": "Every Day Is Flag Day at the Ball Parks," *New York Times*, May 16, 1942.

Chapter 7

219   "Mr Cammeyer again had the grounds": *Brooklyn Daily Eagle*, August 22, 1867.

220   "Harry Stevens always has some new idea": "New York News," *Sporting Life*, February 22, 1896.

220   ham-and-cheese sandwiches: "Ball Fans Must Eat," *New York Times*, April 13, 1924.

221   "threw a chunk of bologna sausage": *Sporting Life*, June 8, 1895, 4.

221   "insatiable appetite for hot roasted peanuts": "Eastern Fare," *Sporting Life*, September 20, 1890.

222   "printing score-cards and selling peanuts": "Washington Whispers," *Sporting Life*, March 28, 1891.

222   "He declines to be a special guest": "Seven to Five," *Boston Daily Globe*, January 18, 1897.

222   "McGinnity's one weakness is peanuts": "Von der Ahe Again," *Brooklyn Daily Eagle*, September 16, 1900.

223   "I saw bush [league] games as a boy": "Author of Game's Song Not Present Until 1940," *Sporting News*, April 27, 1944.

224   "eating a red hot in the first inning": "Series Verifies Fullerton's Dope," *Chicago Daily Tribune*, October 15, 1906.

224   "The redhots warmed with mustard": "Sad Slaughter of Sox," *Chicago Daily Tribune*, October 11, 1906.

224   "Ernie Whelan's 'red-hots'": *Detroit Free Press*, October 12, 1907.

225   "close to the hot dog counter": "E-Yah and A-Las for Tiger," *Chicago Tribune*, October 13, 1907.

225   failed to buy the Brooklyn club: "Niles Man May Buy Brooklyn Club," *Youngstown Vindicator*, June 19, 1908.

225   "fusillade of sandwiches": "Boston Red Sox Take First Game of World's Series," *St. Petersburg Evening Independent*, October 8, 1912.

225   "they keep the money out in the open": United Press International, "Hot Dog This Company Says," *Los Angeles Times*, January 15, 1985.

226   "Harry Stevens giving away his peanuts": "Boston Takes Third Game, 5–4," *New York Times*, October 13, 1914.

226   "He would wrestle a man": "Harry Mozley Stevens," *New York Times*, May 5, 1934.

228   "Ice cream, éclairs and bricklets": "Fans Can Buy Anything," *St. Louis Star,* May 23, 1930.

228   "waiting on, attending in any manner": "Sopranos Gain in Bid to Join Hawking Cry," *New York Times,* April 6, 1977.

228   a succession of luxury hotels: *New York Times,* May 6, 1934.

228   "the importance of the frankfurter": "Harry M. Stevens Dies at Age of 78," *New York Times,* May 4, 1934.

229   Arthur introduced a foot-long hot dog: "Thomas G. Arthur, 84; Made Dodger Dog a Staple of L.A. Stadium Experience," *Los Angeles Times,* June 27, 2006.

229   Cary Grant told Arthur: Ibid.

230   peanut hawker in Triple-A Columbus: From a note archived in the National Baseball Hall of Fame Library.

230   "Hey, lady, wanna buy a goober?": Elmer Dean was profiled in stories by the Associated Press, "Dean Boys' Father Goes to St. Louis," October 3, 1934; the *Milwaukee Journal,* "Dizzy Is Still Hero Down Houston Way," September 23, 1937; the *Sporting News,* "Vaunted Vendor Plays Shell Game," July 4, 1981; the *Lewiston Daily Sun,* "Frisch Reinstates Dizzy Dean," August 17, 1934; and the *Meriden Daily Journal,* "Elmer Dean No Longer Holdout," March 25, 1936.

231   Hal Schiff began selling at Shibe Park: "The Peanut Man Connie Mack Hired," *Philadelphia Inquirer,* October 13, 1974.

231   "Peanut Jim" Shelton: "'Peanut Jim' Forced out of Lineup," *Cincinnati Enquirer,* October 16, 1976.

231   top hat with a working water spigot: "Flag Waver a 'Cheepie,'" *Fort Worth Star-Telegram,* June 30, 1974.

232   Charlie Grimm was a peanut vendor: "Name Doesn't Fit Jolly Charlie Grimm of Cubs," *Beaver County Times,* July 11, 1947.

232   "He is a St. Louis native": Associated Press, "Fred Saigh Agrees to Sell Holdings in St. Louis Club," *Calgary Herald,* January 31, 1953.

232   George (the Peanut Man) Jacobs: "The Disabled List," *Boston Globe,* April 16, 2004.

232   Dan Ferrone sold beer: "Peanut Pitcher," *Chicago Tribune,* April 3, 1989.

232   Manny Gluck, program vendor at Gate 4: "Manny Gluck, 65, Dies; Yankee Vendor No. 1," *New York Times,* May 18, 2005.

233   McNeil unwittingly sold beer: "Jury Acquits Wally the Beer Man," *Minneapolis Star Tribune,* March 22, 2011.

233   "spectators could buy Nachos Grande": "They Had a Hot Night in New Orleans," *St. Petersburg Times,* September 16, 1978.

NOTES

233 "traditional ballpark culinary staple": "Fiesta Bowl 1978 Not USDA Choice," *Kingman Daily Miner* (Arizona), December 26, 1978.
235 "manufactured by the Marsh Candy Company": "The Munificent Mr. Malaprop," *Los Angeles Times,* August 29, 1971.
236 "People like to identify": "If It Has to Do with Baseball, Danny Goodman Sells It," *Christian Science Monitor,* December 28, 1981.
236 "Stick to hot dogs": "The Man Who Made Grand Old Game a Novelty," *Los Angeles Times,* May 20, 1980.
236 "A guy had a choice": "Baseball Novelty," *Los Angeles Times,* May 11, 1971.
236 "novelties will be bigger": "Novelties Big Business," *Sporting News,* July 12, 1980.
237 Goodman bought the candy bars: "The Munificent Mr. Malaprop."
238 Goodman would pitch oil companies: United Press International, "Stars Seek 10-Minute Baseball Intermission," February 10, 1949.
239 dressed in drag and carrying a mop: Associated Press, "Hollywood Sets New Baseball Fad," April 2, 1950.
239 baseball tradition of "dragging the infield": United Press International, "Stars Seek."
240 signature novelty: the bobblehead doll: "Mets' Fans Have Eccentric Habits," *Oxnard Press-Courier* (California), May 22, 1963.
240 "Someone came to me from Japan": "The Munificent Mr. Malaprop."
241 "The collar was low": Gogol, *The Overcoat.*
242 "Turn 'em away, if necessary": "He's for Wrigley Field," *Pasadena Star-News,* December 26, 1957.
242 "If just half his friends show up": "Goodman—That He Is," *Los Angeles Examiner,* February 9, 1958.
242 Dodgers bugles—he ordered twenty thousand: "Events & Discoveries," *Sports Illustrated,* March 23, 1959.
242 "We'll have 12 different hat styles": "Brass Bugles Being Readied for Dodger Games in Coliseum," *Los Angeles Times,* March 10, 1959.
243 devoted double shifts exclusively to plastic baseball hats: "Cronin's Corner," *Los Angeles Times,* May 30, 1958.
243 "you'll think you've bought a new boarder": Ibid.
243 "Dodger fans don't buy hats or jackets": Ibid.
243 "breweries had their own mugs and caps": "The Man Who Made Grand Old Game a Novelty."
244 "concentric rows of novelty and souvenir stands": "Council Rejects O'Malley's Plan," *New York Times,* October 23, 1959.

315

245 **"Danny Goodman Special":** "If It Has to Do with Baseball, Danny Good-man Sells It."

245 **TO HECK WITH HOUSEWORK:** "Rube-Barbs; Wipe Away Scoring Sheet," *Pasadena Star-News,* March 26, 1963.

245 **wipe-clean reusable dry-erase scorecards:** "Can It Wipe Out Bat Muffs Too?," *Pasadena Star-News,* May 27, 1964.

245 **"I turn away more people":** "Danny Goodman's Motto: 'Keep Customers Happy,'" *Long Beach Press-Telegram,* August 21, 1975.

246 **"Why would anyone think it unusual":** "Sideline Business," *Los Angeles Times,* August 12, 1962.

247 **"women represent about 40 percent":** "Novelties Big Business."

247 **Fans were invited to T-Shirt Night:** "Record Number of Promotions Set for 1980," *Los Angeles Times,* April 15, 1980.

247 **twenty-fourth consecutive Hollywood Stars game:** "Star Tracks," *People,* September 21, 1981.

248 **Fernando Valenzuela bumper stickers:** Associated Press, "El Toro Fernando," May 14, 1981.

248 **In 1983, at the age of seventy-four, Danny Goodman:** "Danny Goodman Dies," *Los Angeles Times,* June 19, 1983.

248 **"He is credited with virtually inventing":** *Distinguished Residents of Hillside Memorial Park,* 38.

249 **George Steinbrenner had to withdraw:** *Sporting News,* May 9, 1981.

Chapter 8

251 **cigars in his shirt pocket:** United Press International, "Boy Quizzed in Shooting," *Reading Eagle,* July 5, 1950.

251 **At half past noon, as the Brooklyn Dodgers emerged:** "Mystery Bullet Kills Baseball Fan in Midst of Crowd at Polo Grounds," *New York Times,* July 5, 1950.

251 **sound like a paper bag popping:** United Press International, "Baseball Fan Slain Before 49,316 Crowd," July 5, 1950.

252 **standing-room patrons in the overflow crowd:** "Line of Fire: Independence Day 1950," *New York Daily News,* August 30, 1998.

254 **1939 profile of Gonzales:** "The Cases of Dr. Gonzales," *Life,* November 27, 1939.

255 **"talking more about the shooting":** "Mystery Bullet Kills Baseball Fan in Midst of Crowd at Polo Grounds."

255 **lived with his great-great-aunt:** "Boy, 14, Admits Firing .45 Pistol at Time of Polo Grounds Killing," *New York Times,* July 8, 1950.

255   **police found three .22-caliber weapons:** "Held in Ball Park Death," *New York Times,* July 12, 1950.

255   **Robert Mario Peebles, confessed:** "Boy, 14, Admits Firing .45 Pistol at Time of Polo Grounds Killing"; Associated Press, "Ballpark Death Cleared Up as Boy Confesses," *Yonkers Herald-Statesman,* July 8, 1950.

258   **Flaig died, of a liver ailment:** "Otto Flaig, 55; Teterboro Police Chief," *Bergen County Record* (New Jersey), August 3, 1992.

258   **Joanne Barrett, nearly five months pregnant:** "Bronxville Woman Shot in Hand During Game at Yankee Stadium," *New York Times,* July 5, 1985; Associated Press, "Gunshot Wounds Yankee Fan," *Sarasota Herald-Tribune,* July 5, 1985.

258   **announced her intention to sue the Yankees:** "Woman Shot in Hand at Game Sues the Yankees," *New York Times,* July 11, 1985.

259   **rifling through her handbag:** "Woman Shot at Park Finds Bullet in Purse," *New York Times,* July 8, 1985.

259   **At 3 o'clock in the morning:** Shieber, "That Famous Yankees Logo."

260   **"robbed, beaten, stabbed and shot":** "Crime Blotter Has a Regular: Yankee Caps," *New York Times,* September 15, 2010.

Chapter 9

264   **Born and orphaned in Macon, Missouri:** "She's the Organist at the Garden," *Chillicothe Constitution,* February 22, 1951.

264   **Goodding moved to Manhattan:** Associated Press, "Died Monday," November 20, 1963.

264   **Rickard lay in state on the arena floor:** Associated Press, "Rickard Paid Last Tribute by Thousands," *Spokane Daily Chronicle,* January 9, 1929.

265   **there was no danger of the same:** "Democratic Convention to Be Radiated by Twenty Stations," *New York Times,* June 22, 1924.

265   **the name of the Cleveland organ:** "Preserve Historic Pipe Organ Housed in Public Auditorium," *Cleveland Plain Dealer,* May 10, 2009.

266   **the revolutionary Hammond organ:** Basile, *Fifth Avenue Famous,* 120; "Pipeless Organ," *Time,* April 29, 1935.

266   **"Darling, I Am Growing Old":** *Chicago Tribune,* February 9, 1940.

266   **"Waitin' for the Train to Come In":** "Hawks Late Rally Downs Rangers 9–4," *New York Times,* March 4, 1947.

267   **"My 90-year-old mother":** "Lively Dispute Promised in Flatbush Today," *New York Times,* July 17, 1942.

267   **"a crabbed man":** "Court Asked to Mute Dodgers Calliope," *New York Times,* June 2, 1942.

267   The judge...threw out the case: United Press International, *Windsor Star,* November 20, 1963.

267   before playing "Happy Birthday to You": "Warren Is Not Happy," *New York Times,* April 24, 1951.

268   terrible poignancy in 1951: Associated Press, "Hugh Casey Commits Suicide," *Dubuque Telegraph Herald,* July 3, 1951; "Casey, Ex-Dodger, Is Atlanta Suicide," *New York Times.*

268   Gladys Goodding...died of a heart attack: "Gladys Goodding, Organist, Is Dead," *New York Times,* November 20, 1963.

269   composed that four-note progression: "Organists Enjoy Life on Bench," *Bridgewater Courier-News* (New Jersey), undated clip on file at the National Baseball Hall of Fame Library.

269   briefly alighting on a film scorer: "Peace at Last! K&D Return to Fold," *Los Angeles Times,* March 31, 1966.

269   Kiley had once been a silent-film organist: "John Kiley Now Choir Director at St. Patrick's," *Lowell Sun,* December 23, 1970.

269   The Pirates plucked Vince Lascheid: "Three Rivers Organist Pulls Out the Stops for Blass, Robertson," *Pittsburgh Press,* October 13, 1971.

270   "You Light Up My Life": "Angels Take a Loss After Lights Go Out," *Los Angeles Times,* September 22, 1979.

270   "Hungarian Rhapsody No. 2": "Organist Is Multi-Threat on Sidelines," *Christian Science Monitor,* syndicated in the *Anchorage Daily News,* March 22, 1976.

271   Newman had worked in Vegas and Tahoe: "Ronnie Newman, Who Played Organ for Twins," *Minneapolis Star Tribune,* September 2, 2003.

271   A photo from the middle '50s shows Ellington: The Duke Ellington photograph in the Library of Congress was taken by Charlotte Brooks for *Look* magazine in 1955.

273   Calvin Griffith spoke to the Lions Club: "Griffith Spares Few Targets in Waseca Remarks," *Minneapolis Tribune,* October 1, 1978.

274   "another nigger on his plantation": "Angry Carew Vows He Will Not Play for Griffith's Twins Again," *Minneapolis Tribune,* October 2, 1978.

277   abandoned the Ebbets aesthetic at the bathroom doors: "New Ballpark Statistic: Stadium's Toilet Ratio," *New York Times,* April 12, 2009.

278    $100,000 in dental work: "Baseball's Ban on Tobacco Goes Too Far," *Hartford Courant,* June 19, 1993.

278   selling ice water to Senators fans: "Ice Water Sold at Nats' Game; Griff Is Sorry," *Washington Post,* July 13, 1941.

279   trough-style urinal, which doesn't comply: "Target Field Promises Plenty of Potties, Especially for the Ladies," *City Pages,* April 21, 2009.

281   "The history of every nation": Franklin Roosevelt, on signing the Soil Conservation and Domestic Allotment Act, March 1, 1936.

282   **recruited to fill in for an inebriated groundskeeper:** Smith, "Diamond Cutters."

282   **"We're raising boys, not grass":** Steve Rushin, "Grace and Humility Defined the Great Slugger Harmon Killebrew," SportsIllustrated.com, May 17, 2011, http://sportsillustrated.cnn.com/2011/writers/steve_rushin/05/16/harmon.killebrew/index.html.

282   **Bob Feller's 20-millimeter gun scope:** Smith, "Diamond Cutters."

283   **"Is there another Emil Bossard":** Toma and Goforth, *Nitty Gritty Dirt Man,* 157.

284   **"bases were left out":** Cobb and Stump, *Ty Cobb,* 57.

284   **Mellor mowed a pattern into the outfield:** "Groundskeepers Display Artistry on the Diamond," *New York Times,* September 30, 2008.

287   **trained elephants performing on the lawn:** *The Rotarian,* October 1964, 54.

BIBLIOGRAPHY

Achorn, Edward. *Fifty-nine in '84: Old Hoss Radbourn, Barehanded Baseball & the Greatest Season a Pitcher Ever Had.* New York: HarperCollins, 2010.

Anderson, Bruce. "When Baseballs Fell from the Sky, Henry Helf Rose to the Occasion." *Sports Illustrated* (March 11, 1985).

Bahnsen, John C., Jr., and Wess Roberts. *American Warrior: A Combat Memoir of Vietnam.* New York: Citadel, 2007.

Ballard, Sarah. "Fabric of the Game." *Sports Illustrated* (April 5, 1989).

Basile, Salvatore. *Fifth Avenue Famous: The Extraordinary Story of Music at St. Patrick's Cathedral.* New York: Fordham University Press, 2010.

Broeg, Bob. *Memories of a Hall of Fame Sportswriter.* New York: Sports Publishing LLC, 1995.

Brookes, John. *Manliness.* London: Charles John Ridge, 1875.

Bush, Laura. *Spoken from the Heart.* New York: Scribner, 2010.

Caillault, Jean-Pierre. *A Tale of Four Cities: Nineteenth Century Baseball's Most Exciting Season, 1889, in Contemporary Accounts.* Jefferson, NC: McFarland, 2003.

Callahan, North. *Carl Sandburg: His Life and Works.* University Park, PA: Penn State Press, 1987.

Carson-Gentry, Martha, and Paul Rodebough. *Images of America: West Chester.* Charleston, SC: Arcadia Publishing, 1997.

Chastain, Bill. *Hack's 191: Hack Wilson and His Incredible 1930 Season.* Guilford, CT: Globe Pequot Press, 2012.

Cobb, Ty, and Al Stump. *Ty Cobb, My Life in Baseball: The True Record.* Lincoln, NE: University of Nebraska Press, 1993.

Cohen, Gerald Leonard, and others. *Origin of the Term "Hot Dog."* Gerald Cohen, 2004.

Cramer, Richard Ben. *Joe DiMaggio: The Hero's Life.* New York: Simon & Schuster, 2000.

D'Antonio, Michael. *Forever Blue: The True Story of Walter O'Malley.* New York: Riverhead Books, 2009.

Davis, David. "The Man Behind the MLB Logo." *Wall Street Journal* (October 23, 2008).

DeValeria, Dennis, and Jeanne Burke DeValeria. *Honus Wagner: A Biography.* Pittsburgh: University of Pittsburgh Press, 1998.

Dickson, Paul. *The Dickson Baseball Dictionary,* 3rd ed. New York: W. W. Norton & Company, 2009.

Duren, Ryne, and Tom Sabellico. *I Can See Clearly Now.* Chula Vista, CA: Aventine Press, 2003.

Eig, Jonathan. *Luckiest Man.* New York: Simon & Schuster, 2005.

Eliot, Marc. *Song of Brooklyn: An Oral History of America's Favorite Borough.* New York: Broadway, 2008.

Evers, John. "Teaching the Poilus How to Play Baseball." *Baseball Magazine* (March 1919).

Feldman, Doug. *Dizzy and the Gas House Gang.* Jefferson, NC: McFarland, 2000.

Fetter, Henry D. *Taking On the Yankees.* New York: W. W. Norton & Company, 2003.

Furlong, William Barry. "Johnny Bench: Supercatcher for the Big Red Machine." *New York Times Magazine* (August 30, 1970).

Gammons, Peter. "End of an Era." *Sports Illustrated* (July 24, 1989).

Gant, Tina. *International Directory of Company Histories.* Farmington Hills, MI: St. James Press, 2005.

Gogol, Nikolai. *The Overcoat.* Mineola, NY: Dover, 1992.

Gorman, Robert M., and David Weeks. *Death at the Ballpark: A Comprehensive Study of Game-Related Fatalities of Players, Other Personnel and Spectators in Amateur and Professional Baseball, 1862–2007.* Jefferson, NC: McFarland, 2005.

Greenberg, Hank, and Ira Berkow. *Hank Greenberg: The Story of My Life.* Chicago: Triumph, 2001.

Gutman, Dan. *Banana Bats and Ding-Dong Balls: A Century of Unique Baseball Inventions.* New York: Macmillan, 1995.

Hall, Don C., and Annette Hall. *I Served.* Victoria, BC: Trafford Publishing, 2006.

Hendley, Nate. *Al Capone: Chicago's King of Crime.* Neustadt, ON: Five Rivers Chapmanry, 2006.

Hetrick, J. Thomas. *Chris Von der Ahe and the St. Louis Browns.* Lanham, MD: Scarecrow Press, 1999.

Hill, Bob. *Crack of the Bat: The Louisville Slugger Story.* Champaign, IL: Sports Publishing LLC, 2000.

Hinton, Charles. "A Mechanical Pitcher." *Harper's Weekly* (March 20, 1897).

Hirsch, James S. *Willie Mays: The Life, the Legend.* New York: Scribner, 2010.

Howard, Arlene, and Ralph Wimbish. *Elston and Me: The Story of the First Black Yankee.* Columbia, MO: University of Missouri Press, 2001.

Hynd, Noel. "The Inside Story of Baseball in 1943 Was Less Bounce to the Ounce." *Sports Illustrated* (May 13, 1985).

James, Bill. *The New Bill James Historical Baseball Abstract.* New York: Simon & Schuster, 2003.

Johnson, William Oscar. "Sports and Suds." *Sports Illustrated* (August 8, 1988).

Jordan, David M. *Pete Rose: A Biography.* Westport, CT: Greenwood Publishing Group, 2004.

Kahn, Roger. "Baseball's Secret Weapon: Terror." *Sports Illustrated* (July 10, 1961).

———. *The Era, 1947–1957: When the Yankees, the Giants, and the Dodgers Ruled the World.* Boston: Houghton Mifflin, 1993.

———. *October Men: Reggie Jackson, George Steinbrenner, Billy Martin, and the Yankees' Miraculous Finish in 1978.* Boston: Harcourt, 2003.

Keene, Kerry. *1960: The Last Pure Season.* Champaign, IL: Sports Publishing LLC, 2002.

Kennedy, Kostya. *56: Joe DiMaggio and the Last Magic Number in Sports.* New York: Sports Illustrated Books, 2011.

Knowles, Richard G., and Richard Morton. *Baseball.* London: George Routledge & Sons, 1896.

Kurkjian, Tim. "Old-Fashioned Glove Story." *ESPN The Magazine* (February 17, 2003).

Lamster, Mark. *Spalding's World Tour: The Epic Adventure That Took Baseball Around the Globe—And Made It America's Game.* New York: Public Affairs, 2006.

Lane, F. C. "Ball-players Hands." *Baseball Magazine* (October 1917).

Leavengood, Ted. *Clark Griffith: The Old Fox of Washington Baseball.* Jefferson, NC: McFarland, 2011.

Liberman, Noah. *Glove Affairs: The Romance, History, and Tradition of the Baseball Glove.* Chicago: Triumph Books, 2003.

Lilliefors, James. *Ball Cap Nation: A Journey Through the World of America's National Hat.* Covington, KY: Clerisy Press, 2009.

Lindberg, Michael, and Daniel Todd. *Anglo-American Shipbuilding in World War II: A Geographical Perspective.* Westport, CT: Praeger Publishers, 2004.

Lydston, G. Frank. *The Surgical Diseases of the Genito-Urinary Tract, Venereal and Sexual Diseases.* Philadelphia: F. A. Davis Co., 1899.

Mack, Connie. *My 66 Years in the Big Leagues.* Mineola, NY: Dover, 2009.

Magee, David, and Philip Shirley. *Sweet Spot: 125 Years of Baseball and the Louisville Slugger.* Chicago: Triumph Books, 2009.

McKelvey, G. Richard. *The MacPhails: Baseball's First Family of the Front Office.* Jefferson, NC: McFarland, 2000.

McKenna, Brian. "Global League." Society for American Baseball Research (SABR), http://sabr.org/bioproj/topic/global-league.

Mead, William B. *Baseball Goes to War.* Washington, DC: Broadcast Interview Source, 1998.

Mellor, David R. *The Lawn Bible.* New York: Hyperion, 2003.

Moffi, Larry. *This Side of Cooperstown: An Oral History of Major League Baseball in the 1950s.* Mineola, NY: Dover, 1996.

Morgan, Hal, and Kerry Tucker. *More Rumor!* New York: Penguin Books, 1987.

Morris, Peter. *A Game of Inches: The Stories Behind the Innovations That Shaped Baseball: The Game Behind the Scenes.* Chicago: Ivan R. Dee, 2006.

———. *A Game of Inches: The Stories Behind the Innovations That Shaped Baseball: The Game on the Field.* Chicago: Ivan R. Dee, 2006.

Murphy, Cait. *Crazy '08: How a Cast of Cranks, Rogues, Boneheads, and Magnates Created the Greatest Year in Baseball History.* New York: HarperCollins, 2007.

Nearing, Scott. *Wages in the United States, 1908–1910.* New York: Macmillan, 1911.

Nemec, David. *The Beer & Whiskey League: The Illustrated History of the American Association—Baseball's Renegade League.* Guilford, CT: Lyons Press, 2004.

———. *The Official Rules of Baseball Illustrated.* Guilford, CT: Lyons Press, 2006.

Newman, Barry. "Sultans of Sock: Stirrups Hang On in Minor Leagues." *Wall Street Journal* (April 21, 2009).

Nort, Henry W. "A Message from the War Front." *Baseball Magazine* (December 1918).

Okkonen, Marc. *Baseball Uniforms of the 20th Century.* New York: Sterling Publishing Company, 1991.

Oldenburg, Claes. *Oldenburg: Six Themes.* Minneapolis: Walker Art Center, 1975.

Ritter, Lawrence S. *The Glory of Their Times: The Story of the Early Days of Baseball Told by the Men Who Played It.* New York: Harper Perennial, 1992.

Robinson, Joshua. "A Machine Before Its Time." *Wall Street Journal* (June 21, 2010).

Romaine, Deborah S., and Glenn S. Rothfeld. *The Encyclopedia of Men's Health.* New York: Facts On File, 2005.

Rose, Pete, and Roger Kahn. *Pete Rose: My Story.* New York: Macmillan, 1989.

Rushin, Steve. "Motley Crew." *Sports Illustrated* (September 6, 1999).

Schoendienst, Red, and Rob Rains. *Red: A Baseball Life.* Champaign, IL: Sports Publishing LLC, 1998.

Seidel, Michael. *Ted Williams: A Baseball Life.* Lincoln, NE: University of Nebraska Press, 2003.

Seymour, Harold. *Baseball: The People's Game: Volume 3.* New York: Oxford University Press, 1990.

Shafer, Ronald G. *When the Dodgers Were Bridegrooms.* Jefferson, NC: McFarland, 2011.

Shieber, Tom. "That Famous Yankees Logo." *Baseball Researcher* blog, 2010, http://baseballresearcher.blogspot.com/2010/03/that-famous-yankees-logo.html.

Smith, Gary. "Diamond Cutters." *Sports Illustrated* (September 21, 1998).

Smith, Ron, and the editors of the *Sporting News. Celebrating 70: Mark McGwire's Historic Season.* New York: McGraw-Hill/Contemporary, 1998.

Spalding, Albert Goodwill. *America's National Game.* Point Loma, CA: A. G. Spalding, 1911.

Strasburg, Andy, and others. *Baseball's Greatest Hit: The Story of Take Me Out to the Ball Game.* New York: Hal Leonard Books, 2008.

Sullivan, Dean A., ed. *Early Innings: A Documentary History of Baseball, 1825–1908.* Lincoln, NE: University of Nebraska Press, 1995.

Taylor, Foulproof. *Prizefight Government.* Brooklyn: Foulproof Taylor, 1946.

Toma, George, and Alan Goforth. *Nitty Gritty Dirt Man.* Champaign, IL: Sports Publishing LLC, 2004.

Turbow, Jason, and Michael Duca. *The Baseball Codes: Beanballs, Sign Stealing, and Bench-Clearing Brawls: The Unwritten Rules of America's Pastime.* New York: Anchor Books, 2010.

Veeck, Bill, and Ed Linn. *Veeck as in Wreck.* Chicago: University of Chicago Press, 1962.

Vlasich, James A. *A Legend for the Legendary: The Origin of the Baseball Hall of Fame.* Bowling Green, OH: Bowling Green University Popular Press, 1990.

Von Borries, Philip. *American Gladiator: The Life and Times of Pete Browning.* Bradenton, FL: Booklocker.com, 2007.

Waldo, Ronald T. *Fred Clarke: A Biography of the Baseball Hall of Fame Player-Manager.* Jefferson, NC: McFarland, 2010.

Weintraub, Robert. *The House That Ruth Built: A New Stadium, the First Yankees Championship, and the Redemption of 1923.* New York: Little, Brown, 2011.

Wright, Derrick. *Tarawa 1943: The Turning of the Tide.* Oxford: Osprey Publishing, 2000.

Wulf, Steve. "Glove Story." *Sports Illustrated* (May 7, 1990).

Additional Sources

Distinguished Residents of Hillside Memorial Park and Mortuary. Los Angeles: Hillside Memorial Park and Mortuary, 2011.

The Reach Official American League Base Ball Guide 1910. Philadelphia: A. J. Reach Co., 1910.

Size Matters: How a Growing American Audience Affects the Size and Cost of Performing Arts Spaces. South Norwalk, CT: Theatre Projects Consultants, July 2010.

Sotheby's: The Barry Halper Collection of Baseball Memorabilia: The Early Years. New York: Barry Halper Enterprises, 1999.

Sotheby's: The Barry Halper Collection of Baseball Memorabilia: The Modern Era. New York: Barry Halper Enterprises, 1999.

The United States Patents Quarterly. Washington, DC: Associated Industries Publications, 1977.

INDEX

ABOUT THE AUTHOR

Steve Rushin has written for *Sports Illustrated* for the past twenty-five years and was the 2006 National Sportswriter of the Year. He is the author of a novel, *The Pint Man*, and his work has appeared in *The Best American Sports Writing*, *The Best American Travel Writing*, and *The Best American Magazine Writing*. He lives in Connecticut.